Lecture Notes in Artificial Intelligence 1042

Subseries of Lecture Notes in Computer Science
Edited by J. G. Carbonell and J. Siekmann

Lecture Notes in Computer Science

Edited by G. Goos, J. Hartmanis and J. van Leeuwen

T0236692

Springer
Berlin
Heidelberg
New York
Barcelona
Budapest
Hong Kong
London
Milan
Paris
Santa Clara
Singapore
Tokyo ·

Gerhard Weiß Sandip Sen (Eds.)

Adaption and Learning in Multi-Agent Systems

IJCAI '95 Workshop
Montréal, Canada, August 21, 1995
Proceedings

 Springer

Series Editors

Jaime G. Carbonell
School of Computer Science, Carnegie Mellon University
Pittsburgh, PA 15213-3891, USA

Jörg Siekmann
University of Saarland
German Research Center for Artificial Intelligence (DFKI)
Stuhlsatzenhausweg 3, D-66123 Saarbrücken, Germany

Volume Editors

Gerhard Weiß
Institut für Informatik, Technische Universität München
D-80290 München, Germany

Sandip Sen
Department of Mathematical and Computer Science, University of Tulsa
Tulsa, OK 74104-3189, USA

Cataloging-in-Publication Data applied for

Die Deutsche Bibliothek - CIP-Einheitsaufnahme

Adaption and learning in multi-agent systems : proceedings /
IJCAI '95 workshop, Montréal, Canada, August 1995. Gerhard
Weiss ; Sandip Sen (ed.). - Berlin ; Heidelberg ; New York ;
Barcelona ; Budapest ; Hong Kong ; London ; Milan ; Paris ;
Santa Clara ; Singapore ; Tokyo : Springer, 1996
  (Lecture notes in computer science ; 1042 : Lecture notes in artificial
  intelligence)
  ISBN 3-540-60923-7
NE: Weiss, Gerhard [Hrsg.]; IJCAI <14, 1995, Montréal>; GT

CR Subject Classification (1991): I.2, I.6, D.3.2

ISBN 3-540-60923-7 Springer-Verlag Berlin Heidelberg New York

© Springer-Verlag Berlin Heidelberg 1996
Printed in Germany

Typesetting: Camera ready by author
SPIN 10512570   06/3142 – 5 4 3 2 1 0   Printed on acid-free paper

Preface

This volume contains the revised and extended versions of fourteen papers that were first presented at the workshop on "Adaptation and Learning in Multi-Agent Systems" held August 21, 1995 in Montréal, Canada, as part of the Fourteenth International Joint Conference on Artificial Intelligence (IJCAI-95). The goal of this workshop was to bring together researchers and practitioners with an active interest in adaptation and learning problems in environments co-habited and shared by multiple agents, and to provide a forum for discussing existing approaches and results, exchanging insights and expertise, and developing new ideas and perspectives. The workshop was international and attracted more than 35 participants from seven countries.

Adaptation and learning in multi-agent systems establishes a relatively new but significant topic in Artificial Intelligence (AI). Multi-agent systems typically are very complex and hard to specify in their behavior. It is therefore broadly agreed in both the Distributed AI and the Machine Learning community that there is the need to endow these systems with the ability to adapt and learn, that is, to self-improve their future performance. Despite this agreement, however, adaptation and learning in multi-agent systems has been widely neglected in AI until a few years ago. On the one hand, work in Distributed AI mainly concentrated on developing multi-agent systems whose activity repertoires and coordination mechanisms are more or less fixed and thus less robust and effective particularly in changing environments. On the other hand, work in Machine Learning mainly concentrated on learning techniques and methods in single-agent or isolated-system settings. Today this situation has changed considerably, and there is an increasing number of researchers focussing on this topic.

The papers contained in this volume, each reviewed by three experts, reflect both the broad spectrum of and the progress made in the available work on learning and adaptation in multi-agent systems. They address this topic from different points of view, and describe and experimentally and/or theoretically analyze new adaptation and learning approaches for situations in which several agents have to cooperate or to compete with each other in order to solve a given task or set of tasks.

Additionally, to assist the novice reader, an introductory and motivational article is included which provides a compact guide to this topic. This article takes a general look at multi-agent systems and at adaptation and learning therein, and offers an extensive and interdisciplinary list of pointers to relevant and related work.

This is the first available book on adaptation and learning in multi-agent systems. We hope that the reader will find it both useful and interesting, and that it will foster further investigations on this topic.

We would like to thank all the people who contributed to the success of this workshop. In particular, we are grateful to the authors and workshop participants for submitting papers and for the good atmosphere during and between the sessions, to the committee members for their organizational activities and for carefully reviewing the initial submissions, to the IJCAI-95 organizers for supporting this workshop, and to Springer-Verlag and Alfred Hofmann for the opportunity to publish this volume and for the unbureaucratic cooperation.

January 1996

Gerhard Weiß
Sandip Sen

Workshop Organization

Sandip Sen (Chair)   University of Tulsa, USA

Michael N. Huhns   University of South Carolina, USA
Maja J. Mataric   Brandeis University, USA
Michael J. Shaw   University of Illinois at Urbana-Champaign, USA
Devika Subramanian   Cornell University, USA
Ming Tan   GTE Laboratories Inc., USA
Moshe Tennenholtz   Technion - Israel Institute of Technology, Israel
Gerhard Weiß   Technische Universität München, Germany

Additional Reviewers

Thomas Haynes   University of Tulsa, USA
Tuomas Sandholm   University of Massachusetts at Amherst, USA

Contents

Adaptation and Learning
in Multi-Agent Systems:
Some Remarks and a Bibliography

Gerhard Weiß

Institut für Informatik, Technische Universität München
D-80290 München, Germany
weissg@informatik.tu-muenchen.de

Abstract. In the last years the topic of adaptation and learning in multi-agent systems has gained increasing attention in Artificial Intelligence. This article is intended to provide a compact, introductory and motivational guide to this topic. The article consists of two sections. In the first section, "Remarks", the range and complexity of this topic is outlined by taking a general look at the concept of multi-agent systems and at the notion of adaptation and learning in these systems. This includes a description of key dimensions for classifying multi-agent systems, as well as a description of key criteria for characterizing single-agent and multi-agent learning as the two principal categories of learning in multi-agent systems. In the second section, "Bibliography", an extensive list of pointers to relevant and related work on multi-agent learning done in (Distributed) Artificial Intelligence, economics, and other disciplines is provided.

1. Remarks

Multi-Agent Systems

Multi-agent systems, that is, computational systems composed of several agents capable of mutual and environmental interaction, establish a central research and application area in Distributed Artificial Intelligence (DAI). There are four major reasons for the broad interest in multi-agent systems:

- As distributed systems they offer useful features such as parallelism, robustness and scalability, and therefore are applicable in many domains which cannot be handled by centralized systems. In particular, they are well suited for domains which require the integration of multiple sources of knowledge or activity, the resolution of interest and goal conflicts, the time-bounded processing of very large data sets, or the on-line interpretation of data arising in different geographical locations.
- The concept of multi-agent systems is in accordance with the insight gained over the past decade in disciplines like AI, psychology, and sociology that intelligence and interaction are deeply and inevitably coupled to each other. In particular, multi-agent systems realize this coupling in both directions:

on the one hand, interactivity allows the agents to increase their level of intelligence; and on the other hand, intelligence allows the agents to increase the efficiency of their interactivity.

- The study of multi-agent systems from the perspective of DAI can contribute to our understanding of natural multi-agent systems like insect societies or human teams in general, and to our understanding of complex social phenomena like collective intelligence and emergent behavior in particular.
- Today powerful computers and advanced computing networks provide a solid platform for the realization of multi-agent technology.

In the following, the concept of multi-agent systems will be described in more detail.

Differencing Aspects and their Dimensions. In the DAI literature many multi-agent systems have been described. Taking into consideration that a system always has to be considered in its environmental context in order to really understand its functionality, it can be stated that these systems differ from each other in three key aspects:

- the *environment* occupied by the multi-agent system,
- the agent-agent and agent-environment *interaction*, and
- the *agents* themselves.

For each of these differencing aspects several dimensions can be identified by which multi-agent systems can be classified. With respect to the first differencing aspect, the environment occupied by the multi-agent system, examples of such classifying dimensions (together with attributes that illustrate their spectrum of possible values) are

- the *availability* of environmental resources (ranging from restricted to ample),
- the environmental *diversity* (ranging from poor to rich),
- the environmental *uncertainty and predictability* (ranging from predictable to unpredictable), and
- the environmental *dynamics and status* (ranging from fixed to variable).

It is important to stress that it is not trivial to conclusively define the expression "environment of a multi-agent system". In particular, the widespread definition of this expression as the "sum" of the environments of the individual agents contained in the multi-agent system is problematic: because an agent's environment usually contains other agents, this definition implies that the system itself is contained in its environment. (Another problem results from the fact that an agent's environment containing other agents may be viewed as an agent on its own.) With respect to the second differencing aspect, the agent-agent and agent-environment interaction, examples of classifying dimensions are

- the *frequency* of interaction (ranging from low to high),

- the *persistence* of interaction (ranging from short-term to long-term);
- the *level* of interaction (ranging from signal passing to knowledge exchange),
- the *pattern* of interaction (ranging from unstructured to structured),
- the *variability* of interaction (ranging from fixed to changeable),
- the *type* of interaction (ranging from competitive to cooperative), and
- the *purpose* of interaction (ranging from random to goal-directed).

Finally, with respect to the third differencing aspect, the agents themselves, examples of such classifying dimensions are

- the *number of agents* involved in the multi-agent system (ranging from two upward),
- the *number of goals* an agent has (ranging from one upward),
- the *compatibility of the goals* (ranging from contradicting to complimentary),
- the *uniformity of the agents* (ranging from homogeneous to heterogeneous), and
- the *properties of the individual agents*.

Agent Properties. There has been considerable discussion and fruitful controversy on the last of these items, and the central question addressed is: *"What are the properties that let an object like a software program or an industry robot be an agent?"* Forming the intersection of the many answers which have been given to this question, one obtains something like the following "essence" of kernel properties:

- *perceptual, cognitive and effectual skills;*
- *communicative and social abilities;*
- *autonomy* (self-control).

With that, and in as far as the first two items constitute intelligence in its intuitive meaning, this "essence" implies the concise definition of an agent as an object which in some sense is intelligent and autonomous. Further properties that are often considered to be essential for agency are the following:

- *reactivity* (i.e., the ability to respond to environmental changes in reasonable time);
- *situatedness* (i.e., the ability to continuously interact with – or to be embedded in – its environment);
- *pro-activeness and deliberation* (i.e., the ability to act in a foreseeing, goal- or plan-oriented manner);
- *rationality* (i.e., the ability to always behave in a way which is suitable or even optimal for goal attainment);
- *mobility* (i.e., the ability to change the physical position);
- *introspection* (i.e., the ability to examine and self-reflect its own thoughts, ideas, plans, etc);

- *veracity* (i.e., the property of not knowingly communicating false information);
- *benevolence* (i.e., the property of always doing what is asked to do).

(Some of these terms are differently used by different authors, and the explanations provided in brackets are only intended to approximately describe their meanings.) In addition to the properties mentioned above, sometimes properties are ascribed to agents which describe their internal states. Examples of such properties or so-called *mental attitudes* are the following:

- belief, knowledge, etc, which describe *information or cognitive states*;
- intention, commitment, plan, etc, which describe *deliberative or conative states*;
- desire, goal, choice, preference, etc, which describe *motivational or affective states*.

Each of the properties listed above concerns, in one way or another, a significant aspect of agency and, with that, represents a classifying dimension for multi-agent systems.

The System-Application Assignment Problem. Clearly, it is not the attribute value of a single dimension but the combination of the attribute values of all dimensions that characterizes a multi-agent system. An understanding of the relationships between these dimensions would provide a valuable guideline for deciding which type of multi-agent system is best or at least sufficiently well suited to a given application task, and which type of application task can be best solved by a given multi-agent system. The problem of making this decision is sometimes called the (bidirectional) *multi-agent system-application assignment problem*. To solve this problem is one of the most important long-term challenges in DAI.

Topics of Current Research and Practice. There are many topics that are of relevance to the specification, implementation, handling, and assessment of multi-agent systems. These include, for instance, agent theories and architectures, communication languages, coordination mechanisms, negotiation and cooperation strategies, organization design, multi-agent planning and diagnosis, and multi-agent problem decomposition and synthesis. To discuss these topics and the specific issues raised by them would be beyond the scope and intention of this article. As a survey of the readings recommended below shows, current research and practice on agents and multi-agent systems simultanously focusses on these topics from different points of view and at different levels.

Adaptation and Learning

Adaptation and learning in multi-agent systems constitutes a further example of such a relevant topic, and it is commonly agreed by the DAI as well as the Machine Learning community that this topic deserves particular attention. As the above considerations suggest, multi-agent systems typically are of considerabe complexity with respect to both their structure and their functionality. For most application tasks, and even in environments that appear to be more or less simple, it is extremely difficult or even impossible to correctly determine the behavioral repertoire and concrete activities of a multi-agent system a priori, that is, at the time of its design and prior to its use. This would require, for instance, that it is known a priori which environmental requirements will emerge in the future, which agents will be available at the time of emergence, and how the available agents will have to interact in response to these requirements. This kind of problems resulting from the complexity of multi-agent systems can be avoided or at least reduced by endowing the agents with the ability to adapt and to learn, that is, with the ability to improve the future performance of the total system, of a part of it, or of a single agent. The rest of this section takes a closer look on the notion of adaptation and learning in multi-agent systems. In doing so, no explicit distinction is made between adaptation and learning; instead, it is assumed that "adaptation" is covered by "learning". This is in accordance with common usage, according to which the term "adaptation" is only applied to those self-modifications that enable a system to survive in a changed environment. (In its most general meaning, the term "adaptation" denotes all changes of a system so that it becomes suitable for a given situation or purpose. This meaning, however, is too broad to be of value from the viewpoint of Machine Learning.)

Categories of Learning. Learning in multi-agent systems is more than a mere magnification of learning in single-agent systems. On the one hand, learning in multi-agent systems comprises learning in single-agent systems, because an agent, although embedded in a multi-agent system, can learn in a solitary way and completely independent of the other agents. This is what can be called *single-agent or isolated learning*: learning that does not rely on the presence of multiple agents. On the other hand, learning in multi-agent systems extends learning in single-agent systems, because agents in a multi-agent system can learn in a communal way inasmuch as their learning is influenced (e.g., initiated, redirected, or made possible at all) by exchanged information, shared assumptions, commonly developed viewpoints of their environment, commonly accepted social and cultural conventions and norms which regulate and constrain their behaviors and interaction, and so forth. This is what can be called *multi-agent or interactive learning*: learning that relies on or even requires the presence of multiple agents and their interaction. Single-agent and multi-agent learning constitute the *principal categories* of learning in multi-agent systems. (There are borderline situations which make it difficult to draw clear boundaries between these two learning categories; for instance, one might think of an agent that learns about or models other agents.)

When people talk about learning in multi-agent systems, they usually think of multi-agent instead of single-agent learning. Two usages of the term "multi-agent learning" can be distinguished:

– In its stronger and *more specific meaning*, "multi-agent learning" refers only to situations in which several agents collectively pursue a common learning goal.

– In its weaker and *less specific meaning*, "multi-agent learning" additionally refers to situations in which an agent pursues its own learning goal, but is affected in its learning by other agents, their knowledge, beliefs, intentions, and so forth.

Independent of its underlying meaning, multi-agent learning is a many-faceted activity, and therefore it is not surprising that many synonyms of this term can be found in the literature. Examples of such synonyms, each stressing another facet, are mutual learning, cooperative learning, collaborative learning, co-learning, shared learning, team learning, social learning, pluralistic learning, and organizational learning. Whereas single-agent learning has been studied in AI since decades, multi-agent learning constitutes a relatively young field of study. Compared to its age, however, this field has already reached a considerable stage of development. Multi-agent learning is the subject of the bibliography presented in the second section.

The Credit-Assignment Problem. The basic problem any learning system is confronted with is the *credit-assignment problem*, that is, the problem of properly assigning credit or blame for overall performance changes (increase and decrease) to each of the system activities that contributed to that changes. Although this problem has been traditionally considered in the context of single-agent learning, it is also existent in the context of multi-agent learning. Taking the standard AI view according to which the activities of an agent are given by the external actions carried out by it and its internal decisions implying these actions, the credit-assignment problem can be usefully decomposed into two subproblems:

– the assignment of credit or blame for an overall performance change to external actions, and
– the assignment of credit or blame for an action to the corresponding internal decisions.

The first subproblem, which might be called the *inter-agent credit-assignment problem*, is particularly difficult for multi-agent systems, because here an overall performance change may be caused by external actions of several agents. This subproblem requires that the agents answer the question "What action carried out by what agent contributed to the performance change?" The second subproblem, which might be called the *intra-agent credit-assignment problem*, is equally difficult in single-agent and multi-agent systems. This sub-problem requires that an agent answers the question "What decisions led to a contributing action?" Any approach to multi-agent learning has to attack both the inter-agent and the intra-agent subproblem in order to succeed. How difficult it is to solve these subproblems and, with that, the total credit-assignment problem, depends on the concrete learning situation.

Forms of Learning. There is a great variety in the possible forms of learning in multi-agent systems, and there are several key criteria that may be applied in order to structure this variety. Two standard examples of such criteria, which are well known in the field of ML, are the following:

- The *learning method* or strategy used by a learning entity (a single agent or several agents). The following methods are usually distinguished:

  - rote learning (i.e., direct implantation of knowledge and skills without requiring further inference or transformation from the learner);

  - learning from instruction and by advice taking (i.e., operationalization – transformation into an internal representation and integration with prior knowledge and skills – of new information like an instruction or an advice that is not directly executable by the learner);

  - learning from examples and by practice (i.e., extraction and refinement of knowledge and skills like a general concept or a standardized pattern of motion from positive and negative examples or from practical experience);

  - learning by analogy (i.e., solution-preserving transformation of knowledge and skills from a solved to a similar but unsolved problem);

  - learning by discovery (i.e., gathering new knowledge and skills by making observations, conducting experiments, and generating and testing hypotheses or theories on the basis of the observational and experimental results).

  A major difference between these methods lies in the amount of learning efforts required by them (increasing from top to bottom).

- The *learning feedback* that is available to a learning entity and that indicates the performance level achieved so far. This criterion leads to the following usual distinction:

  - supervised learning (i.e., the feedback specifies the desired activity of the learner and the objective of learning is to match this desired action as closely as possible);

  - reinforcement learning (i.e., the feedback only specifies the utility of the actual activity of the learner and the objective is to maximize this utility);

  - unsupervised learning (i.e., no explicit feedback is provided and the objective is to find out useful and desired activities on the basis of trial-and-error and self-organization processes).

  In all three cases the learning feedback is assumed to be provided by the system environment or the agents themselves. This means that the environment or an agent providing feedback acts as a "teacher" in the case of supervised learning and as a "critic" in the case of reinforcement learning; in the case of unsupervised learning, the environment and the agents just act as passive "observers".

It is important to see that different agents do not necessarily have to learn on the basis of the same learning method or the same type of learning feedback. Moreover, in the course of learning an agent may employ different learning methods and types of learning feedback. Both criteria directly or indirectly lead to the distinction between learning and teaching agents, and they show the close relationship between multi-agent learning on the one hand and teaching and tutoring on the other. Examples of other than these two standard criteria, together with a brief description of their extreme values, are the following:

- The *purpose and goal of learning*. This criterion allows to distinguish between the following two extremes (and many graduations in between them):
  - Learning that aims at an improvement with respect to one single agent, its skills and abilities.
  - Learning that aims at an improvement with respect to the agents as a unit, their coherence and coordination.

  This criterion could be refined with respect to the number and compatibility of the learning goals pursued by the agents. Generally, an agent may pursue several learning goals at the same time, and some of the learning goals pursued by the agents may be incompatible while others are complementary.
- The *decentralization* of a learning process (where a learning process consists of all activities carried out by one or more agents in order to achieve a particular learning goal). This criterion concerns the degree of distribution and parallelism, and there are two obvious extremes:
  - only one of the available agents is involved in the learning process, and the learning steps are neither distributed nor parallelized;
  - all available agents are involved, and the learning steps are "maximally" distributed and parallelized.

  Of course, the degree of dentralization may vary for different learning processes.
- An *agent's involvement* in a learning process. With respect to the importance of involvement, one can identify the following two extremes:
  - the involvement of the agent under consideration is not a necessary condition for achieving the pursued learning goal (e.g., because it can be replaced by another equivalent agent);
  - the learning goal cannot be achieved without the involvement of exactly this agent.

  Other aspects of involvement that could be applied in order to refine this criterion are its duration and intensity. It also has to be taken into consideration that an agent may be involved in several learning processes, because it may pursue several learning goals.
- The *agent-agent and agent-environment interaction* required for realizing a learning process. Two obvious extremes are the following:

- learning requires only a minimal degree of interaction;
- learning would not be possible without extensive interaction.

This criterion could be further refined with respect to the frequency, persistence, level, pattern and type of interaction.

Many combinations of different values for these criteria are possible. For instance, one might think of a small group of agents that intensively interact (by discussing, negotiating, etc) in order to understand why the overall system performance has decreased in the past, or of a large group of agents that loosly interact (by sometimes giving advices, sharing insights, etc) in order to enhance the knowledge base of one of the group members.

Challenging Research Issues. The above criteria characterize learning in multi-agent systems at the single-agent and the total-system level, and they define a large space of possible forms of multi-agent learning. Each point in this space represents a form of multi-agent learning having its specific characteristics and its specific demands on the skills and abilities of the individual agents. Research and practice in DAI and ML has just started to explore this space. Considerable progress has been made especially in the last few years, but there are still many open questions and unsolved problems. Examples of challenging issues for future research are the following:

- requirements for learning in multi-agent systems;
- principles and concepts of learning in multi-agent systems;
- models and architectures of multi-agent systems capable of learning;
- extension and transformation of single-agent learning approaches to multi-agent learning approaches;
- parallel and distributed inductive learning in multi-agent systems;
- multi-strategy and multi-perspective learning in multi-agent systems;
- learning in multi-agent systems as organizational self-design;
- theoretical analysis of learning in multi-agent systems.

In attacking these and other issues, it is likely to be very useful and inspiring to take also related work from other disciplines than (D)AI into consideration. A number of references to such work are given in the "Bibliography" section.

Selected Pointers to Related Literature

In the following, some standard pointers to the literature on DAI, agency, multi-agent systems, and single-agent learning are provided.

There is wealth of literature on DAI in general. Standard DAI books are (Bond & Gasser, 1988; Huhns, 1987; Gasser & Huhns, 1989). The first chapter of (Bond & Gasser, 1988) offers a broad overview of important aspects and problems in DAI. Traditionally, two types of DAI systems are distinguished, namely, multi-agent systems and distributed problem solving systems (see, e.g., Durfee & Rosenschein, 1994).

Those specifically interested in the various aspects of agency are referred to (Wooldridge & Jennings, 1995). The first chapter of this book, written by the book editors, provides a valuable survey of the state of the art in (D)AI research on intelligent agents. A recent agent-oriented introductory textbook on AI is presented in (Russell & Norvig, 1995).

Work on multi-agent systems can be found, e.g., in the Proceedings of the First International Conference on Multi-Agent Systems (ICMAS, 1995) as well as in the Proceedings of the European Workshops on Modelling Autonomous Agents in a Multi-Agent World (Demazeau & Müller, 1990, 1991; Werner & Demazeau, 1992; Castelfranchi & Werner, 1994; Castelfranchi & Müller, 1995).

There are many books on single-agent ML; see, e.g., the established series (Kodratoff & Michalski, 1990; Michalski, Carbonell & Mitchell, 1983, 1986; Michalski & Tecuci, 1994). A recent textbook on ML is (Langley, 1995). Actual work on ML can be found, e.g., in the Proceedings of the European and the International Conferences on Machine Learning. The credit-assignment problem of learning was first mentioned in (Minsky, 1961).

Acknowledgements

I would like to thank Daniel Hernández, Heinz-Jürgen Müller and Sandip Sen for their suggestions and comments on an earlier draft of this article.

References

Bond, A.H., & Gasser, L. (Eds.) (1988). *Readings in distributed artificial intelligence*. Morgan Kaufmann.

Castelfranchi, C., & Müller, J.-P. (Eds.) (1995). *From reaction to cognition*. Lecture Notes in Artificial Intelligence, Vol. 957. Springer-Verlag.

Castelfranchi, C., & Werner, E. (Eds.) (1994). *Artificial social systems*. Lecture Notes in Artificial Intelligence, Vol. 930. Springer-Verlag.

Demazeau, Y., & Müller, J.-P. (Eds.) (1990). *Decentralized A.I.* North-Holland.

Demazeau, Y., & Müller, J.-P. (Eds.) (1991). *Decentralized A.I. 2* North-Holland.

Durfee, E.H., & Rosenschein, J.S. (1994). Distributed problem solving and multi-agent systems: Comparisons and examples. *Proceedings of the 13th International Workshop on Distributed Artificial Intelligence* (pp. 94–104).

Gasser, L., & Huhns, M. N. (Eds.) (1989). *Distributed artificial intelligence, Vol. 2*. Pitman.

Huhns, M.N. (Ed.) (1987). *Distributed artificial intelligence*. Pitman.

ICMAS (1995). *Proceedings of the First International Conference on Multiagent Systems*. AAAI Press/MIT Press.

Kodratoff, Y., & Michalski, R.S. (Eds.) (1990). *Machine learning, Vol. III*. Morgan Kaufmann.

Langley, P. (1995). *Elements of machine learning*. Morgan Kaufmann.

Michalski, R.S., Carbonell, J.G., & Mitchell, T.M. (Eds.) (1983). *Machine learning, Vol. I*. Morgan Kaufmann.

Michalski, R.S., Carbonell, J.G., & Mitchell, T.M. (Eds.) (1986). *Machine learning, Vol. II*. Morgan Kaufmann.

Michalski, R.S., & Tecuci, G. (Eds.) (1994). *Machine learning, Vol. IV*. Morgan Kaufmann.

Minsky, M. (1961). Steps towards artificial intelligence. *Proceedings of the IRE* (pp. 8–30). Reprinted in E.A. Feigenbaum & J. Feldman (Eds.) (1963), *Computers and thought* (pp. 406–450), McGraw-Hill.

Russell, S., & Norvig, P. (1995). *Artificial intelligence: A modern approach*. Prentice Hall.

Werner, E., & Demazeau, Y. (Eds.) (1992). *Decentralized A.I. 3*. North-Holland.

Wooldridge, M.J., & Jennings, N.R. (Eds.) (1995). *Intelligent agents*. Lecture Notes in Artificial Intelligence, vol. 890. Springer-Verlag.

2. Bibliography

This is a bibliography of multi-agent learning. It contains a number of references to relevant reports, articles, and books, and is intended to be an aid and service to those interested in this field.

Providing a bibliography of multi-agent learning is not without problems for three major reasons. First, multi-agent learning constitutes a relatively young but rapidly developing field of research and application. As a response to this, not only pointers to completed work, but also to work on novel ideas and of exploratory content have been included. Second, multi-agent learning constitutes a field without clear boundaries, and there are very close relationships to several other fields like single-agent learning, organizational design and adaptive systems theory. As a consequence, and apart from a few exceptions, only pointers to work that primarily deals with multi-agent learning or essential aspects of it have been included. And third, multi-agent learning constitutes a field of highly interdisciplinary nature. Therefore, not only pointers to work in (D)AI, but also to related work conducted in other disciplines have been included.

The bibliography consists of three parts. Part I contains references to work in (D)AI. (In order to avoid unnecessary redundancy, the papers in this volume are not referenced.) This part is roughly divided into two categories: "Principles, Algorithms, Applications, Tools" and "Theory". The first category contains references to work concentrating on multi-agent learning from a more practical point of view and being centered, in one or another way, around the question how learning and interaction (cooperation, communication, and so forth) in multi-agent systems are related to each other. The second category contains references to work dealing with the computational theory of team learning, which addresses the questions of efficiency and complexity of multi-agent learning from a theoretical point of view.

Part II contains references to work in economics. In this discipline multi-agent learning constitutes a traditional and well-established subject of study, where the focus of attention is on learning in organizations like business companies and state institutions. Learning in organizations, or organizational learning, is seen as a fundamental requirement for an organization's competitiveness, productivity, and innovativeness in uncertain and changing technological and market circumstances. With that, organizational learning is considered to be essential to the flexibility and sustained existence of an organization. It is likely that AI can considerably profit from the extensive knowledge about and experience with multi-agent learning that is available in economics.

Finally, part III contains a few references to work on multi-agent learning steeming from disciplines like psychology and sociology. This part is by no means complete, and the references should be just viewed as starting points for an exploration of the related literature available in these disciplines.

PART I: Work in Distributed Artificial Intelligence

Principles, Algorithms, Applications, Tools

1. Asada, M., Uchibe, E., & Hosoda, K. (1995). Agents that learn from other competitive agents. In (WS-IMLC95).
2. Boyan, J.A., & Littman, M.L. (1993). Packet routing in dynamically changing networks: A reinforcement learning approach. In J.D. Cowan, G. Tesauro & J. Alspector (Eds.), *Advances in Neural Information Processing Systems* (Vol. 6, pp. 671–678). San Fransisco: Morgan Kaufmann.
3. Brazdil, P., Gams, M., Sian, S., Torgo, L., & van de Velde, W. (1991). Learning in distributed systems and multi-agent environments. In Y. Kodratoff (Ed.), *Machine learning - EWSL-91* (pp. 412–423). Lecture Notes in Artificial Intelligence, vol. 482. Berlin: Springer-Verlag.
4. Brazdil, P., & Muggleton, S. (1991). Learning to relate terms in a multiple agent environment. In Y. Kodratoff (Ed.), *Machine Learning - EWSL-91* (pp. 424–439). Berlin: Springer-Verlag.
5. Byrne, C., & Edwards, P. (1995). Collaborating to refine knowledge. In (WS-IMLC95).
6. Chan, P.K., & Stolfo, S.J. (1993). Toward parallel and distributed learning by meta-learning. *Working Notes AAAI Workshop Know. Disc. Databases* (pp. 227–240).
7. Chan, P.K., & Stolfo, S.J. (1993). Meta-learning for multistrategy and parallel learning. *Proceedings of the Second International Workshop on Multistrategy Learning* (pp. 150–165).
8. Chan, P.K., & Stolfo, S.J. (1993). Toward multistrategy parallel and distributed learning in sequence analysis. *Proceedings of the First International Conference on Intelligent Systems for Molecular Biology* (pp. 65–73).
9. Chan, P.K., & Stolfo, S.J. (1993). Experiments on multistrategy learning by meta-learning. *Proceedings of the Second International Conference on Inform. Know. Management* (pp. 314–323).
10. Clouse, J.A. (1995). Learning from an automated training agent. In (WS-IMLC95).

11. Davies, W., & Edwards, P. (1995). Distributed learning: An agent-based approach to data-mining. In (WS-IMLC95).

12. Dorigo, M., & Gambardella, L.M. (1995). *Ant-Q. A reinforcement learning approach to combinatorial optimization*. Technical Report 95-01. IRIDIA, Université Libre de Bruxelles.

13. Dorigo, M., Maniezzo, V., & Colorni, A. (1996). The ant system: Optimization by a colony of cooperating agents. Appears in *IEEE Transactions on Systems, Man, and Cybernetics*, 26(2).

14. Dowell, M.L. (1995). *Learning in multiagent systems*. Dissertation. Department of Electrical and Computer Engineering, University of South Carolina.

15. Dowell, M.L., & Bonnell, R.D. (1991). Learning for distributed artificial intelligence. *Proceedings of the Twenty-Third Southeastern Symposium on System Theory* (pp. 218–221).

16. Dowell, M.L., & Stephens, L.M. (1994). MAGE: Additions to the AGE algorithm for learning in multi-agent systems. *Proceedings of the Second International Working Conference on Cooperating Knowledge Based Systems (CKBS94)*.

17. Edwards, P., & Davies, W. (1993). A heterogeneous multi-agent learning system. In S.M. Deen (Ed.), *Proceedings of the Special Interest Group on Co-operating Knowledge Based Systems* (pp. 163–184).

18. Findler, N.V. (1991). Distributed control of collaborating and learning expert systems for street traffic signals. In Lewis & Stephanon (Eds.), *IFAC Distributed Intelligence Systems* (pp. 125-130). Pergamon Press.

19. Gil, Y. (1995). Acquiring knowledge from users in a reflective architecture. In (WS-IMLC95).

20. Grosof, B. (1995). Conflict resolution in advice taking and instruction for learning agents. In (WS-IMLC95).

21. Huhns, M.N., Mukhopadhyay, U., Stephens, L.M., & Bonnell, R.D. (1987). DAI for document retrieval: The MINDS project. In M.N. Huhns (Ed.), *Distributed Artificial Intelligence* (pp. 249–283). Pitman.

22. Humphrys, M. (1995). *W-learning: Competition among selfish Q-learners*. Technical Report no. 362. Computer Laboratory, University of Cambridge.

23. Kinney, M., & Tsatsoulis, C. (1993). Learning communication strategies in distributed agent environments. Working Paper WP-93-4. Intelligent Design Laboratory, University of Kansas.

24. Littman, M.L. (1994). Markov games as a framework for multi-agent reinforcement learning. *Proceedings of the 1994 International Conference on Machine Learning* (pp. 157–163).

25. Littman, M.L., & Boyan, J.A. (1993). *A distributed reinforcement learning scheme for network routing*. Report CMU-CS-93-165. School of Computer Science, Carnegie Mellon University.

26. Maes, P. (1994). Social interface agents: Acquiring competence by learning from users and other agents. In O. Etzioni (Ed.), *Working Notes of the 1994 AAAI Spring Symposium on Software Agents*.

27. Markey, K.L. (1993). Efficient learning of multiple degree-of-freedom control

problems with quasi-independent Q-agents. *Proceedings of the 1993 Connectionist Models Summer School.* NJ: Lawrence Erlbaum Associates, Inc.

28. Matarić, M.J. (1994). Learning to behave socially. *Proceedings of the 3rd International Conference on Simulation of Adaptive Behavior – From animals to animats* (pp. 453–462).

29. Michalski, R., & Tecuci, G. (1995). *Machine learning. A multistrategy approach.* San Francisco, CA: Morgan Kaufmann.

30. Nagendra Prasad, M.V., Lander, S., & Lesser, V.R. (1995). *Experiences with a Multi-agent Design System.* Technical Report. Department of Computer Science, University of Massachusetts.

31. Nagendra Prasad, M.V., Lesser, V., & Lander, S. (1995). *Learning organizational roles in a heterogeneous multi-agent system.* Technical Report TR-95-35. Department of Computer Science, University of Massachusetts.

32. Nagendra Prasad, M.V., Lesser, V., & Lander, S. (1995). Learning experiments in a heterogeneous multi-agent system. In *Working Notes of the IJCAI95 Workshop on Adaptation and Learning in Multiagent Systems* (pp. 59–64).

33. Ohko, T., Hiraki, K., & Anzai, Y. (1995). LEMMING: A learning system for multi-robot environments. *Proceedings of the 1993 IEEE/RSJ International Conference on Intelligent Robots vand Systems* (Vol. 2, pp. 1131–1146).

34. Parker, L. (1993). Adaptive action selection for cooperative agent teams. *Proceedings of the Second International Conference on Simulation of Adaptive Behavior* (pp. 442–450).

35. Parker, L. (1993). Learning in cooperative robot teams. Paper presented at *IJCAI93 Workshop on Dynamically Interacting Robots.*

36. Payne, T.R., Edwards, P., & Green, C.L. (1995). Experience with rule induction and k-nearest neighbour methods for interface agents that learn. In (WS-IMLC95).

37. Pearson, D., & Huffman, S. (1995). Combining learning from instruction with recovery from incorrect knowledge. In (WS-IMLC95).

38. Provost, F.J. (1995). Scaling up inductive learning with massive parallelism. *Machine Learning.*

39. Provost, F.J., & Hennessy, D. (1994). Distributed machine learning: Scaling up with coarse-grained parallelism. *Proceedings of the Second International Conference on Intelligent Systems for Molecular Biology.*

40. Sandholm, T.W., & Crites, R.H. (1995). Multiagent reinforcement learning in the iterated prisoner's dilemma. *Biosystems*, Special Issue on the prisoner's dilemma.

41. Schaerf, A., Shoham, Y., & Tennenholtz, M. (1995). Adaptive load balancing: A study in multi-agent-learning. *Journal of Artificial Intelligence Research*, 2, 475–500.

42. Sekaran, M., & Sen, S. (1994). Multi-agent learning in non-cooperative domains. *Proceedings of the 12th National Conference on Artificial Intelligence* (Vol. 2, pp. 1489). Menlo Park, CA: AAAI Press/MIT Press.

43. Sen, S., Sekaran, M., & Hale, J. (1994). Learning to coordinate without shar-

ing information. *Proceedings of the 12th National Conference on Artificial Intelligence* (Vol. 1, pp. 426–431). Menlo Park, CA: AAAI Press/MIT Press.

44. Shavlik, J., & Maclin, R. (1995). Learning from instruction and experience in competitive situations. In (WS-IMLC95).

45. Shoham, Y., & Tennenholtz, M. (1992). Emergent conventions in multi-agent systems: initial experimental results and observations. *Proceedings of the Third International Conference on Principles of Knowledge Representation and Reasoning* (pp. 225–231).

46. Shoham, Y., & Tennenholtz, M. (1994). *Co-learning and the evolution of social activity.* Technical Report STAN-CS-TR-94-1511. Department of Computer Science, Stanford University.

47. Shoham, Y., & Tennenholtz, M. (1995). Social Laws for Artificial Agent Societies: Off-line Design. Appears in *Artificial Intelligence, 73.*

48. Sian, S.S. (1990). The role of cooperation in multi-agent learning. *Proceedings of the International Working Conference on Cooperating Knowledge Based Systems.* (pp. 164–177). Springer-Verlag.

49. Sian, S.S. (1991). Adaptation based on cooperative learning in multi-agent systems. In Y. Demazeau, & J.-P. Müller (Eds.), *Decentralized A.I. 2* (pp. 257–272). Amsterdam: North-Holland.

50. Sian, S.S. (1991). Extending learning to multiple agents: issues and a model for multi-agent machine learning (MA-ML). In Y. Kodratoff (Ed.), *Machine learning – EWSL-91* (pp. 440–456). Berlin: Springer-Verlag.

51. Sikora, R., & Shaw, M.J. (1990). *A double-layered learning approach to acquiring rules for financial classification.* Faculty Working Paper No. 90-1693. College of Commerce and Business Administration, University of Illinois at Urbana-Champaign.

52. Sikora, R., & Shaw, M.J. (1991). *A distributed problem-solving approach to inductive learning.* Faculty Working Paper 91-0109. College of Commerce and Business Administration, University of Illinois at Urbana-Champaign, Illinois.

53. Tan, M. (1993). Multi-agent reinforcement learning: Independent vs. cooperative agents. *Proceedings of the Tenth International Conference on Machine Learning* (pp. 330–337).

54. Tennenholtz, M. (1995). On Computational Social Laws for Dynamic Non-Homogeneous Social Structures. Appears in *Journal of Experimental and Theoretical Artificial Intelligence.*

55. Weiß, G. (1993). Collective learning and action coordination. *Proceedings of the 13th International Conference on Distributed Computing Systems* (pp. 203–209).

56. Weiß, G. (1993). Learning to coordinate actions in multi-agent systems. *Proceedings of the 13th International Conference on Artificial Intelligence* (Vol. 1, pp. 311–316).

57. Weiß, G. (1993). Action selection and learning in multi-agent environments. *Proceedings of the Second International Conference on Simulation of Adaptive Behavior* (pp. 502–510).

58. Weiß, G. (1993). Lernen und Aktionskoordinierung in Mehragentensystemen. In J. Müller (Ed.), *Verteilte Künstliche Intelligenz – Methoden und Anwendungen* (pp. 122–132). Mannheim: BI Verlag.

59. Weiß, G. (1994). *Some studies in distributed machine learning and organizational design*. Techn. Rep. FKI-189-94. Institut für Informatik, TU München.

60. Weiß, G. (1995). Distributed reinforcement learning. *Robotics and Autonomous Systems*, 15, 135–142.

61. Weiß, G. (1995). *Distributed machine learning*. Sankt Augustin: Infix-Verlag.

62. WS-IMLC95 (1995). Workshop "Agents that learn from other agents" held at the 1995 International Machine Learning Conference. (Proceedings are ALSO available at http://www.cs.wisc.edu/~shavlik/ml95w1/pubs.html.)

Theory

63. Daley, R.P., Kalyanasundaram, B., & Velauthapillai, M. (1992). Breaking the probability 1/2 barrier in fin-type learning. *Proceedings of the Fifth Annual Workshop on Computational Learning Theory* (pp. 203–217), Pittsburgh, Pennsylvania. ACM Press.

64. Daley, R.P., Kalyanasundaram, B., & Velauthapillai, M. (1992). The power of probabilism in popperian finite learning. *Proceedings of the Third International Workshop on Analogical and Inductive Inference* (pp. 151–169). Dagstuhl Castle, Germany.

65. Daley, R.P., Kalyanasundaram, B., & Velauthapillai, M. (1993). Capabilities of fallible finite learning. *Proceedings of the Sixth Annual Conference on Computational Learning Theory* (pp. 199–208), Santa Cruz, CA. ACM Press.

66. Daley, R.P., Pitt, L., Velauthapillai, M., Will, T. (1991). Relations between probabilistic and team one-shot learners. In L. Valiant & M. Warmuth (Eds.), *Proceedings of the Workshop on Computational Learning Theory* (pp. 228–239). Morgan Kaufmann.

67. Jain, S., & Sharma, A. (1990). Finite learning by a team. In M. Fulk & J. Case (Eds.), *Proceedings of the Third Annual Workshop on Computational Learning Theory* (pp. 163–177). Morgan Kaufmann.

68. Jain, S., & Sharma, A. (1990). Language learning by a team. In M.S. Paterson (Ed.), *Proceedings of the 17th International Colloquium on Automata, Languages and Programming* (pp. 153–166). Springer-Verlag.

69. Jain, S., & Sharma, A. (1993). *Computational limits on team identification of languages*. Technical Report 9301. School of Computer Science and Engineering, University of New South Wales.

70. Jain, S., & Sharma, A. (1993). Probability is more powerful than team for language identification. *Proceedings of the Sixth Annual Conference on Computational Learning Theory* (pp. 192–198). ACM Press.

71. Jain, S., & Sharma, A. (1994). *On aggregation teams of learning machines*. SCS&E Report no. 9405. School of Computer Science and Engineering, University of New South Wales.

72. Jain, S., & Sharma, A. (1995). Team learning of formal languages. In (WS-IMLC95).

73. Jain, S., Sharma, A., & Velauthapillai, M. (1994). *Finite identification of functions by teams with success ratio 1/2 and above. Journal of Computer and System Sciences.*

74. Pitt, L. (1984). A characterization of probabilistic inference. *Proceedings of the 25th Symposium on the Foundations of Computer Science.*

75. Pitt, L. (1989). Probabilistic inductive inference. *Journal of the ACM*, 36, 383–433.

76. Pitt, L., & Smith, C. (1988). Probability and plurality for aggregations of learning machines. *Information and Computation*, 77, 77–92.

77. Smith, C. (1982). The power of pluralism for automatic program synthesis. *Journal of the ACM*, 29, 1144–1165.

78. Velauthapillai, M. (1989). Inductive inference with bounded number of mind changes. *Proceedings of the Workshop on Computational Learning Theory* (pp. 200–213).

PART II: Work in Economics

79. Adler, P. (1990). Shared learning. *Management Science*, 36/8, 938–957.

80. Argyris, C. (1982). *Reasoning, learning and action: individual and organizational.* San Fransisco: Jossey-Bass.

81. Argyris, C. (1993). *On organizational learning.* Cambridge, Mass: Blackwell.

82. Argyris, C., & Schön, D.A. (1978). *Organizational learning.* Reading, MA: Addison-Wesley.

83. Arrow, K. (1962). The implications of learning by doing. *Review of Economic Studies*, 29, 166-170.

84. Bennis, W., & Nanus, B. (1985). Organizational learning: The management of the collective self. *New Management*, 3, 6–13.

85. Brown, J.S., & Duguid, P. (1991). Organizational learning and communities-of-practice: Toward a unified view of working, learning, and innovation. *Organization Science*, 2(1), 40–57.

86. Cangelosi, V.E., & Dill, W.R. (1965). Organizational learning: Observations toward a theory. *Administrative Science Quaterly*, 10, 175–203.

87. Cohen, M.D. (1986). Artificial intelligence and the dynamic performance of organizational designs. In J.G. March & R. Weissinger-Baylon (eds.), *Ambiguity and command* (pp. 53–71). Marshfield, Mass.: Pitman.

88. Cohen, M.D. (1991). Individual learning and organizational routine: Emerging connections. *Organization Science*, 2(1), 135–139.

89. Cohen, M.D. (1992). When can two heads learn better than one? Results from a computer model of organizational learning. In M. Masuch & M. Warglien (Eds.), *Artificial intelligence in organization and management theory* (pp. 175–188), Amsterdam: North-Holland.

90. Cohen, W., & Levinthal, D. (1990). Absorptive capacity: A new perspective on learning and innovation. *Administrative Science Quaterly*, 35, 128–152.

91. Cohen, M.D., March, J.G., & Olsen, J.P. (1972). A garbage can model of organizational choice. *Administrative Science Quaterly*, 17(1), 1–25.

92. Cohen, M.D., & Sproull, L.S. (1991) (Eds.). *Organization Science*, 2(1) [Special Issue on Organizational Learning].

93. Daft, R.L., & Huber, G.P. (1987). How organizations learn: A communication framework. *Research in the Sociology of Organizations*, 5, 1–36.

94. Derry, D. (1983). Decision-making, problem-solving, and organizational learning. *Omega*, 11, 321–328.

95. Dixon, N.M. (1990). Action learning, action science and learning new skills. *Industrial & Commercial Training*, 22(4), 1–16.

96. Dixon, N.M. (1992). Organizational learning: A review of the literature with implications for HRD professionals. *Human Resource Development Quaterly*, 3(1), Spring, 29–49.

97. Dodgson, M. (1993). Organizational learning: A review of some literatures. *Organization Studies*, 14/4, 375–394.

98. Duncan, R., & Weiss, A. (1979). Organizational learning: Implications for organizational design. In B.M. Staw (Ed.), *Research in organizational behavior* (Vol. 1, pp. 75–123). Greenwich, Conn.: JAI Press.

99. Easterby-Smith, M. (1990). Creating a learning organisation. *Personal Review*, 19(5), 24–28.

100. Epple, D., Argote, L., & Devadas, R. (1991). Organizational learning curves: A method for investigating intra-plant transfer of knowledge acquired through learning by doing. *Organization Science*, 2(1), 58–70.

101. Fiol, M., & Lyles, M.A. (1993). Organizational learning. *Academy of Management Review*, 10, 803–813.

102. Friedlander, F. (1983). Patterns of individual and organizational learning. In Shrivastava and Associates (Eds.), *The executive mind: New insights on managerial thought and action* (pp. 192–220). San Fransisco: Jossey-Bass.

103. Garratt, B. (1990). *Creating a learning organization: A guide to leadership, learning and development.*

104. Garratt, B., & Burgoyne, J.G. (1987). *The learning organization.* London: Fontana/Collins.

105. Grantham, C. (1994). The learning organization. In S.A. Katsikides (Ed.), *Informatics, organization and society* (pp. 228–250). Wien: Oldenbourg.

106. Hall, D.T., & Fukami, C.V. (1979). Organization design and adult learning. In B.M. Staw (Ed.), *Research in organizational behavior* (Vol. 1, pp. 125–167). Greenwich, Conn.: JAI Press.

107. Hedberg, B. (1981). How organizations learn and unlearn. In P.C. Nystrom & W.H. Starbuck (Eds.), *Handbook of organizational design* (Vol. 1, pp. 1–27). New York: Oxford University Press.

108. Herriott, S. R., Levinthal, D., & March, J. G. (1985). Learning from experience in organizations. *The American Economic Review*, 75(2), 298–302.

109. Huber, G.P. (1991). Organizational learning: The contributing processes and the literatures. *Organization Science*, 2(1), February, 88–115.

110. Hutchins, E. (1991). Organizing work by adaptation. *Organization Science*, 2(1), 14–39.

111. Jelinek, M. (1979). *Institutionalizing innovations: A study of organizational learning systems*. New York: Praeger.

112. Kim, D. (1993). The link between individual and organizational learning. *Sloan Management Review*, Fall, 37–50.

113. Lant, T. (1994). Computer simulations of organizations as experiential learning systems: Implications for organization theory. In K.M. Carley & M.J. Prietula (Eds.), *Computational organization theory*, Lawrence Erlbaum Associates, Inc.

114. Lant, T., & Mezias, S. (1990). Managing discontinuous change: a simulation study of organizational learning and entrepreneurship. *Strategic Management Journal*, 11, 147–179.

115. Lant, T., & Mezias, S. (1990). An organizational learning model of convergence and reorientation. *Strategic Management Journal*, 11, 147–179.

116. Levinthal, D.A. (1991). Organizational adaptation and environmental selection –Interrelated processes of change. *Organization Science*, 2(1), 140–145.

117. Levitt, B., & March, J.G. (1988). Organizational learning. *Annual Review of Sociology*, 14, 319–340.

118. Lounamaa, P.H., & March, J.G. (1987). Adaptive coordination of a learning team. *Management Science*, 33, 107–123.

119. Lundberg, C. (1989). On organizational learning: Implications and opportunities for expanding organizational development. *Research in Organizational Change and Development*, 3(6), 126–182.

120. March, J.G. (1991). Exploration and exploitation in organizational learning. *Organization Science*, 2(1), 71–87.

121. March, J.G., & Olsen, J.P. (1975). The uncertainty of the past: Organizational learning under ambiguity. *European Journal of Political Research*, 3, 147–171.

122. March, J.G., Sproull, L.S., & Tamuz, M. (1991). Learning from samples of one or fewer. *Organization Science*, 2(1), 1–13.

123. Marsick, V. (Ed.) (1987). *Learning in the workplace*. New York: Croom Helm.

124. Masuch, M., & Lapotin, P. (1989). Beyond garbage cans: An AI model of organizational choice. *Administrative Science Quaterly*, 34(1), 38–67.

125. Miles, R.H., & Randolph, W.A. (1980). Influence of organizational learning styles on early development. In J.R. Kimberly & R.H. Miles (Eds.), *The organizational life cycle: Issues in the creation, transformation, and decline of organizations* (pp. 44–82). San Francisco: Jossey-Bass.

126. Mills, D.Q., & Friesen, B. (1992). The learning organization. *European Management Journal*, 10(2), 146–156.

127. Mody, A. (1990). *Learning through allianes*. Washington: The World Bank.

128. Normann, R. (1985). Developing capabilities for organizational learning. In J.M. Pennings & Associates (Eds.), *Organizational strategy and change: New views on formulating and implementing strategic decisions* (pp. 217–248). San Francisco: Jossey-Bass.

129. Nystrom, P.C., & Starbuck, W.H. (1984). To avoid organizational crises, unlearn. *Organizational Dynamics*, 53–65.

130. Pautzke, G. (1989). *Die Evolution der organisatorischen Wissensbasis: Bausteine zu einer Theorie des organisatorischen Lernens*. Herrsching: Verlag Barbara Kirsch.

131. Pedler, M., Boydell, T., & Burgoyne, J. (1989). Towards the learning company. *Management Education and Development*, 20, 1–8.

132. Perelman, L. (1984). *The learning enterprise: Adult learning, human capital and economic development*. Washington, DC: Council of State Planning Agencies.

133. Probst, G.J.B., & Büchel, B.S.T. (1994). *Organisationales Lernen. Wettbewerbsvorteil der Zukunft*. Wiesbaden: Gabler.

134. Pucik, V. (1988). Strategic alliances, organizational learning, and competitive advantage: The HRD agenda. *Human Resource Management*, 27(1), 77–93.

135. Reinhardt, R. (1993). Das Modell organisationaler Lernfähigkeit und die Gestaltung lernfähiger Organisationen. Frankfurt am Main: Peter Lang.

136. Reber, G. (1992). Lernen, organisationales. In E. Frese (Ed.), Handwörterbuch der Organisation (pp. 1240–1255).

Revans, R.W. (1980). *Action learning: New techniques for management*. London: Blond & Briggs.

137. Sattelberger, T. (Ed.) (1994). *Die lernende Organisation. Konzepte für eine neue Qualität der Unternehmensführung*. Wiesbaden: Gabler.

138. Schein, E.H. (1993). How can organizations learn faster? The challenge of entering the green room. *Sloan Management Review*, Winter, 85–92.

139. Senge, P. (1990). *The Fifth Discipline: The art and practice of the learning organization*. New York: Doubleday.

140. Simon, H.A. (1991). Bounded rationality and organizational learning. *Organization Science*, 2(1), February, 125–134.

141. Shrivastava, P. (1983). A typology of organizational learning systems. *Journal of Management Studies*, 20, 7–28.

142. Starbuck, W.H., & Dutton, J.M. (1973). Designing adaptive organizations. *Journal of Business Policy*, 3, 21–28.

143. Stata, R. (1989). Organizational learning – The key to management innovation. *Sloan Management Review*, 30(3), 63–74.

144. Warglien, M. (1992). Exit, voice, and learning: Adaptive behavior and competition in a hotelling world. In M. Masuch & M. Warglien (Eds.), *Artificial intelligence in organization and management theory* (pp. 189–214), Amsterdam: North-Holland.

145. Weick, K.E. (1991). The nontraditional quality of organizational learning. *Organization Science*, 2(1), 116–124.

146. Wolff, R. (1982). *Der Prozeß des Organisierens: Zu einer Theorie des organisationellen Lernens*. Spardorf: Wilfer.

147. Yelle, L.E. (1990). The learning curve: Historical review and comprehensive survey. *Decision Sciences*, 10, 302–328.

PART III: Others

148. Bandura, A. (1977). *Social learning theory*. Englewood Cliffs, NJ: Prentice-Hall,
149. Dillenbourg, P., Mendelsohn, P., & Schneider, D. (1994). The distribution of pedagogical roles in a multi-agent learning environment. In R. Lewis & P. Mendelsohn (Eds.), *Lessons from Learning* (pp. 199–216). Amsterdam: North-Holland. .
150. Dillenbourg, P., Baker, M., Blaye, A., & O'Malley, C. (1995, to appear). The evolution of research on collaborative learning. In H. Spada & P. Reimann (Eds.), *Learning in Humans and Machines*.
151. Laughlin, P.R. (1988). Collective induction: group performance, social combination processes, and mutual majority and minority influence. *Journal of Personality and Social Psychology*, 54(2), 254–267.
152. Mandl, H., & Renkl, A. (1992). A plea for "more local" theories of cooperative learning. *Learning and Instruction*, 2, 281–285.
153. Roschelle, J. (1992). Learning by collaboration: Convergent conceptual change. *Journal of the Learning Sciences*, 2, 235–276.
154. Slavin, R.E. (1983). *Cooperative learning*. New York: Longman.

Refinement in Agent Groups

Ciara Byrne and Peter Edwards
{byrne, pedwards}@csd.abdn.ac.uk

Department of Computing Science,
King's College,
University of Aberdeen,
Aberdeen,
Scotland AB9 2UE

Abstract. A group of intelligent agents may work together in order to solve a problem or achieve a common goal. If the group fails to achieve a goal, it may be able to adapt its behaviour so that such a goal can be achieved in the future. One of the ways in which the behaviour of the agent group can be changed is by refining the knowledge of individual agents. We are developing a distributed refinement system called DRAMA (Distributed Refinement Among Multiple Agents) to perform this task. The system makes use of a special type of agent called a refinement facilitator which coordinates the refinement process within the agent group.

1 Motivation

Suppose that a group of people want to cook Christmas dinner. They divide up the work in some manner: one person is to prepare the turkey, another to make the Christmas cake, etc. The goal of the group is to produce the meal at an appropriate time on Christmas day and this goal can only be achieved if all members of the group contribute. The person who is supposed to make the Christmas cake doesn't start preparing it until Christmas morning. He reads the recipe and discovers that he doesn't have all the required ingredients and since there are no shops open, he is unable to make the cake. In a different case, he may make the cake but find that he can't cook it because the oven is already being used to cook the turkey. Another possibility is that another member of the group sleeps in and therefore fails to carry out his task. These are some examples of how a group goal fails due to the actions of one or more of the participants. How can the same group of agents ensure that it will succeed if it attempts to cook Christmas dinner next year? In other words, how can the group ensure that it will be able to achieve a similar goal in the future?

A group of intelligent agents should be able to ensure that a failure is not repeated by adapting their behaviour. Adaptation can be achieved by using machine learning techniques to refine the knowledge of agents. The aim of learning in any intelligent system should be the improvement of the performance of that system. Where the system consists of a number of interacting intelligent agents, performance may be evaluated by the coherence of the agent group or from the point of view of individual agents' success in achieving their goals. "Coherence will refer to how well the system behaves as a unit" [1]. Coherence may be measured along several dimensions including the quality of the solutions which the system produces, the efficiency with which solutions are produced and how gracefully performance degrades in the presence of failure or uncertainty.

This paper is concerned with failure-driven learning, i.e. learning is prompted by the failure of the agent group to achieve a goal. Performance is rated by solution quality in the sense that the agent group either finds a solution (achieves the group goal) or fails to find one (the group goal fails). The process of refining the knowledge of agents attempts to improve solution quality by allowing the agent group to avoid failures in the future.

2 The Refinement Problem

Techniques for refining the knowledge held in a single knowledge base have already been extensively investigated [2] [3] [4] [5]. The process of refining the multiple related knowledge bases of a group of cooperating agents presents unique challenges. In addition to their domain knowledge, social agents have knowledge that allows them to interact with others. Agents may represent knowledge in different ways. Since agents each have their own knowledge base, finding the failure point (or failure points) in the group's knowledge is a much more complex problem than in a single knowledge base. Refining one agent's knowledge may change its behaviour in a manner that affects other agents-who will need to react to these changes in an appropriate manner. It may be also be desirable to maintain consistency between the knowledge bases of various agents.

2.1 The Knowledge of Agents

An agent which interacts with other agents needs two distinct types of knowledge: domain knowledge and social knowledge. The agent's domain knowledge concerns its problem-solving domain and environment. An agent's social knowledge allows it to interact with other agents. This knowledge may include the following:

Communication: Knowledge about the physical means of inter-agent communication (e.g. information about communication channels and the locations of agents) and an inter-agent communication language.

Interaction: How to interact with other agents in order to procure services, perform tasks for others, etc. An agent may, for example, know how to use a cooperation strategy such as the Contract Net Protocol [6]).

Agent Models: An agent can use these models to identify other agents with whom it is useful to interact, and to make this interaction more effective. For example, an agent may wish to determine which agents have the skills necessary to perform a particular task. A model may contain information such as the skills of other agents and their level of authority in the group.

2.2 Failures

Agents may have different knowledge bases and disparate views of their environment. Since social agents interact with other agents as well as the environment, the possibilities for failure increase. There are three basic phases in the process of achieving a group goal: task decomposition, task allocation and the coordination of tasks while they are being carried out. Failures may occur if agents commit errors during any of these phases. Task decomposition may be incorrect or insufficient. In the case of insufficient decomposition, the agent to whom the task is allocated may have the skills necessary to perform the task but cannot relate the task description to these skills. For example, if one agent is allocated the task "make a Christmas cake", that agent may be able to measure ingredients, mix them, use the oven, etc. but does not have a recipe for Christmas cake. Task decomposition and allocation may not take into account dependencies between tasks, e.g. the ingredients for the meal must be purchased before the cooking can be done. Failures may also be caused by allocating a task to an agent which cannot perform it or by failing to allocate a task redundantly when agents are unreliable. During the execution of subtasks, an agent may fail to complete a task. This may prohibit another agent from performing its task, e.g. by using a cooking utensil which that agent needs and not returning it. An agent may fail to share important information in a timely fashion, e.g. by not informing other agents that it has finished using the oven (if this would be appropriate). These are just some examples of the new range of failures that are possible when a group of agents attempt to achieve group goals as opposed to individual ones.

2.3 Faults in Knowledge Bases

Any of the failures described above are the result of faults in the knowledge of one or more agents in a group. Faults in a knowledge base include incorrectness, incompleteness, inconsistency, redundancy and intractability. The meaning of these terms may require some reinterpretation when applied to the collective knowledge of a group of agents rather than a single knowledge base.

Incorrectness: Some part of the knowledge is inaccurate. The question of context is important here as the same piece of knowledge may be correct in some contexts and not in others. As different agents may use the same knowledge in different contexts this issue is even more important in an agent system.

Incompleteness: Some necessary knowledge is missing. In the case of social agents, incompleteness in social knowledge is an additional problem.

Inconsistency: While this is a fault in the knowledge of a single agent, it may not always be necessary to maintain consistency between the knowledge bases of group members.

Redundancy: While redundancy in a knowledge base may not actually cause failures, it is usually desirable to make a knowledge base as compact as possible. On the other hand, redundancy is *necessary* in an agent group if the agents share a common environment or have similiar abilities.

Intractability: It is too expensive to achieve the goal using the current knowledge. For example, an agent group may use an interaction protocol which means that the group uses too many resources (e.g. time) when attempting to achieve a goal. In this case, social knowledge may need to be refined in order to allow agents to interact in a more efficient manner.

3 Designing a Distributed Refinement System

Refinement systems generally execute a cycle similar to the following (based on EITHER [2]): Recognise that a fault has occurred, locate the failure point (or postulate several possible failure points) and determine what refinements need to be made to the faulty knowledge. The existing knowledge and examples of the concept whose definition is considered to be faulty may be used to guide the choice of refinements. Examples of concepts defined in the knowledge base are classified as either positive (an example of the concept) or negative (not an example of the concept). Classification is usually performed by an oracle. An oracle may also be used to detemine when a failure has occurred and to help locate the failure point. We hypothesise that while oracles may exist for each individual agent, there may not always be a single oracle that can evaluate the knowledge of the entire agent group. As a starting point for designing any refinement system for multiple agents, it is therefore useful to consider a number of questions:

1. How will the system recognise that a failure has occurred?
2. How will the failure point be located?
3. Where do the examples originate and how are they classified?
4. What is the form of an example?
5. How are refinements generated?
6. If there are several possible refinements, how are the final refinement(s) chosen?
7. When the knowledge of one agent is refined, will other agents in the group need to have their knowledge updated in some way?
8. Will an autonomous agent accept refinements to its knowledge which originate from some external entity?

3.1 The Argument Against Centralisation

One possible solution to the refinement problem would involve collecting the knowledge of all agents and refining it in a similar manner to that employed for a single knowledge base. Of course, consideration would need to be given to the fact that the knowledge originated from several different agents. However, we would predict several problems with this approach. Agents may represent knowledge in different ways and still be able to cooperate. Therefore, the knowledge bases of individual agents would have to be translated into a common representation before refinement could occur and the refined knowledge retranslated into the agents' individual representations. How would knowledge be reassigned to agents once it had been refined in conjunction with the knowledge of other agents? How would the refinement system determine when inconsistency and redundancy between agent knowledge bases is necessary and when it is a problem? If the knowledge of different agents is contradictory how can it be determined which is correct? In addition, a centralised refinement system would require access to the internal structure of agents and this may not always be desirable. In conclusion, we feel that this would constitute a centralised solution to a distributed problem and we consider a distributed solution to be more appropriate.

3.2 A Distributed Approach

We believe that a group of agents can determine the causes of a failure and implement an effective set of refinements if they cooperate by sharing their knowledge and different perspectives on a failure. Our refinement system DRAMA (Distributed Refinement Among Multiple Agents) consists of two parts: a refinement module within agents and a refinement facilitator. Agents use the refinement module to generate refinements to their own knowledge. This can be regarded as an extra skill which agents possess in addition to the skills which they use in problem-solving. The facilitator coordinates the refinement process within the group but does not itself generate refinements [1]. Agents recognise that a failure has occurred and inform the facilitator which then gathers refinement proposals from relevant agents. The facilitator evaluates the proposed refinements and chooses a subset for implementation; in other words it acts as a filter for refinements.

We believe that this approach has several advantages. It allows agents to retain their autonomy by letting them propose refinements to their own knowledge rather than having refinements imposed upon them. Difficulties arise in the refinement process because individual agents only have a limited view of any failure which arises in the achievement of a group goal. The facilitator attempts to solve this problem by considering the views of all agents who may have contributed to the failure. The capabilities of the facilitator could possibly be distributed among the agents in the group but the use of a single facilitator agent reduces

---

[1] One of the problem-solving agents in the group may also act as a facilitator.

the amount of inter-agent communication and negotiation that would otherwise be necessary.

4 GOAL

We decided to test this approach to refinement by applying it to agents written in an agent-oriented programming language called GOAL (Goal-Oriented Agent Language). Agent-oriented programming [7] is a new programming paradigm which attempts to use mentalistic concepts such as beliefs, desires and intentions to formally describe the properties of agents. GOAL is based on Agent-K [8]. An Agent-K agent is specified in terms of its capabilities, a set of initial beliefs and a number of commitment rules. An agent's *capabilities* are the actions which it can perform. A *belief* is a logical statement which the agent "believes" to be true at a particular point in time. An agent's beliefs may change over time. When an agent decides to carry out an action, it forms a *commitment* to do so. A commitment to perform an action may be made in response to a request from another agent. One of the ways in which commitments can be formed is by the firing of a commitment rule. A commitment rule's conditions are matched against incoming messages and the agent's current mental state. If the rule fires, then a commitment is formed to perform the action requested by the message sender. Agents use KQML (Knowledge Query and Manipulation Language) [9] messages for inter-agent communication.

4.1 The Test Domain

We have implemented a simple hunter-prey scenario using agents programmed in GOAL. We chose this domain because it has previously been used in the DAI literature [10] and both agents and their environment can be defined at various levels of complexity. During experimentation, the environment may be made progressively more realistic and complex, thereby making it more difficult for agents to achieve their goals. The domain has the characteristics that it is dynamic, ongoing and unpredictable. The aim of refinement is the improvement of the performance of the agent group. In our test domain, performance is measured by the quality of solution produced. In the simple scenarios discussed here, there are only two possible evaluations of solution quality: either a solution is found, i.e. the group goal is achieved, or it is not. Agents are hunters who seek and kill prey. Some hunters have the ability to initiate cooperation in order to achieve goals such as the killing of a large prey by a group of hunters. Unless they are involved in cooperation, hunter agents execute a very simple cycle of actions: find a prey, move to the prey if it is not in the current location, attack the prey and eat it. A special world agent simulates the environment by periodically updating agents with new sets of beliefs about the environmental state. How much of the world a hunter can "see" depends on a vision-range parameter which is set in the world agent. We expect this test scenario to become more complex as our work proceeds.

4.2   The GOAL Language

In addition to beliefs, capabilities and commitment rules, GOAL also allows an agent's individual goals to be specified in the form of a simple goal tree. The structure of a GOAL agent is shown in Fig.1. High-level goals are decomposed into subgoals and eventually primitive actions. Some goals require the cooperation of other agents. These group goals are described by the number and types of agents needed to achieve them and the actions which each of the agents will be required to take. When an agent wants to achieve a group goal, it requests the cooperation of appropriate agents. If they agree to participate, it sends them instructions during cooperation and dissolves the group either when the group goal has been achieved or cannot be achieved. All agents except the agent which initiated cooperation suspend their own goals during cooperation. As a result, agents must either be altruistic or believe implicitly that they will benefit from cooperation.

Fig. 1. A GOAL Agent

Associated with each action are various preconditions which must be satisfied before it can be performed. Two types of preconditions are defined: a *constraint set* and a set of *immediate preconditions*. The constraint set includes constraints on the characteristics of the agents with which the agent is currently cooperating (Wholist); when (When) and why (Why) the goal or action is being performed; and the arguments of the action (Arglist). Since there may be several precondition sets associated with a particular action, an index number is used to distinguish between them. A constraint set thus has the form given in Fig.2.

The *precond* field here consists of the set of immediate preconditions associated with the constraint set. The constraints are evaluated when an action or goal is under consideration. If a constraint set is satisfied, then the agent forms an instantiation [2] of the goal or action and forms a commitment to perform it.

```
constraints(Action,
            When,
            Arglist,
            Wholist,
            Why,
            Index,
            precond(Arg-names, Precond-sets))
```

Fig. 2. The syntax of a precondition set

Even when an agent has decided to take an action, additional preconditions concerning the mental state of the agent and the state of the world may need to be evaluated immediately before the execution of an action. We call this type of precondition an *immediate precondition*. The total precondition set shown in Fig.3 means that *Hunter1* will not form an instantiation of the action *eat(X)* unless its argument is an object of type *prey* and the action is being requested by another agent. Whether the agent is cooperating or not is irrelevant. The immediate preconditions indicate that the agent will not attempt to execute the action unless it is in the same position as the prey and the prey is dead. The reason for this separation of constraints and immediate preconditions is to differentiate the factors taken into consideration when making a commitment to perform an action, and the world state immediately before the action is attempted. The world state may change in the time between the formation of the commitment and its execution.

An agent may also have knowledge in the form of domain hierarchies. A hierarchy will describe a particular aspect of the agent's task or environment. For example, in the hunter-prey domain there may be a hierarchy which defines the prey in the environment as either small or large prey. Hierarchies are used to evaluate constraints, e.g. the constraint set of an action such as *attack(Object)* may contain a constraint which specifies that *Object* should be a small prey.

5 Refinement Within Agents

Agents propose refinements to their own knowledge. In theory, refinements could be made to any of the types of knowledge which GOAL agents possess, i.e. definitions of goals and group goals, domain hierarchies, capabilities and commitment

---

[2] Examples of instantiations are given later in this paper.

```
constraints(eat,
            time (−),
            [prey(−)],
            −,
            other-request(−),
            1,
            precond([Prey],
                    [[believes(hunter1, [Now, object-position(hunter1, Here)], t),
                      believes(hunter1, [Now, object-position(Prey, Here)], t),
                      believes(hunter1, [Now, object-status(Prey, dead)], t)]])).
```

Fig. 3. Example precondition set from the hunter-prey domain

rules. The form which a refinement will take depends on the type of knowledge being refined. For example, knowledge about capabilities may be changed by adding or deleting a belief about the capabilities of a particular agent, whereas the definition of a group goal may be modified by reallocating an action to an agent or increasing the number of cooperating agents. Initially, we have given agents the ability to refine precondition sets. The agent gathers information relevant to the fault in order to guide refinement, determines which type of knowledge needs to be refined (if refinements to several types of knowledge are possible) and applies refinement operators in order to generate a refinement. In the case of preconditions, GOAL allows agents to record information about the circumstances in which actions have been taken in the past. In order to participate in the refinement process an agent needs to know the following: how to describe faults to the facilitator and understand descriptions of faults, how to generate refinements and describe them, and how to update its knowledge if modifications are required due to the refinement of another agent's knowledge.

To generate refinements to preconditions, agents need information about the context in which a particular action has been performed in the past. Records of the circumstances in which actions are taken, i.e. the evaluation of constraints and preconditions, are continuously generated during an agent's execution. Such a record is termed an *instantiation* and has the form given in Fig. 4. The instantiation of a successful action can be seen as a positive example and an unsuccessful one as a negative example. If there are multiple precondition sets for a particular action, we need to identify which set has been satisfied. *C-set* indicates the constraint set that was satisfied by this instantiation and *P-set* the set of immediate preconditions that was satisfied.

In general, existing refinement systems work by applying generalisation operators when the fault involves the misclassification of a positive example and specialisation operators when a negative example is misclassified. In this context, a positive example of an action is one which was successful, e.g. an attempt to take the action *move-to([1,2])* results in the agent's new position being [1,2]. A inst(Action, When, Arglist, Wholist, Why, C-set, P-set, Evals)

inst(move-to, [2,8,95,9,20,3], [[1,3]], [], hunter1, 1, 2, [t,t,t])

Fig. 4. The syntax of an instantiation

negative example would be the execution of an action in inappropriate circumstances, e.g. *attack(X)* where X is another hunter. Because there are two distinct types of precondition (constraints and immediate preconditions) in our system, we use the following set of refinement operators:

1. Specialise an existing constraint set.
2. Delete a constraint set.
3. Generalise an existing constraint set.
4. Add a new constraint set.
5. Delete an immediate precondition from an existing set.
6. Add a new set of immediate preconditions.
7. Add an immediate precondition to an existing set.
8. Delete a set of immediate preconditions.

An agent may apply some combination of these operators in order to generate a suitable refinement. Although these refinement operators may be used in any domain, a number of characteristics of the hunter-prey domain will determine exactly how they will function and what strategy is used to control their application. For example, we are assuming that a hunter's example set will consist largely of positive examples with few, if any, negative examples of actions. Therefore, refinement operators must be able to use positive example sets effectively. Obviously, this condition may not apply in other problem domains. Therefore, evaluating the generality of results obtained in this particular domain may be problematic. However, from the perspective of the facilitator the manner in which operators generate refinements is an internal implementation detail of the agents. The important thing from the point of view of the agent group is that refinements *are* generated and that they are presented in an appropriate manner to the refinement facilitator.

6 The Refinement Facilitator

A facilitator coordinates interaction between agents. For example, KQML [9] communication facilitators are used to manage message traffic among other agents by routing messages to appropriate agents, providing buffering and translation facilities, etc. The task of the refinement facilitator is to coordinate refinement by processing refinement requests from agents, soliciting refinement proposals, choosing the refinements which will eventually be implemented and informing agents of changes to the knowledge of other agents. Much of the facilitator's knowledge will be domain-independent because it is concerned with general issues such as types of refinements and the relationships between them. It will also require some domain-specific knowledge in order to work with a particular group of agents. The refinement facilitator requires the following types of knowledge:

Information about agents: Names and URLs (Universal Resource Locators) of agents.

Descriptions of faults and refinements: The facilitator needs to know how faults are described so that it can correctly interpret and process descriptions received from agents. Similarly, the facilitator must correctly interpret descriptions of proposed refinements.

Refinement types: Refinements can be divided into categories depending on the type of knowledge being modified, e.g. precondition sets or a definition of a group goal.

Fault decomposition: The facilitator must know how to use a fault description provided by an agent to identify possible failure points and solicit refinements from appropriate agents.

Relationships between refinement types: We have proposed a number of possible relationships between refinements: refinements can be equivalent, complementary or conflicting. Two different refinements may have the same effect as regards correcting a fault, but involve different changes to the knowledge of agents. These refinements can be considered to be equivalent. Refinements conflict if they negate each other's effects and complement each other if both (or several) are needed to repair a fault.

Rating refinements: If there are alternative sets of refinements which may be applied to correct a fault, then the facilitator needs to have some way of choosing between them. A rating scheme is used to calculate ratings for refinements and the refinement set that achieves the best overall rating is approved.

Knowledge update rules: When an agent makes changes to its knowledge, other agents may need to be informed. This may be necessary in order to maintain consistency between the knowledge bases of agents. In other cases, agents may need to be informed about a refinement because of the changes this will cause to the future behaviour of an agent. A knowledge update rule thus defines a list of agents which should receive messages describing the refinement which occurred.

7 An Example

To illustrate our ideas, we present an account of how DRAMA would rectify a simple fault from the hunter-prey domain. The domain knowledge in this scenario consists of hierarchies which classify agents and prey objects, locations, and reasons for performing actions. For example, *Hunter1* has the domain knowledge shown in Fig.5. The agent's environment is divided into squares, each of which are referenced by x and y coordinates. Each square is characterised by the dominant type of terrain in that square, e.g. marshland. Prey animals in the environment are classified as large or small. Finally, agents may perform actions under their own initiative or because of a request from another agent.

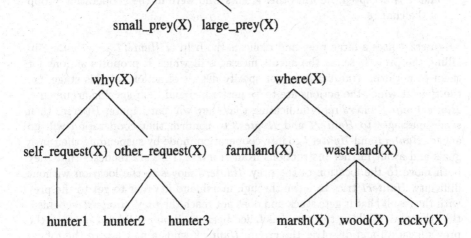

Fig. 5. Domain Hierarchies of Hunter1

All hunters have the ability to generate refinements that modify the precondition sets of particular actions. In addition, *Hunter2* can propose refinements involving changes to its beliefs about the capabilities of an agent. The simple refinement facilitator used in this example has the following knowledge:

Information about agents: *Hunter1, Hunter2, Hunter3* and their respective URLs.

Refinement types:

modify-preconds: An agent modifies the set of preconditions (either a constraint set or immediate preconditions) associated with one of its actions.

modify-capabilities: An agent modifies its view of the capabilities of another agent, e.g. by adding or removing an action from the list of actions that it believes another agent is capable of performing.

Relationships between refinements: If a *modify-preconds* refinement proposed by agent A is concerned with action X and a *modify-capabilities* refinement is concerned with the ability of A to perform X, the two refinements are considered equivalent.

Rating strategies: A refinement to a precondition set receives a better rating than a refinement to knowledge about capabilities.

Knowledge update rules: If the agent which initiated cooperation (i.e. the owner of the group goal) proposed a refinement of type *modify-capabilities* and it is accepted, inform other agents who were in the cooperating group of the change.

Hunter2 senses a large prey and requests the help of *Hunter1* and *Hunter3* in killing the prey. It sends the agents messages in which it proposes actions for them to perform. *Hunter2* does not specify details of actions at this stage, i.e. the time at which the actions are to be performed and their specific arguments. *Hunter1* and *Hunter3* reply indicating that they will participate. *Hunter2* then sends messages to *Hunter1* and *Hunter3* to confirm that cooperation will go ahead. *Hunter1* and *Hunter3* go into cooperation mode by suspending their own goals and await further instructions from *Hunter2*. *Hunter2* requests that they both move to the location of the prey. *Hunter3* moves to the location without difficulty. *Hunter1* tries to move through marshland in order to get to the prey with the result that it gets stuck and does not reach the prey. *Hunter2* recognises that the goal of killing the prey has failed because *Hunter1* did not move to the prey's location and dissolves the group. *Hunter2* sends a message to the refinement facilitator which names the agents involved in cooperation and describes the nature of the failure. In this case there is only one failure point. In more complex scenarios, there may be multiple failure points. The type of fault involved is the non-performance of an agreed action by *Hunter1*. The facilitator requests refinement proposals from both *Hunter1* and *Hunter2*. The facilitator will have determined from the failure description that *Hunter3* was not responsible for the failure since it carried out the requested actions.

As *Hunter1* can only generate refinements of type *modify-preconds*, it attempts to find a refinement of this type. On receipt of the request for refinement proposals, *Hunter1* examines its actions. Agents move from one location to another by executing a series of *next-location* primitive actions. *Next-location(Loc)* causes the agent to move one square in a given direction. *Hunter1* plotted a route through marshland because this was the most direct route to its target location and the precondition set for next-location allowed it to do so. The total precondition set for *next-location(Loc)* is shown in Fig.6.

```
constraint(next-location,
           time(−),
           [wasteland(−)],
           −,
           why(−),
           1,
           precond([Loc], []))
```

Fig. 6. Hunter1's precondition set for the *next-location* action

Because this is an example of an action being performed in the wrong circumstances, the agent applies a specialisation operator. In this case, *Hunter1* does not know whether the constraint set or the set of immediate preconditions is at fault. The constraint set is specialised due to the existence of a heuristic which

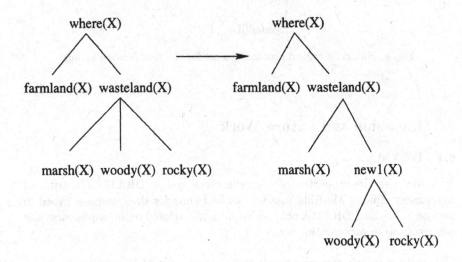

Fig. 7. Changes to the domain hierarchies

specifies that it is better to refine a constraint set than a set of immediate preconditions. This is because the agent has more information (i.e. evaluations of constraint sets in previous actions) on which to base refinements of the former type. The refinement operator finds the first constraint in the set which can be specialised sufficiently to exclude the failing example. In this case, the *where* constraint of the *next-location* action is specialised sufficiently to exclude moves through marshland. The specialised constraint should allow the agent to move through any type of wasteland except marshland. The domain hierarchy for the *where* constraint must be changed in order to allow this. A new predicate, *new1*, is created that covers woodland and rocky areas but not marshland. The new domain hierarchies are shown in Fig.7. The new predicate replaces the old *where* constraint in the specialised constraint set (shown in Fig.8).

Having found this possible refinement, *Hunter1* suggests it to the facilitator. Since *Hunter2* has the ability to generate refinements of type *modify-capability*, it may suggest a change in its belief that *Hunter1* can move to a given location. The facilitator decides that the two refinements are equivalent. By using the rating strategy it chooses the refinement proposed by *Hunter1*. The facilitator informs *Hunter1* that it can carry out the refinement.

```
constraints(next-location,
            time(−),
            [new1(−)],
            -,
            why(−),
            1,
            precond([Loc], []))
```

Fig. 8. Hunter1's refined precondition set for the *next-location* action

8 Discussion and Future Work

8.1 DRAMA

To summarise the properties of our refinement system DRAMA (Distributed Refinement Among Multiple Agents), we will consider the questions raised in Section 3. To date, DRAMA only addresses faults related to incompleteness and incorrectness in precondition sets.

How will the system recognise that a failure has occurred? In general, the leader of a group goal will recognise that a failure has occurred because the goal has not been achieved. It will then inform the refinement facilitator that a failure has occurred.

How will the failure point be located? Agents analyse their own knowledge, postulate possible failure points and propose refinements to correct their knowledge.

What is the form of an example? Examples take the form of instantiations of actions.

Where do examples come from and how are they classified? Agents continuously gather examples of the use of actions. The agent observes the results of its actions and thereby classifies examples as successful or unsuccessful. Classification may also originate from an external source, e.g. the leader of a group goal (the agent which initiated cooperation).

If there are several possible refinements, how are refinements chosen? The facilitator uses its knowledge of the relationships between refinements in order to sort refinements into sets and then uses a rating strategy to choose the "best" set. In essence, it acts as a filter for refinements.

When the knowledge of one agent is refined, will other agents in the group need their knowledge updated in some way? Knowledge update rules fulfill this function by informing agents of changes to the knowledge of other agents. Agents which receive updates can use this information to change their own knowledge so that it remains consistent with the knowledge of others.

Will an autonomous agent accept refinements to its knowledge which originate from some external entity? Agents suggest refinements to their own knowledge and therefore refinements do not originate from an external source.

8.2 Evaluating Generality

Our ultimate aim is to design an approach to refinement that is generally applicable in two different senses; namely that it can be used in multiple domains and with agents which are written in diverse languages.

Agents work together in order to solve problems from a particular problem domain. A refinement scheme should be independent of any particular domain. We are currently designing a domain-independent framework for a refinement facilitator. This framework will need to be instantiated with some domain-specific knowledge in order to function with agents in a particular problem domain, e.g. the hunter-prey domain. The basic refinement cycle outlined above, the types of knowledge which a facilitator needs and the way in which the facilitator uses its knowledge should remain broadly the same regardless of the domain.

Designing a refinement system that is effective when applied to agents written in languages other than GOAL is a longer term objective, and may prove too complex to achieve. A language-independent facilitator is possible if agents can describe faults and refinements in a manner that is independent of the language in which they are written. Such a facilitator would need to be able to interpret these high-level descriptions.

8.3 Future Work

There are many issues, in addition to those outlined in earlier sections, which we plan to explore. These include the use of knowledge update rules, side-effect refinements, maintaining consistency between the knowledge of agents, more direct exchange of knowledge between agents, and increasing agents' input into the selection of refinements by the facilitator. A side-effect refinement is one which does not directly contribute to the resolution of the current failure but could allow the agent to avoid different types of failure in the future. Suppose an agent is asked to move to a particular location by the leader of a group goal. For some reason moving to this location has a detrimental effect on the agent. During the refinement phase it is determined that this action was not necessary in order to achieve the goal so it is removed from the definition of the group goal. However, it would also be beneficial to the agent to refine its precondition set so that it will not move to this location again. This is a side-effect refinement. Another type of side-effect refinement could occur when one agent modifies a precondition set for an action and other agents update their precondition sets with the refined one. Performance may also be improved by allowing agents to suggest refinements to each other's knowledge, provide confidence factors for refinements proposed by other agents and exchange information (such as instantiations) which can be used to guide the generation of refinements.

It should be emphasised that this is very much work in progress and our ideas will develop as we put them into practice. To date, we have concluded that agents need information on the context in which they take actions in order to generate refinements to precondition sets. We have made a first attempt to facilitate the continuous generation of such information by extending an existing agent language. We have implemented a basic hunter-prey scenario by programming a group of agents in this language. Our aims in the immediate future include building a prototype refinement facilitator and expanding the range of refinements which an agent can make. We also intend to test the refinement scheme in progressively more complex versions of the hunter-prey domain and eventually in a completely new domain.

References

1. A. H. Bond and L. Gasser, *An Analysis of Problems and Research in DAI*, Readings in Distributed Artificial Intelligence (1988), Morgan-Kaufmann, 3–35.
2. D. Ourston and R.J. Mooney, *Changing the Rules: A Comprehensive Approach to Theory Refinement*, Proceedings of the Eighth International Conference on Machine Learning (1991), 485–489.
3. G. Towell, J. Shavlik and M. Noordewier, *Refinement of Approximate Domain Theories by Knowledge-Based Neural Networks*, Proceedings of the Eighth National Conference on Artificial Intelligence (1990), 861–866.
4. B.L. Richards and R.J. Mooney, *Learning Relations by Pathfinding*, Proceedings of the Tenth National Conference on Artificial Intelligence (1992), 723–738.

5. S. Craw and D. Sleeman, *The Flexibility of Speculative Refinement*, Machine Learning: Proceedings of the Eighth International Workshop (1991), 28–32.

6. R.G. Smith, *The Contract Net Protocol: High-Level Communication and Control in a Distributed Problem Solver*, IEEE Transactions on Computers, C-29:12 (1980), 1104–1113.

7. Y. Shoham, *Agent-Oriented Programming*, Technical Report STAN-CS-1335-90 (1990), Department of Computer Science, Stanford University.

8. W. Davies and P. Edwards, *Agent-K: An Integration of AOP and KQML*, CIKM Workshop on Intelligent Information Agents (1994), Y. Labrou and T. Finin (Eds), National Institute of Standards and Technology, Gaithersburg, Maryland.

9. T. Finin, R. Fritzson, D. McKay et al, *An Overview of KQML: A Knowledge Query and Manipulation Language*, Technical Report (1992), Department of Computer Science, University of Maryland.

10. M. Tan, *Multi-Agent Reinforcement Learning: Independent vs. Cooperative Agents*, Machine Learning: Proceedings of the Tenth International Conference (1993), 330–337.

Opponent Modeling in Multi-Agent Systems

David Carmel and Shaul Markovitch

Computer Science Department,
Technion, Haifa 32000, Israel,
{carmel|shaulm}@cs.technion.ac.il

Abstract. Agents that operate in a multi-agent system need an efficient strategy to handle their encounters with other agents involved. Searching for an optimal interactive strategy is a hard problem because it depends mostly on the behavior of the others. In this work, interaction among agents is represented as a repeated two-player game, where the agents' objective is to look for a strategy that maximizes their expected sum of rewards in the game. We assume that agents' strategies can be modeled as finite automata. A *model-based* approach is presented as a possible method for learning an effective interactive strategy. First, we describe how an agent should find an optimal strategy against a given model. Second, we present a heuristic algorithm that infers a model of the opponent's automaton from its input/output behavior. A set of experiments that show the potential merit of the algorithm is reported as well.

1 Introduction

One of the central issues of research in Multi-Agent Systems (MAS) deals with the development of effective interactive mechanisms among selfish and rational autonomous agents. Agents that operate in MAS must consider the existence of other agents involved and need an efficient interactive strategy to handle their encounters with others. For example, a *software agent* that searches for information in the Internet may benefit from cooperating with other software agents that share similar goals. The agent might agree to retrieve information for other agents in exchange for information retrieved by them.

When looking for an efficient strategy for interaction, an agent must consider two main outcomes of its behavior. First, the direct reward for its action during the current encounter with others. Second, the effect of its behavior on the expected future behavior of the other agents. Going back to the example, cooperation may increase the cost of the current search due to the overhead of helping others, but it may also increase cooperation in the future.

Designing an optimal strategy for interaction is a hard problem because its effectiveness depends mostly on the strategies of the other agents involved. However, the agents are autonomous and selfish, hence their strategies are private. One way to deal with this problem is to endow agents with the ability to learn the strategies of others based on their interaction experience. Recent studies

[Lit94, SSH94, ST94, SC95] describe various methods for incorporating learning into MAS. In this work, we suggest a *model-based* approach for learning an efficient interactive strategy.

In our framework interactions among agents are represented as a repeated two-player game. The objective of each agent is to look for an interaction strategy that maximizes its expected sum of rewards in the game. We assume that each agent is indifferent to the rewards of its opponents (from now on we call the other agents *opponents*).

According to our model-based learning approach, at any stage of interaction the learning agent holds a model of its opponent's strategy. In this work we assume that the opponent's strategy can be modeled as a finite automaton following Rubinstein's model [Rub86]. The agent exploits the current opponent model in order to predict its behavior and chooses its own action according to that prediction. When the model's prediction is wrong, the agent updates the opponent model in order to make it consistent with the new counterexample. In a previous work [CM94], we use a similar approach for model-based learning in zero-sum two-player games.

In Section 2 we describe our basic framework. In Section 3 we describe how an agent should find an optimal strategy against a given model. In Section 4 we present a heuristic algorithm that infers a model of the opponent's automaton from its input/output behavior, and report some experimental results.

2 Interaction as a Repeated Game

We assume that interaction between two agents can be described as a sequence of encounters. An encounter between two agents is described as a two-player game $G = < R_1, R_2, u_1, u_2 >$, where R_i is a finite set of alternative moves for player i. $u_i : R_1 \times R_2 \rightarrow \Re$ is the utility function of player i. R_1, R_2 are *common knowledge* while u_1, u_2 are *private*.

A sequence of meetings among agents is described as a repeated game $G^{\#}$, based on the repetition of G an indefinite number of times. At any stage t of the game, the players choose their moves, $(r_1^t, r_2^t) \in R_1 \times R_2$, simultaneously. A history $h(t)$ of $G^{\#}$ is a finite sequence of joint moves chosen by the agents until the current stage of the game.

$$h(t) = [(r_1^0, r_2^0), (r_1^1, r_2^1), \ldots, (r_1^{t-1}, r_2^{t-1})] \tag{1}$$

H is the set of all finite histories for $G^{\#}$.
A player's strategy S_i for $G^{\#}$ is a function from the set of histories of the game to the set of the player's moves.

$$S_i : H \rightarrow R_i \tag{2}$$

$\mathcal{S}_i$ is the set of all possible strategies for player i in $G^{\#}$.
We distinguish between a *stationary player* that selects its strategy at the beginning of the game and does not change it afterwards, and an *adaptive player* that can change its strategy at any stage of the repeated game.

While the history of the game is *common knowledge*, each player predicts the future course of the game differently. Agent i chooses its moves against agent j in order to maximize its expected sum of rewards in the game. Agent i uses its own strategy, S_i, and its opponent model, S_j^i, to predict an infinite sequence of joint moves .

$$[(r_i^t, r_j^t), (r_i^{t+1}, r_j^{t+1}), \ldots, (r_i^{t+k}, r_j^{t+k}) \ldots] \tag{3}$$

We define the expected sum of rewards for $G^\#$ as

$$U_i(S_i, S_j^i) = \sum_{k=t}^{\infty} \gamma_{ij}^{k-t} u_i(r_i^k, r_j^k) \tag{4}$$

$0 \leq \gamma_{ij} < 1$ is a discount factor that describes how agent i estimates the probability of re-meeting with agent j. It is easy to show that $U_i(S_i, S_j^i)$ converges for any $\gamma_{ij} < 1$. We assume that the player's objective is to maximize the expected sum of rewards in the repeated game $G^\#$.

S_i^{opt} will be called an *optimal strategy* for player i, with respect to strategy S_j, if $\forall S \in \mathcal{S}_i$, $U_i(S_i^{opt}, S_j) \geq U_i(S, S_j)$.

Generally, searching for an optimal strategy in the space of strategies is too complicated for an agent with limited computational resources. In this work we adopt a common convention that strategies can be represented by deterministic finite automata [Rub86].

A DFA (*Moore machine*) is defined as a tuple $M = (Q, \Sigma_{in}, q_0, \delta, \Sigma_{out}, F)$ where Q is a non empty finite set of states, Σ_{in} is the machine input alphabet, q_0 is the initial state, and Σ_{out} is the output alphabet. $\delta : Q \times \Sigma_{in} \rightarrow Q$ is a transition function. δ is extended to the range $Q \times \Sigma_{in}^*$ in the usual way:

$$\begin{aligned} \delta(q, \lambda) &= q \\ \delta(q, s\sigma) &= \delta(\delta(q, s), \sigma) \end{aligned} \tag{5}$$

λ is the null string. $F : Q \rightarrow \Sigma_{out}$ is the output function. $M(s) = F(\delta(q_0, s))$ is the output of M for a string $s \in \Sigma_{in}^*$. $|M|$ denotes the number of states of M.

A strategy for player i against opponent j is represented by a DFA M_i where $\Sigma_{in} = R_j$ and $\Sigma_{out} = R_i$. Given a history $[(r_i^0, r_j^0), (r_i^1, r_j^1), \ldots, (r_i^{t-1}, r_j^{t-1})]$, the move selected by M_i is $M_i(r_j^0 r_j^1 \ldots r_j^{t-1})$.

3 An optimal strategy against a given opponent model

Assume that the agent has a model $\overline{M}$ of its opponent's DFA. How should it play against it optimally? The next theorem shows that for any opponent model $\overline{M}$, there is a dominant strategy for the agent, M^{opt}, and also shows how it can be computed.

Theorem 1. *For any DFA $\overline{M}$ there exists a DFA M^{opt} such that $|M^{opt}| = |\overline{M}|$ and M^{opt} is optimal in respect to $\overline{M}$.*

Proof. Given $\overline{M} = (\overline{Q}, R_i, \bar{q}_0, \bar{\delta}, R_j, \overline{F})$. For every $\bar{q} \in \overline{Q}, r_i \in R_i$, the expected sum of rewards can be computed as follows:

$$W(\bar{q}, r_i) = u_i(r_i, \overline{F}(\bar{q})) + \gamma_{ij} \max_{r'_i \in R_i} W(\bar{\delta}(\bar{q}, r_i), r'_i) \tag{6}$$

Computation of W is a Markovian problem with a stable solution that can be computed by *dynamic programming* [Ber87]. The best response for player i, given any state of the opponent model, is

$$opt(\bar{q}) = arg \max_{r_i \in R_i} W(\bar{q}, r_i) \tag{7}$$

An optimal player's DFA, $M^{opt} = (Q, R_j, q_0, \delta, R_i, F)$ can be constructed as follows:

- $Q = \overline{Q}$,
- $q_0 = \bar{q}_0$,
- $F(q_i) = opt(\bar{q}_i)$,
- $\delta(q_i, \overline{F}(\bar{q}_i)) = \bar{\delta}(\bar{q}_i, F(q_i))$.

M^{opt} is always in a parallel state to $\overline{M}$ and it always reacts optimally against it. Therefore, $\forall M \in \mathcal{S}$, $U_i(M^{opt}, \overline{M}) \geq U_i(M, \overline{M})$. □

The above theorem shows how to use an opponent model. The next section discusses methods for acquiring such a model.

4 Opponent modeling

Under the assumption that the opponent's strategy can be modeled as a DFA, the learning agent has to infer a DFA from a sample of the opponent's behavior in the past. Finding the smallest finite automata consistent with a given sample has been shown to be NP-Hard [Gol78, Ang78]. It has also been shown that the minimal consistent automata cannot be approximated within any polynomial-time algorithm [Pit89]. Thus, passive modeling of a given automaton from an arbitrary sample seems to be infeasible.

Angluin [Ang87] describes an algorithm that efficiently infers an automaton model using a 'minimal adequate teacher', an oracle that answers membership and equivalence queries. For a membership query, the algorithm asks for the machine's output for a given string of input actions. For an equivalence query, the algorithm conjectures that the model and the machine are equivalent. The teacher replies by 'Yes' for a right conjecture, or provides a counterexample on which the model and the machine disagree. This algorithm, named L^*, is an efficient inference procedure that constructs a minimal DFA consistent with the learned machine. The computational time is polynomial in the number of states of the machine and the longest counterexample supplied by the teacher.

Another alternative was studied by Rivest and Schapire [RS89]. Their procedure simulates iterated interactions of a robot with an unknown environment and is based on L^*. Instead of an *adequate teacher* that answers queries, the learner is permitted to experiment with the environment (machine). When the learner is requested by L^* to simulate a membership query for a specific input, it operates the machine and observes the result. If the model's prediction is different from the actual behavior of the machine, the learner treats it as a counterexample.

4.1 Identifying a DFA from a Given Sample

An *example* of a DFA's behavior is a pair (s, r) where $s \in \Sigma_{in}^*$, $r \in \Sigma_{out}$. $r = M(s)$ annotates the output of the machine M for an input sequence s. A *Sample D* is a finite set of examples of the machine's behavior. For any example $(s, r) \in D$, we mark r as $D(s)$. We say that a model M is consistent with a sample D iff for any example $(s, r) \in D$, $M(s) = D(s)$.

Gold [Gol78] studied the problem of identifying a DFA from a given sample by representing the machine using an observation table (S, E, T). $S \subseteq \Sigma_{in}^*$ is a prefix-closed set of strings. $E \subseteq \Sigma_{in}^*$ is a suffix-closed set of strings called *tests*. T is a two dimensional table with one row for each element of $S \cup S\Sigma$, where $S\Sigma = \{s\sigma | s \in S, \sigma \in \Sigma_{in}\}$, and one column for each element of E. The table entries, $T(s, e) \in \Sigma_{out}$.

A table is *closed* iff for any given $s \in S\Sigma$ there is a string $s' \in S$ such that $row(s) = row(s')$. A table is *consistent* iff for any two strings, $s_1, s_2 \in S$ such that $row(s_1) = row(s_2)$, and for any $\sigma \in \Sigma_{in}$, $row(s_1\sigma) = row(s_2\sigma)$. We say that a DFA M is consistent with an observation table (S, E, T) iff for any entry (s, e) in T, $M(se) = T(s, e)$.

A DFA M, that is consistent with a closed and consistent table $M = M(S, E, T)$, can be constructed as follows [Ang87]:

- $Q = \{row(s) : s \in S\}$
- $q_0 = row(\lambda)$
- $\delta(row(s), \sigma) = row(s\sigma)$
- $F(row(s)) = T(s, \lambda)$

Theorem 2 (Angluin). If (S, E, T) *is a closed and consistent observation table, then the DFA* $M(S, E, T)$ *is consistent with the table* T, *and any other DFA consistent with* T *but not equivalent to* $M(S, E, T)$, *must have more states.*

We say that a table (S, E, T) *covers* a sample D if for any $d \in D$ there is an entry $(s, e) \in T$ such that $d = (se, \sigma)$ and $T(s, e) = \sigma$. We say that a table entry (s, e) is *supported* by a sample D if there is an example $d \in D$ such that $d = (se, \sigma)$, and $T(s, e) = \sigma$.

Given a closed and consistent table (S, E, T) that covers D, we can construct $M(S, E, T)$ consistent with D. Thus, the problem of finding a DFA consistent with D is reduced to the problem of finding a closed and consistent observation table that covers D. Given a sample D, it is easy to find S and E such that for any $d \in D$, there are $s \in S$, $e \in E$, and $d = (se, \sigma)$. Table identification forces the learner to fill all table entries. Table entries supported by D must be filled by $T(s, e) = D(se)$. The main question remaining is how to fill entries not supported by D.

An entry (s, e) of the table (S, E, T) is called a *permanent entry* if it is supported by D. (s, e) is called a *hole* entry if it is not supported by D. Two table entries, (s_1, e_1) and (s_2, e_2), are called *tied* if $s_1 e_1 = s_2 e_2$. An *assignment* is a vector over Σ_{out}^* that assigns an output value to each *hole* of a table. An assignment is *legal* iff tied holes receive the same value.

Finding a legal assignment for a given table is easy. For example, the assignment that inserts the same output value for all the holes must be legal. We call it the *trivial assignment*. The problem becomes much harder if we look for a legal assignment that yields a closed and consistent table. We call it the *optimal assignment*.

Theorem 3 (Gold). *The problem of finding an optimal assignment for an observation table that covers a given sample is NP-hard.*

The L^* algorithm [Ang87] uses a 'minimal adequate teacher' to directs the learner to fill hole values optimally by answering membership queries. The L^* algorithm maintains an observation table (S, E, T) for representing the learned DFA. Initially, $S = E = \{\lambda\}$ and all table entries are filled by membership queries. In the main loop, L^* tests the current table for closeness and consistency. In the case of a failure, L^* extends the table to become closed and consistent, where new table entries are filled by membership queries. When the table becomes closed and consistent, L^* constructs $M(S, E, T)$ and asks for equivalence. If a counterexample is provided by the teacher, the table is extended to include the new example. The algorithm continues until 'YES' is replied by the teacher for the conjectured model. Figure 2 shows an example for an observation table used by L^*.

Theorem 4 (Angluin). L^* *eventually terminates and outputs a minimal DFA equivalent to the Teacher's DFA. Moreover, if n is the number of states of the teacher's DFA, and m is an upper bound on the length of the longest counterexample provided by the teacher, then the total running time of L^* is bounded by a polynomial in n and m.*

4.2 A Heuristic Algorithm for Learning DFA

The L^* algorithm is not suitable for opponent modeling due to the unavailability of a teacher. Also, in contrast to Rivest and Schapire's procedure, experiments with the opponent might be too expensive or even destructive for the learner. We propose to deal with this problem by considering heuristic approaches; following the 'Occam razor' principle, we search for the minimal DFA consistent with the opponent's behavior. By using heuristics that try to control the growth of the model during the interaction, and by making some limiting assumptions on the given data, we show that a reasonable solution may be found. This method is analogous to the famous classification problem of constructing a decision tree from a set of pre-classified examples. Finding the smallest decision tree consistent with a given data is known to be NP-Hard [QR89]. However, using heuristic methods such as those described by Quinlan [Qui86], a 'reasonable' consistent decision tree can be constructed. This method has been shown to be efficient in many practical applications.

During encounters with the environment, the learning agent holds a consistent model with the environment's behavior in the past, and exploits the model to predict the environment's behavior in the future. When a new example arrives, it can be a *supporting example* or a *counterexample*. For the first case, the algorithm does not change the model. For a *counterexample*, the algorithm constructs a new table that covers the data, including the new *counterexample*. Following that, it arranges the table to become closed and consistent, and constructs a new model consistent with the new table.

The algorithm named US-L^*, (unsupervised L^*), maintains the same observation table as L^* does. At the beginning, the algorithm inserts all the prefixes of the examples into S, and constructs $S\Sigma$ to include all their extensions. E is initialized to include the empty test λ. Entries of the table are filled as follows: When an entry (s, e), is supported by a past example, it gets the example's output value and it is marked as a *permanent* entry. When a table entry is not supported by a past example, it gets an output value predicted by the previous model, and it is marked as a *hole* entry.

Following that, the algorithm arranges the table to become consistent. At first, it attempts to change the hole assignment to solve inconsistency without the necessity to add new tests. In the case of inconsistency, there are two S-rows, s_1 and s_2, $\sigma \in \Sigma_{in}$, and $e \in E$, such that $row(s_1) = row(s_2)$, but $T(s_1\sigma, e) \neq T(s_2\sigma, e)$. The original L^* solves this inconsistency by adding a new test σe into E, an extension that separates $row(s_1)$ and $row(s_2)$ and causes an addition of at least one new state to the model. US-L^* tries to solve the inconsistency by changing the hole assignment. When $T(s_1\sigma, e) \neq T(s_2\sigma, e)$, if one entry is a *hole* and one is *permanent*, the *hole* entry gets the output value of the *permanent*. When both are *hole* entries, the longer one gets the output value of the shorter one. Changing a value of a *hole* entry causes all its tied entries to get the same value for keeping the legality of the assignment. In order to prevent an infinite loop, any changed entry is marked and can not be changed again. Adding of a new test is done only in the case of a failure to solve inconsistency by changing *hole* assignment (if both entries are *permanent* or both entries were changed already). Finally, the algorithm arranges the table to become closed exactly as L^* does. When the table is not closed, there is $s \in S\Sigma$ such that for any $s' \in S$, $row(s') \neq row(s)$. US-L^* moves s from $S\Sigma$ to S and for each $\sigma \in \Sigma_{in}$ adds $s\sigma$ into $S\Sigma$. Figure 1 shows a pseudo code of the algorithm and Figure 2 shows an example of a closed and consistent observation table and the corresponding DFA.

Algorithm: US-$L^*(D, M, t)$
  D: a set of past examples of the machine's input/output behavior.
  M: The current model.
  $t = (s, \sigma)$: a new example of the machine's behavior

  $D \leftarrow D \cup \{t\}$
  if $D(s) \neq M(s)$, $\{t$ is a *counterexample* $\}$
    Init (S, E, T):
      $S \leftarrow$ all prefixes of D
      for each $s \in S$ and $\sigma \in \Sigma_{in}$
        if $s\sigma \notin S$, $S\Sigma \leftarrow S\Sigma \cup \{s\sigma\}$
      $E \leftarrow \{\lambda\}$
      for each $s \in S \cup S\Sigma$, $T(s, \lambda) \leftarrow Query(s, \lambda)$
    Consistency:
      While not Consistent(S, E, T)
        find two equal rows $s_1, s_2 \in S$, $\sigma \in \Sigma_{in}$, $e \in E$, such that $T(s_1\sigma, e) \neq T(s_2\sigma, e)$
        if both $(s_1\sigma, e)$ and $(s_2\sigma, e)$ are permanent
        or both have been changed before $\{$we must distinguish between rows s_1 and $s_2\}$
          $E \leftarrow E \cup \{\sigma e\}$
          for each $s \in S \cup S\Sigma$, $T(s, \sigma e) \leftarrow Query(s, \sigma e)$
        else
          if one entry is a *hole* which was not changed before (assume $(s_2\sigma, e)$)
          or both entries are *holes* which were not changed before and assume $s_1 \leq s_2$
          $T(s_2\sigma, e)$ (and its tied entries)$\leftarrow T(s_1\sigma, e)$
          mark $(s_2\sigma, e)$ (and its tied entries) as changed
    Closeness:
      While not Closed(S, E, T)
        find $s \in S\Sigma$ such that $\forall s' \in S$, $row(s') \neq row(s)$
        move s into S
        for each $\sigma \in \Sigma_{in}$
          $S\Sigma \leftarrow S\Sigma \cup \{s\sigma\}$
          for each $e \in E$, $T(s\sigma, e) \leftarrow Query(s\sigma, e)$
    $M \leftarrow M(S, E, T)$
  return M

$Query(s, e)$:
  if (s, e) is *supported* by D
    mark (s, e) as a *permanent* entry, return $D(se)$
  else
    mark (s, e) as a *hole* entry
    if (s, e) has a tied entry (s', e') $\{s'e' = se\}$
      return $T(s', e')$
    else
      return $M(se)$

Fig. 1. US-L^*: Unsupervised learning algorithm of a DFA

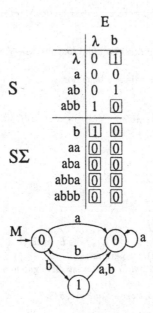

	E	
	λ	b
S λ	0	1
a	0	0
ab	0	1
abb	1	0
SΣ b	1	0
aa	0	0
aba	0	0
abba	0	0
abbb	0	0

Fig. 2. A closed and consistent observation table (S, E, T) and $M(S, E, T)$

4.3 Correctness of US-L^*

Theorem 5. *If D is a set of examples of the machine's behavior, M is a DFA consistent with D, and t is a new example. Then US-$L^*(D, M, t)$ eventually terminates and outputs a model consistent with $D \cup \{t\}$. Moreover, if k is the size of the set of all prefixes of the examples in $D \cup \{t\}$, then the total running time, and the size of the observation table used by US-L^*, are bounded by a polynomial in k and $|M|$.*

To prove the theorem we need the following two lemmas:

Lemma 6. *The consistency loop terminates after at most $k^2(1 + |\Sigma_{in}|) + k$ iterations and outputs a consistent table.*

Proof. During the consistency loop there are two kinds of iterations. In the first one, we add a test to E. In the second, we change the hole assignment of the table. Let us define $row(S) = \{row(s) | s \in S\}$. Adding of a test to E increases the number of distinct rows in $row(S)$ by at least one. There can be at most k distinct rows in $row(S)$. Therefore, the number of 'adding-test' iterations is bounded by k. This bound holds also for the size of E. For the second kind of iterations, since any hole can be changed only once, the number of such iterations is bounded by the table size $|S \cup S\Sigma| \times |E| \le k^2(1 + |\Sigma_{in}|)$. The total number of iterations is bounded by the sum of the two bounds, $k^2(1 + |\Sigma_{in}|) + k$. Termination occurs only when the table is consistent so the loop is terminated and outputs a consistent table. □

Lemma 7. The closeness loop at the end of the algorithm, terminates after at most $2k^3(1+|\Sigma_{in}|)+|M|$ iterations, does not change the consistency of the table, and outputs a closed table.

Proof. When the loop begins, $S\Sigma$ includes at most $k|\Sigma_{in}|$ elements. At each iteration, $S\Sigma$ is extended with $|\Sigma_{in}|$ elements. E is not extended during the loop. New entries are filled by the old model or by tied entries that were changed during the consistency loop. There are at most $k^2(1 + |\Sigma_{in}|)$ changed entries, and each one has at most $2k$ tied entries. Therefore, at most $2k^3(1 + |\Sigma_{in}|)$ new rows can be changed by old tied entries. New rows that are not changed by old values, are filled by the model, hence, at most $|M|$ distinct such rows can be added during the loop. The number of iterations can be bounded by counting the number of distinct rows that might be added during the loop, $2k^3(1 + |\Sigma_{in}|) + |M|$. Termination occurs only when the table is closed so the loop is terminated and output a closed table. Consistency of the table is not changed during the closeness loop because any row that is moved into $row(S)$ is distinct from any other rows in $row(S)$. Thus, inconsistency can not be added to the table. □

Now we can prove the correctness of the algorithm.

Proof (of Theorem 5). If t is a supporting example the proof is trivial.
If t is a counterexample, the algorithm constructs (S, E, T) to cover $D \cup \{t\}$. During table construction, any permanent entry is filled with the value of its supporting example, and any hole entry is filled with an old tied entry or by the current model. This filling strategy assures the legality of the assignment. All operations during the consistency and closeness loops are polynomial in k and $|M|$. Thus, the two previous lemmas show that the consistency and the closeness loops at the end of the algorithm terminate and output a closed and consistent table, in time bounded by a polynomial in k and $|M|$. The size of E is bounded by k. The size of $S \cup S\Sigma$ is bounded by a polynomial in k and $|M|$. Therefore, table size is also bounded by a polynomial in k and $|M|$. □

4.4 An Example Run of the Algorithm

Assume that $\Sigma_{in} = \{a, b\}$, $\Sigma_{out} = \{0, 1\}$. Figure 3 shows the target DFA and Figure 4 describes an example of a learning session of the algorithm.

Fig. 3. DFA1

The first example $(\lambda, 1)$ is a *supporting example* and does not change the model. The second example $(a, 0)$ is a counterexample. Table entries are changed

and the new model has two states. The third example, $(ab, 0)$, is also a counterexample. The algorithm adds aba and abb into $S\Sigma_{in}$ and the observation table
becomes inconsistent, because $row(a) = row(ab)$ but $row(aa) \neq row(aba)$ and
$row(ab) \neq row(abb)$. Unlike to the original L^*, by changing the holes $T(aba, \lambda)$
to be equal to $T(aa, \lambda)$ and $T(\mathring{a}bb, \lambda)$ to be equal to $T(ab, \lambda)$, the table becomes
consistent without further extension. As a result, the third model is equivalent
to the learned machine.

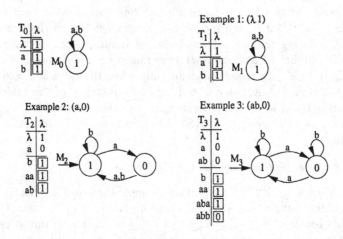

Fig. 4. A learning session of DFA1. Holes are marked by squares. After three examples,
the learned model is equivalent to the target machine.

The size of the model is mostly effected by the set of examples. The correctness proof also shows that for an arbitrary sample the observation table
can increase in size to become polynomial in the size of the given sample. We
hypothesize that the algorithm is best suited for prefix-closed samples. This is
the case in opponent modeling because any given history includes all its prefixes as examples. We conducted an experiment where random DFAs of various
sizes were created and were modeled by US-L^* using various sizes of random
prefix-closed samples of their behavior. A random machine DFA with a given
number of states was constructed by choosing a random transition function and
by choosing a random output function. 100 experiments were conducted for each
pair of sample size and machine size. It is important to clarify that the randomly
built DFA are not necessarily minimal.

Figure 5 shows the average size of the learned models as a function of the
sample size and as a function of the DFA size. It is quite clear that the average
size of the learned models is similar to the size of the machines and is not affected
by the sample size. These results suggest that US-L^* has a strong ability to detect
the common pattern of the sample.

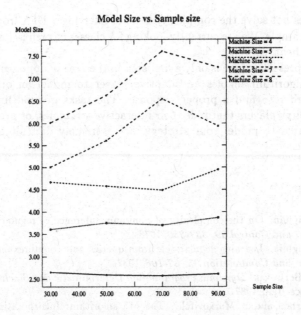

Fig. 5. Average model size learned by US-L^* as a function of the sample size, for different sizes of the target machine.

5 Summary

Finding an optimal strategy for interaction in MAS is a hard problem because it depends mostly on the strategies of the other agents involved. Therefore, adaptation and learning abilities are essential for an intelligent agent that interacts with other selfish agents. In this work, we treat the process of interaction as a repeated game where agents adapt their strategy according to the history of the game. We suggest a *model-based* approach where an agent learns a model of its opponent's strategy based on its past behavior, and uses the model to predict its future behavior. To make learning feasible we restrict our attention to opponent strategies that can be represented by a DFA.

Learning a minimal DFA without a teacher was proved to be hard. We present a heuristic algorithm, US-L^*, that is based on Angluin's L^* algorithm. The algorithm maintains a model consistent with its past examples. When a new counterexample arrives it tries to extend the model in a minimal fashion. We conducted a set of experiments where random automata that represent different strategies were generated, and the algorithm tried to learn them based on prefix-closed samples of their behavior. The algorithm managed to learn very compact models that agree with the samples. The size of the sample had a small effect on the size of the model.

The experimental results suggest that for random prefix-closed samples the algorithm behaves well. However, following Angluin's result on the difficulty of learning almost uniform complete samples [Ang78], it is obvious that our algorithm does not solve the complexity issue of inferring a DFA from a general prefix-closed sample. We are currently looking for classes of prefix-closed samples where US-L^* behaves well.

The work presented here is only a first step in the area of opponent modeling. The US-L^* algorithm enables an adaptive player to model an other agent's strategy in order to find a proper response. The tasks of modeling adaptive players, modeling players that hide their interactive strategies, or avoiding other agent's attempts to model your strategy, are extremely difficult and deserve further research.

References

[Ang78] D. Angluin. On the complexity of minimum inference of regular sets. *Information and Control 39, 337-350*, 1978.

[Ang87] D. Angluin. Learning regular sets from queries and counterexamples. *Information and Computation 75, 87-106*, 1987.

[Ber87] D. P. Bertsekas. *Dynamic Programming: Deterministic and Stochastic Models.* Prentice-Hall, 1987.

[CM94] D. Carmel and S. Markovitch. The M* algorithm: Incorporating opponent models into adversary search. Technical Report CIS report 9402, Technion, March 1994.

[Gol78] E. M. Gold. Complexity of automaton identification from given data. *Information and Control 37, 302-320*, 1978.

[Lit94] Michael L. Littman. Markov games as a framework for multi-agent reinforcement learning. *Proceedings of the eleventh International Conference on Machine Learning*, pages 157–163, July 1994.

[Pit89] L. Pitt. Inductive inference, DFAs and computational complexity. In K. P. Jantke, editor, *Analogical and Inductive Inference, Lecture Notes in AI 397*, pages 18–44. Springer-Verlag, 1989.

[QR89] J. R. Quinlan and R. L. Rivest. Inferring decision tree using the minimum description length principle. *Information and Computation 80,227-248*, 1989.

[Qui86] J. R. Quinlan. Induction of decision trees. *Machine Learning 1, 81-106*, 1986.

[RS89] R. L. Rivest and R. E. Schapire. Inference of finite automata using homing sequences. In *Proceedings of the 21th ACM Symposium on Theory and Computing*, pages 411–420, 1989.

[Rub86] A. Rubinstein. Finite automata play the repeated prisoner's dilemma. *Journal of Economic Theory 39, 83-96*, 1986.

[SC95] T. W. Sandholm and R. H. Crites. Multiagent reinforcement learning and the iterated prisoner's dilemma. *Biosystems Journal, (Submitted)*, 1995.

[SSH94] S. Sen, M. Sekaran, and J. Hale. Learning to coordinate without sharing information. In *Proceeding of the Twelfth National Conference on Artifical Intelligence (AAAI-94)*, pages 426 – 431, 1994.

[ST94] Y. Shoham and M. Tennenholtz. Co-Learning and the evolution of social activity. Technical Report STAN-CS-TR-94-1511, Stanford Univrsity, Department of Computer Science, 1994.

A Multi-Agent Environment for Department of Defense Distribution

Laurence Glicoes   Richard Staats   Michael Huhns

Logistics Management Institute
2000 Corporate Ridge
McLean, Virginia 22102-7805
rstaats@lmi.org

Abstract

The United States Department of Defense (DoD) requires an effective, economic method for utilizing the available distribution system to move its personnel, equipment and supplies in support of military operations world wide. Recent reductions in the DoD budget have placed a premium on leveraging technologically innovative solutions to accomplish this requirement. This paper examines the integration of cooperative autonomous computational agent technology with cost effective Low-Earth Orbit (LEO) satellite communications capability. Under this concept, Intelligent Agents (IA) would be developed and integrated into the spectrum of transportation actions DoD wide. The IA would be divided into two categories, static (attached to intermodal sites) and mobile (attached to shipments). The IA act as economic competitors in routing the shipments through the DoD transportation network. The result being effective and efficient transportation of goods and personnel for both routine operations and unforeseen contingencies. The global communication system offered by the LEO satellites would be used to track shipment status and continually update the shared intermodal knowledge base.

1. Introduction and Overview of the Existing System

The end of the Cold War heralded many changes for the United States Department of Defense (DoD). Smaller budgets and additional active deployments to more diverse locations strain DoD readiness. DoD has shifted from being primarily a forward deployed (i.e. large forces deployed in likely conflict areas) to a force projection organization (i.e. reliant on strategic mobility assets to reach contested areas). At its core, force projection means having the ability to deploy a large military force from the United States to anywhere in the world in a limited amount of time. A premium has been placed on finding innovative methods to increase the efficiency and effectiveness of DoD's transportation system. Any innovations to the logistics system must, at a minimum, satisfy requirements for efficiency and effectiveness.

This paper explores the use of Intelligent Agent (IA) technology in conjunction with a Low Earth Orbiting (LEO) satellite communications backbone as a methodology for DoD to increase both the efficiency and effectiveness of the DoD transportation system. Our solution is based on an artificial intelligence, limited horizon approach to distribution, made possible through the integration of emerging technologies. These emerging technologies include: long life batteries, advances in artificial intelligence shells and routines, improvements in microchip capabilities, enhancements in data compression and coding, dramatic increases in data transmission spectrums, advancements in data fusion and extremely large database management, innovations in real time optimization techniques, and availability and reliability of electronic storage methods. Before examining our concept for integrating IA and LEO technologies, we will describe the DoD transportation system in more detail.

1.1 Problem Overview The DoD transportation system, used in both routine and crisis situations, is referred to as the Defense Transportation System (DTS). The DTS specifies the procedures used by the military to request and for commercial industry to provide necessary transportation services. The basic process incorporated in the DTS is specified in various military regulations and the US federal code.

The DTS is composed of both military owned and private commercial transportation assets. While reliant on commercial operators to move the bulk of its passengers and cargo, the military maintains the basic transportation capability it needs to meet unique military requirements. For example, U.S. Air Force C-5A Galaxy aircraft has the volume and payload capacities required to move military cargoes which are too large or too heavy to be transported in commercial aircraft. However, DoD does not maintain a fleet of passenger aircraft, because it is more cost effective to use existing capacity in the commercial sector. Likewise, the military relies on commercial transportation sources to move household goods for military families. The commercial sector is better suited to perform these services for DoD. The system achieves a balance between the capabilities the military must maintain and those which can be obtained from the commercial sector.

The system works well in practice, because numerous commercial firms offer redundant capabilities for the bulk of military transportation requirements. Thus, DoD is able to transport its cargo and passengers while leveraging commercial sector innovations. In this partnership with industry, DoD constantly seeks better methods to meet its peacetime and wartime transportation requirements at the lowest overall cost.

1.2 Current and Ongoing Innovation The procedures underlying the system are detailed in various regulations and public law. The movement process in wartime is called a "deployment". To oversee the $6B a year DTS expenditures, the United States Congress authorized the creation of the United States Transportation Command (USTC) in 1989 which is located at Scott Air Force Base, Illinois. The mission of USTC is to manage the transportation system for the DoD in both peace and war. The outline of USTC's approach to accomplishing this task is contained in the "Re-engineering the Defense Transportation System Action Plan (DTSAT)", recently published by USTC [USTRANSCOM 1994]. A key provision of the DTSAT is ensuring automation technology is available to all personnel involved with the DTS to assist them in performing their jobs more efficiently and effectively. Examples of this automation technology include: the Global Transportation Network (GTN), the World-wide Port System (WPS), and others.

After the Gulf War DoD embarked upon a number of logistics initiatives directed at eliminating problems in the movement and tracking of personnel and equipment. Two of the major problems encountered during this large scale deployment of forces were the constant changes in the physical location of the ultimate destination where cargo was to be delivered, and inability to determine the status and location of shipments within the transportation and distribution network. In an effort to achieve a permanent fix to this and other problems, DoD has initiated several programs to overcome the most recent deficiencies of the Gulf War. Total Asset Visibility (TAV) is an effort whose goal is to know what equipment and supplies DoD owns, and where they are located. The goal of the next effort, Intransit Visibility (ITV), is to be able to identify and track equipment and supplies within the transportation and distribution system. The final initiative, the Total Distribution Advanced Technology Demonstration (TDATD), seeks to provide DoD personnel the integrated automation technology necessary to be able to bring logistics (supply, maintenance and transportation) information together in a manner that facilitates a structured decision making process to support military operations. As these initiatives have evolved, the DoD transportation community has become more aware of how *difficult* coordination and communication between the various developing systems will be.

2. Background and Description of System

The concept of decentralized logistics control based on the use of autonomous computational agents was initially submitted to the Logistics Management Institute (LMI) by Dr. Michael N. Huhns, in response to a solicitation appearing in the Commerce Business Daily publication [CBD 1994]. In the solicitation, LMI was seeking new and emerging technology applications to improve the strategic mobility of United States Armed Forces. This paper expands Dr. Huhns' initial concept.

2.1 General Approach Our proposed solution takes a non-traditional approach to DoD transportation. The conventional military wisdom is that results are achieved through *positive control*. Some *individual* must always be in charge and be held accountable at each step in the operation. But the transportation process has become too large and complex for any *one* person to manage.

Consider recent military operations in Somalia. The efficient and orderly movement of large amounts of personnel and equipment within a short time frame presents a massive problem in planning and scheduling. Previous DoD efforts at obtaining a solution were primarily centralized and top-down, with a strategy based on hierarchical decomposition. Unfortunately, centralization cannot take advantage of opportunities for synergism that often arise among tasks assigned to different nodes of the hierarchical plan.

We propose an innovative and entirely different approach, a primarily decentralized implementation based on cooperating autonomous computational agents or IAs augmented by *the capacity* to *monitor* the location of shipments in route and *change shipments' destinations*. Our IAs would come in two varieties. Mobile IAs would be attached to shipment units such as containers, pieces of bulk equipment or passenger compartments. Potentially each item of materiel, each box of ammunition, each piece of artillery, could be an "intelligent" entity whose sole objective is to reach its destination in a timely fashion in the best possible condition. Our second type of IAs would be the static IAs. These IAs would be located at the intermodal decision points. Examples of decisions made by static IAs would include: which mode of transportation to assign to shipment units, how to contend for limited transportation, storage, and material handling resources, and how to avoid or resolve conflicts with other IAs.

The use of the IAs would free the human managers to do what they do best, manage the exceptional and crisis situations. The IAs have other advantages too. They are able to perform calculations much faster and more accurately and recall more information for longer periods than the human managers. This will enable the transportation system to achieve economies of scale currently inconceivable by transportation managers.

An analogy for understanding our approach is the case where a large number of commuters manage to travel from their homes to their workplaces each day. They each have a goal (e.g. to arrive at their destination by a certain time), shared limited resources (e.g. roads, planes and trains), and, most importantly, can make local decisions about when and how to make use of the resources. Imagine instead someone with a large computer attempting to coordinate the travel and work schedules of all of the commuters in a city. They would have to: (1) schedule when each commuter should leave their homes, (2) plan all routes, (3) schedule when each should stop or go or turn at every intersection, etc. The planning task would be enormous and, even if an optimally efficient plan could be generated, it would fail when the inevitable exceptions occurred. However, millions of people manage to get to their workplaces each day without any central plan or control. They succeed by autonomously coordinating their actions with those of the other commuters, and making local decisions in the furtherance of their individual goals.

A critical segment of our scheme is that performance information for the distribution system would be centrally gathered, allowing key managers to make informed decisions concerning steps necessary to improve the entire process. Thus, the complex, exception basis decisions concerning the distribution system, would be acted upon by an informed management, where the authority and responsibility to make resource and funding commitments resides.

Cooperative machine learning is a key portion of our envisioned design. Learning and adaptability are crucial in the case of the commuter example. This is because commuters not only make reactive decisions about traffic, but also learn various routes and their availability or effectiveness at different times of the day and week. Those with flexible schedules can trade time of departure preferences with time spent on the road. Other commuters can factor the expected traffic problems in deciding where they want to live. People learn from others' experiences as well as their own.

2.2 System Description In the future DTS cargo and passengers will move through a system composed of four elements: the transportation and material storage assets, the human managers, the IAs, and the communications system with a LEO satellite backbone. By combining autonomous computational agent technology with low cost global communications capability of LEO satellites, our concept envisions cooperative Intelligent Agents (IA) strategically placed and integrated throughout the DTS [Gasser 1991]. Under this concept, the distribution network would be optimized sub-locally at each node using a limited look ahead, based on stochastic, historical approximations of the global state of the system [Lee & Cohen 1985]. Each node in the distribution network and the shipment units themselves, e.g. major weapons systems, containers, etc., function as IA.

The process of decentralized implementation would occur in two phases; a strategic and a tactical phase. The strategic phase, in which destination and transit goals are assigned to each entity by a central authority, is implemented by the *static IA*. The static IA, normally attached to facilities such as depots, sea ports, operation centers, etc., would be capable of communicating with adjacent transportation nodes (other static IA) and scheduling or arranging for transportation services within their authority for each shipment unit. The tactical phase, in which shipment units make local, autonomous decisions about their route and resource usage enroute to destination, would be made possible by what we call mobile IA. The mobile IA, attached to individual or groups of items being shipped, would be capable of communicating with the static IA as well as other mobile IA and would negotiate their transportation according to their priorities and the available transportation assets (Figure 1).

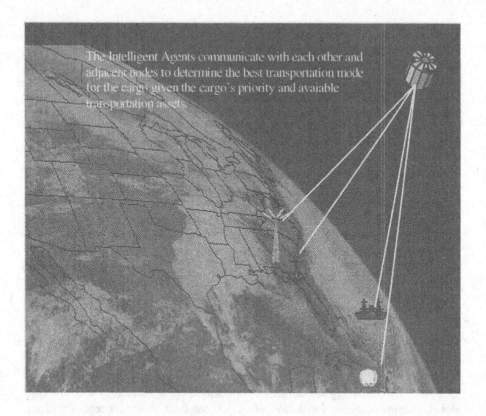

The Intelligent Agents communicate with each other and adjacent nodes to determine the best transportation mode for the cargo given the cargo's priority and avaiable transportation assets.

Figure 1

All requests for DoD shipments must initially be processed through a Transportation Office. This is the first activity which has the authority to commit Government funds for the movement of DoD personnel and materiel. The procedures for obtaining transportation services are essentially the same for both peacetime and wartime shipments. We believe that the transportation information system, located in the Transportation Office, would constitute the first static IA. At this time, there is no standard automated system among the Army, Navy, Air Force, or Marines which could be enhanced or upgraded to perform this IA function.

Within the transportation office, the purpose of these static IA would be to facilitate the process of receiving requests for transportation and arranging for the movement of the associate cargo or passengers. The human manager would inform the static IA when transportation assets such as trucks, trains, etc. became available. Examples of the types of shipments include: household goods, privately owned vehicles, general freight, individual and group moves. The job of the Transportation Officer and subsequently the IA, will be made easier through the use of electronic data interchange (EDI). Once EDI is fully implemented, shipment requests will be routinely made in electronic format, lending themselves to being acted upon by an IA. The static IA would be developed and expected to perform the following tasks:

process routine requests for movement under established guidelines (priority of shipment, type of service, mode of transportation, least costs for requested service, etc.); develop the ability to gradually assist with more complicated shipment procedures (e.g. shipment consolidations, mode selection, etc.); interface with the next higher echelon of control for unit moves, with respect to granting approval of the shipment to begin moving (port call phasing to prevent port congestion); acquiring information about previous shipment movement performance for the purpose of optimizing future shipments (faster service, better carrier, less cost, etc.).

The next location of static IA would be at the designated operations center or centers for the DTS. For example, one logical candidate to perform an operations center function would be the United States Transportation Command (USTC), for as we mentioned earlier, it is the designated command to manage the DTS. Other logical candidates would include regional transportation headquarters in the theater of operations and other transportation managers such as the Military Traffic Management Center and the Military Sealift Command. We view the operations center as providing the "central authority" by which destination and transit goals are assigned to each shipment entity. This assignment is based solely on broad performance criteria established for the DTS whereby shipment transit times are established for specific routes and system performance is measured against these standards. This does not constitute an assignment of a required delivery date (RDD) for each shipment unit, as that function is the responsibility of the shipper. These destination and transit goals merely specify for example, that an air cargo shipment from the east coast of the United States to Germany should take no longer than a total of 5 days once the cargo reaches the air terminal on the east coast.

Transit goals are of particular significance when deployments are involved. The military strategy of the United States revolves around the ability to project a force anywhere in the world in a given number of days. To achieve the desired deployment timeline, performance criteria must be established for each "segment" of the deployment. This means, for example, that so many days are allocated to the cargo to move from its origin to the designated sea port of embarkation, and a given number of days are allocated for staging at the seaport and loading aboard a ocean going vessel. The vessel is allowed a given number of days for ocean transit (based on the deployment distance and speed of the ship), where after the cargo is allowed a given number of days for offloading and staging at the port of debarkation and movement to its final destination. Individual segment performance is essential in bounding collective system performance. Collectively, one goal of our IA's will be to ensure the deployment timeline is met.

The remaining static IA would be assigned to other fixed locations, such as supply depots, transit points, air and sea ports and installations where personnel and equipment reside. These IA would essentially be associated with the "nodes" of a distribution network and their function would be to assist the mobile IA in reaching their destination according to schedule. Static IA would also be found at receiving points located in overseas areas. They would be attached permanently to locations where DoD cargo activity would normally occur or be temporary, established to support specific operations, such as the role U.S. Forces recently played in Somalia.

Mobile IA would accompany the shipment units themselves. This concept is what was initially envisioned by Dr. Huhns [Huhns 1994], where cargo would actually route itself through the distribution network. At this point, it is important to understand a few basic facts about the DTS. The system is a combination of transportation services DoD purchases from the commercial sector and transportation services DoD provides to itself using military transportation assets. An example of services DoD purchases is the movement of military personal property or household goods. In this case, DoD pays a carrier to move the household goods from origin to destination. What route the household goods travel is left to the carrier, provided the goods reach destination as prescribed in the required delivery date (RDD). An example of services DoD provides to itself would be an air shipment of cargo from a military installation to an overseas location when the goods travel aboard a U.S. Air Force cargo plane.

With a commercial shipment, DoD has little control over the route the cargo takes to reach destination and how many intermediate carriers may handle the cargo before it is finally delivered. All that is important is that it reaches destination in undamaged condition by the RDD. On the other hand, shipments that move entirely by military transport are somewhat visible to DoD. There is control over the routing, so there is a fair amount of information available about the shipment and the performance of the system. With commercial shipments, all DoD knows is that the shipment was picked up and it was delivered. What happened to it between origin and destination is unknown. This makes establishing performance goals for the "nodes" of the system difficult, when trying to optimize the entire DTS. So initially, we envision the mobile IA as leading the first attempt to determine what happens to DoD cargo that is in the hands of the commercial sector. How does their system work and interface with the DTS? Many shipments are a combination of commercial transportation services and military provided transportation services. Such is the case with many deployments. Cargo moves to a commercial port by commercial truck or rail, to be loaded aboard a DoD transportation asset for movement to destination. Understanding the integration of commercial capability with military capability is key to maximizing performance to meet military objectives.

2.3 Systemic Challenges Our proposed decentralized solution for the DTS requires that several technical difficulties be surmounted. The major one is that such a decentralized implementation must still be controlled, and decentralization makes control more difficult. Another is how the agents cooperate within the distribution network and compete for limited movement resources. Dr. Huhns suggested a method for achieving control and concomitantly efficiency, by making use of a market mechanism [Wellman 1992]. In this technique, each intelligent entity would be given a sum of "money" that it can use to "purchase" transportation, storage, or whatever other resources it might need. The amount of "money" available would vary with the priority of the shipment unit within the distribution network, and could change dynamically. More important items would be allocated proportionately more money. Items in conflict or contending for the same resource would bid for it, with the highest bidder winning the rights to the resource, but then having less money left to bid in the future. For example, a pallet of food that spent a lot of its "money" to be on the first aircraft to an operation might then have to wait longer for a truck at a subsequent staging depot to take it to final destination, because it did not have enough money left to out-bid contending pallets.

The ability to dynamically change shipment priority while it is enroute is critical to the success of the DTS system of the future. Consider the following example. A natural disaster occurs in Puerto Rico, and the US military is alerted to offer relief to the citizens of the island. A container of repair parts is moving through the distribution system as a routine "general resupply" shipment when suddenly the priority of the shipment is elevated to "critical commodity" to support systems' repair for the pending military operation.

The LEO satellite network can function as an interrogator of the mobile IA for information on each shipment unit. If a manager identified the need to upgrade the priority of a shipment, he or she could send a priority upgrade to the mobile IA through the LEO network in real time *as they move to destination*. Likewise, the system, through the LEO communications capability, could affect a lessening of a shipment priority.

2.4 Technological Enablers   Current technology, with some research and development, could make such a system feasible today at relatively low cost. First, it is easy to label each item with a bar-code or its equivalent, to identify it. This practice is now common throughout DoD. Second, microprocessor technology now enable inexpensive "smart cards" to be programmed and interrogated about the information they maintain. This technology, in basic form, is currently being adapted by DoD. Concurrent with progress in microcomputer technology, are advances in miniaturization of components and battery technology. With developmental effort, miniaturized microprocessors could be attached to each shipment item, where they could provide the intelligence needed by the item for its decision making. Existing strides in information technology such as data mining and database wrapping are opening up global information interchanges. Low cost global communications capability, which is currently being developed commercially using low-earth-orbit (LEO) satellites, could provide the means for passing information and data among the various system components. The resultant logistics system would be robust, adaptive, and efficient. It would not be vulnerable to any single-point failures. The key question now is how would the IA fit within the system architecture.

3. Description of IA and System Architecture

The IA, whether static or mobile, consist of a microprocessor and a communications device (hardware) and the algorithms (software). The static IAs would exist on larger computer platforms, while mobile IA would have to be much smaller in size (miniaturized) to be able to accompany its cargo from origin to destination. In general, the IA act as expert systems which update their knowledge base with each transaction. Each IA makes decisions based on its perceived state of the distribution system.

3.1 IA System Perception The IA perception of the system comes from three sources: exogenous parameters, historical data, and information being passed in real time from other IA, static or mobile (see Figure 2 below). For example, during routine (peacetime) conditions, the collective goal of the static and mobile IA might be to ensure delivery of needed materiel using the most efficient transportation means available, consistent with customer priorities. During crisis situations, such as military operations, IA emphasis might shift from efficiency to increasing the throughput without creating a saturation condition. As the ability of IAs to determine and react to the current and projected state of the distribution system improves through the learning process, the IA will become drivers which enable an efficient, responsive and cost effective Defense Distribution System, capable of supporting United States Forces around the world.

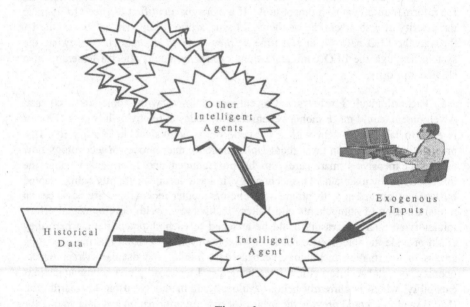

Figure 2

3.2 Roles and Functions of Mobile and Static IA The mobile and static IAs have distinct roles and functions. The mobile IAs are responsible for monitoring the location and condition of the cargo to which they are attached. Further, the mobile IA are required to perform two additional tasks. First, they must be able to *query and respond to the queries of other IA* in the distribution system. Second, as *rules surrounding their shipments are violated, the IA must identify those violations to decisions makers.* For example, IA might complain if: the shipment needed to be refrigerated and it was too hot; it was fragile, and it was at the bottom of a stack; or the shipment has exceeded its required delivery date.

The static and mobile IA would vary in complexity as well as function. Generally, the static IA would be expected to be the most functionally developed, having to perform repetitive shipment processing and control within its geographic area of responsibility. It would be able to select the proper modes for the various shipping units originating or as required, transiting its area of responsibility. Further, the static IA would be responsible for maintaining the inferential data. Each time a transaction or shipment was completed, the static IA would refresh its associate database.

The mobile IA would be relatively simple. They could carry a database consisting of only a few essential elements. For example, a mobile IA might contain: a unique identifier, such as the DoD Transportation Control Number or TCN; shipper and consignee information; a pointer to the detailed contents (manifest) if it is a container; brief aggregate description of its contents; current location; destination; priority; and condition. The unique identifier or TCN, is the distribution system's method of distinguishing shipping units. The shipping unit does not need to implicitly have all of its cargo identified in great detail, but it must be able to tell the user where the information is. The brief description helps human managers when intervention is required. Current location of the shipping unit and its destination are used to aid in routing decisions. The priority is the relative importance of the shipment. Condition covers special storage and cargo handling issues such as: explosive, requires refrigeration, fragile, etc.

The mobile IA could be programmed relatively simply at the beginning of each mission. The destination, special conditions and other information would be fed into the IA, and the IA would query its surroundings during the journey to obtain real time information about its current location or interim destinations. For purposes of this paper, we will define an *action* for a mobile IA to consist of notifying a manager of a situation which requires intervention or bidding of its credits to improve its de facto priority.

The static IA has a much more complex job than that of the mobile IA. A static IA must assign numerous shipments to transportation media such as planes, ships and rail assets. The static IAs will have a plethora of data available to them to include all aspects of past system performance. To properly perform its function, the static IA will have to consist not only of a high powered computational system, but the static IA must have access to an extensive database. The static IA will be in constant communications with its neighboring static IA, and this will necessitate a more sophisticated communications system than that used by the mobile IAs.

We envision each static IA as having a neural net and a genetic algorithm at its heart which helps to determine the mode selections. At a fundamental level, the assignments of cargo to transportation platforms can be viewed as a matching problem (see Figure 3 below).

Transportation Mode Assignments viewed as a Matching Problem

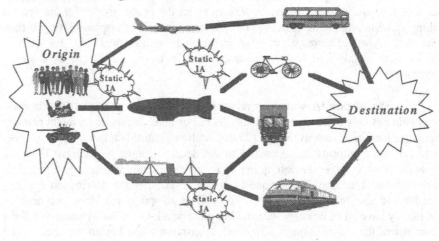

Figure 3

Each item of cargo can be viewed as a vector while the vector elements represent transportation mode assignments made by static IAs. For example, a case of whole blood might have the following assignment vector **[35, 27, 18, 1]** which represents shipment by Allied Van lines truck A34218 **(35)** from Fort Riley to Kansas City. From Kansas where it flew on United Flight 2381 **(27)** to Frankfurt. At Frankfurt International Airport, the blood was transported by Hamstein Gmbh truck 27B-562 **(18)** to Germersheim where the case of blood was placed in refrigerated storage **(1)**.

We will define an *action* as taken by a static IA as being: the assignment of a cargo to a specific transportation platform (e.g. train, plane or truck), sending cargo to holding areas, or requesting assistance from human transportation managers. We have defined the basic role of the static IA, but it is important to understand how the static IA's neural net will be trained to adequately handle the tasks it has been assigned.

3.3 Static IA Learning Cycle We anticipate the static IA-human interface to evolve through four distinct processes (see Figure 4 below). Initially, the knowledge base would have to be "seeded". The rules governing the DTS would be extracted from the various regulations and directives that govern movement under the DTS. Equally important would be obtaining input from functional experts in the field. The extracted system processes and performance standards would provide the foundation from which machine learning would occur. It should be noted that currently *a comprehensive, real time model of the **entire** Defense Transportation System does not exist*, and no one knows, on a daily basis, the overall status of the "system", e.g., its workload, bottlenecks, disruptions, etc. Recognition of this leads us to require an extensive learning phase where the ability to communicate in real time with both static and mobile IA, makes it possible to address system-wide performance and initiate the necessary changes and modifications to improve service and reduce costs.

The next phase of the learning cycle would be an inductive phase. We start with the assumption that the *human managers are, by and large, making the best decisions possible given their current state of knowledge about the DTS*. The static IA will observe the human manager as he or she makes actual transportation assignments. By monitoring the human manager, the static IA observes cause (i.e. the shipments entering the node and the transportation mode selections available for the onward movement of the cargo) and the effects (i.e. which cargoes are assigned to which modes). From these inputs, the static IA will inductively determine the "rules" behind the human managers decision. To test the state of the static IA progress, the static IA will predict what the human manager will do and then compares this estimation of what happened in practice. With each transaction the static IA will update its apriori estimate and dynamically establish an aposteri knowledge base. When the static IA is accurate in its estimations at a certain level (e.g. 80% of the static IA's estimates match human decisions), the static IA begins the next phase of the learning process.

The third phase of the learning process is a certification process. The static IA receives the same information the human manager does on incoming cargo, e.g. transportation modes available, etc. The static IA then prepares a draft manifesting and slating list for assignment of the cargo to the various transportation modes. Most important, the static IA identifies those decisions which it believes differ significantly from the decisions which would have been made by the human manager *and clearly identifies the rationale for these decisions*. At this point, the human manager reviews the proposed slatings and manifests and determines whether the static IA is making reasonable decisions. If the human manager certifies the static IA, the process moves into the last, steady-state phase. If the manager determines the static IA is making unreasonable assignments, the identified problems are corrected, and the static IA returns to the induction phase of the learning process.

In the steady-state phase the static IA is the primary manager at the node for purposes of mode selection. The static IA receives information on the cargo and passengers awaiting shipment and on the transportation assets available to carry the shipment units on toward their destinations. Based on its objectives and the static IA's extensive database, the static IA assigns the shipment units to the transportation platforms. The static IA is constantly receiving information about the state of the DTS from other IA both static and mobile (see Figure 5 below). Based on this information, the static IA updates its database. Thus, as the state of the system changes, the static IA responds by modifying its decision criteria.

The DTS Static Intelligent Agent Learning Cycle

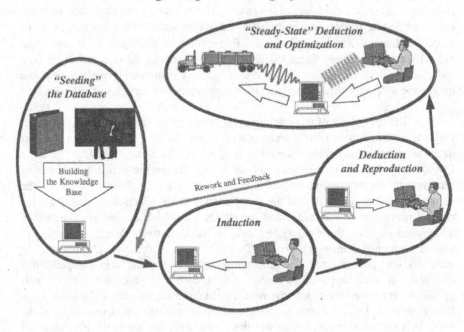

Figure 4

Examples of IA Communications

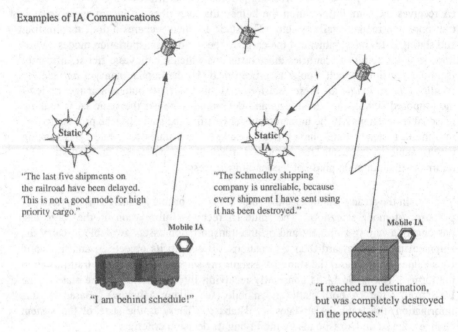

"The last five shipments on
the railroad have been delayed.
This is not a good mode for high
priority cargo."

"The Schmedley shipping
company is unreliable, because
every shipment I have sent using
it has been destroyed."

Mobile IA

Mobile IA

"I am behind schedule!"

"I reached my destination,
but was completely destroyed
in the process."

Figure 5

There are several key instances when the mobile IA communicate with the static IA. As the mobile IA begin to be delayed, they will notify an appropriate static IA. Also, if the cargo in the mobile IA's care is damaged or violated while enroute, the mobile IA must notify appropriate authorities (including static IA). Finally, when the shipments reach their destinations, the shipments send back status reports indicating their arrival times and condition on arrival.

The human manager will continue to have access to a record of the static IA's decisions, and the human manager retains the ability to override specific assignments. The steady-state phase will be a learning experience for both the static IA and the manager. If the human manager believes the static IA to be acting in error or to have become unstable, the manager may request the static IA be returned to the inductive phase of the learning process, but these requests should be rare. In general, they would occur only in circumstances where the environment had changed in a wholly unanticipated way.

3.4 Adaptive Learning Algorithm In this section we will explore the internal dynamics of the IA's learning algorithm (see figure 6 below).

The data inputs for a static IA come from three sources: human managers, the historical and rules database, and other IA. These data inputs provide three types of information to the system (see figure 7 below).

Adaptive Learning Algorithm Components

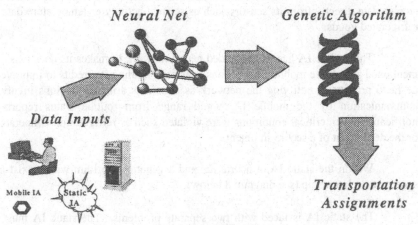

Neural Net *Genetic Algorithm*

Data Inputs

Mobile IA Static IA

Transportation Assignments

Figure 6

Adaptive Learning Algorithm Components

Data Inputs   *Current State of the System*
· **Priorities for Shipments**
· **Destinations for Shipments**
· **Available Transportation**
    Assets

Mobile IA   Static IA

Real Time Exception Data

Historical Information
· **Past Performance of Carriers**
· **Distinctions in priority**
· **Shipping Times**

Figure 7

The human manager lets the static IA know when transportation assets such as planes and trucks are available as well as giving the system real time exception data. The other IA inform the decision making IA of the current state of the system including the priorities, destinations and special requirements of competing shipments, and the state of the system. Finally, the database informs the IA of past performance of the system, anticipated delays and recorded distinctions in priority (i.e. de facto priorities for otherwise equally valuable assets).

The mobile IA would receive data from the same sources, but it would also receive data directly from its sensors such as seismic activity or temperature data on refrigerated goods.

The mobile IA has an embedded neural network to makes its decisions. As mentioned above, the mobile IA's actions consist of bidding its credits to improve its de facto priority or notifying the network as situations arise. Situations involving communication by the mobile IA would range from routine status reports to notification when critical conditions were violated such as refrigeration temperatures or the defilement of a secure shipment.

Within the static IA, a neural net and a genetic algorithm will coexist in a synergistic relationship (see diagram 8 below).

The static IA is faced with two separate problems. The static IA must be able to perform pattern recognition for the recognizing the hierarchy of priorities which exist in the DTS. The static IA must be able to learn from each transaction which occurs. This is work well suited for the capabilities of a neural net. More

Adaptive Learning Algorithm Components

Neural Net   *Sets coefficients for optimization*

Specifies Initial Solution for GA

Learns from Each Transaction

Genetic Algorithm

*Selects Optimal Solution for
Transportation Assignment
Matching Problem*

Figure 8

specifically, the neural net will set the coefficients for the optimization and specify an initial (not necessarily feasible) solution for the genetic algorithm.

Recall we described the transportation assignment problem in terms of a matching problem. We can further characterize this problem as a discontinuous, integral optimization problem. The genetic algorithm is well suited to solve this type of problem. The genetic algorithm uses the objective function described in the following section.

3.5 IA Mathematical Description of Objectives Rather than focus on specific functional forms for the objectives of the IA, we have taken a more heuristic approach to the problem description. From a macroeconomics standpoint, we can view each of the IA as a producer. Each producer attempts to maximize its utility, and given a sufficiently competitive system, the overall system achieves a stable, optimal macroscopic solution [Hahn 1982]. *In the context of this problem, sufficiently competitive means a relatively large number of shipments with varying priorities and adequate, available transportation modes (surface and air) and assets (ships, trains, trucks, airplanes) at the distribution systems decision points.* These decision points refer to nodes in the distribution system where shipment units can change their mode of transportation, e.g., move from an ocean going vessel to an airplane. The modal interchange locations do not have to be collocated, but merely accessible to one another. For example, a diversion of a shipment from ocean carriage to air cargo means that the seaport must be linked to the airport by either rail or truck transport.

In both the case of the static and the mobile IA, the IA will be making inferential decisions, i.e. the IA's objective functions are not fully determined until the shipments all reach their destinations, but the IA make decisions in real time while the shipment units are still in the transportation pipeline. Therefore, the IA are forced to make inferences about what the optimal decisions are from an objective function standpoint. The IA will base these decisions on the three sources of information previously mentioned: exogenous parameters, historical data, and information being passed in real time from other IA. Of particular note here is the historical data; as IA complete transactions the historical data base will be updated, and future IA decisions will be modified based on these updates. For example, imagine a situation where a particular carrier is very unreliable. Every time an IA assigns a shipment unit to the carrier, the shipment unit is lost. Very quickly the system would start to avoid this carrier, because the expected value for the shipment unit cost would rise.

The objectives assigned to different items would be augmented with appropriate utility functions to optimize different requirements. For example, most items would seek to minimize the difference between *actual* and *scheduled* arrival at final destination, whereas selected items might seek to move concurrently with other shipment units such as maintaining the shipment integrity of the components of a weapons system. A good example would be all of the different types of ammunition needed to reload a main battle tank. In later, more sophisticated versions, objectives could be assigned *collectively to groups of items*, such that each item would seek the success of its group, possibly through altruistic decisions.

A default assumption is that a shipment unit's utility is inversely related to the time it takes it to reach its destination in a safe, undamaged condition. The static IAs' utility is measured in terms of minimizing cost under routine conditions and a function of shipment priorities and arrival times under crisis situations [Ferguson, et. al. 1989].

We could describe the objective of the mobile IA to be:

$$\underset{\forall Action}{Min} \{Arrival\ Date + M\phi\}$$

Equation 1

where **Arrival Date** is the date the shipping unit arrives at its destination, f represents the condition of the shipment (e.g. the smaller is the better), and M is the penalty for delivery of the shipment in less than perfect condition. (*M also contains a normalizing factor so that the objective function is uniform in appropriate units.*) A major criteria for the shipment is that it arrives on time (not late or early) at the destination. *Arrival Date* may be a function of scheduled and actual arrival date. An example of such a function would be equation 2 shown below. Note that in this example we assign differing weights for lateness or being early, but in both cases *some* type of penalty *would be* applied.

$$\alpha \cdot Max\big[(Actual - Scheduled),0\big] + \beta \cdot Max\big[(Scheduled - Actual),0\big]$$

Equation 2

The function Φ represents the *condition* of the shipment at its destination. This is initially an estimation, but as the cargo approaches its terminal point, the estimate becomes its true state. The function Φ varies in value from 1 (destroyed) to 0 (perfect). There is no requirement for Φ to be linear. Another portion of Φ would be any monetary amount spent during the journey to expedite movement.

The static IA have an objective function which is dependent on both the cargo flowing through their areas of responsibility and the transportation assets the IA assign to that cargo. A sample objective function for a static IA is given below in Equation 3.

$$\underset{\forall Action}{Min} \left\{ \underbrace{\Pi \cdot \Psi}_{\text{Shipment Units}} + \underbrace{\beta\Phi(\bullet)}_{\text{Condition Violations}} + \gamma \cdot \underbrace{\sum Cost}_{\substack{\forall \text{Shipping Unit} \\ \text{Shipping Costs}}} \right\}$$

where $\Pi \triangleq \{P_1, P_2, \cdots \}$ a vector of weightings (or priorities)

for the various shipments, $\Psi \triangleq \begin{Bmatrix} \{Arrival\ Date + M\phi\}_1 \\ \{Arrival\ Date + M\phi\}_2 \\ \vdots \end{Bmatrix}$,

$\beta \equiv$ weighting for the condition violations, $\Phi(\bullet) \equiv$ a function relating violations of shipping and storage conditions to a numerical value (e. g. storing ammunition at too great a density, sending refrigerated goods in non - refrigerated vehicles), $\gamma \equiv$ weighting for shipping costs, and Cost $\equiv$ cost of shipping from this node forward

Equation 3

The quantity *shipment units* is a weighted sum of the objective functions for the mobile IA. . The weightings in the Pi vector are influenced by the specified priority of the shipment *and* the amount of credits the mobile IA bids to improve its chances for premium transportation. The term *Condition Violations* represents a combination of factors relating to the condition of the cargo in both storage and in transit. Examples of factors include: refrigeration for perishable goods, ensuring system components arrive at the same time and place, and storing volatile substances away from each other. The last term, *Shipping Costs*, refer to the estimated cost to DTS to ship the cargo using a specific set of assignments from the decision node forward to the destination; previous assignments are viewed as sunk costs.

The location of the various IA and their interaction, will be discussed in the following paragraphs.

4. Modeling the Transportation Infrastructure

It will be useful to explore the extent of the IA domain by examining the transportation network in more detail. The Advanced Research Projects Agency (ARPA) has a four year program called TransTech which will explore modeling the transportation infrastructure to include both information, transportation asset and cargo flow. The priciple focus of TransTech is to investigate and demonstrate technology that will make a fundamental difference in transportation. The program will capitalize on the revolutionary advances made in communications, simulation, planning, presentation, retrieval, and visualization technology, as well as seek mechanical systems to improve the intermodal system performance and efficiency. Within this context, a broad network will be created that links transportation/logistics suppliers and uses in a common operating enviornment where powerful new tools can be used to efficiently and flexibly manage the logistics 'war' of the 21st century. The TransTech enviornment will facilitate distributed real-time visualization and interaction with all elements of the military and commercial infrastructure. Not only will Transtech link operational users, but will create a parallel synthetic virtual world that replicates the real operational world, allowing users to switch from one to the other. The vitual world will be used to test new designs of equipment or infrastructure, what-if questions, and execution related problem solving without having to make costly investments in the real-world. The objective of TransTech is to develop a comprehensive transportation and logistics operations, planning and simulations environment. This program will focus heavily on Total Asset Visibility efforts, since much of the TransTech network will rely on real-time feeds of actual operations information as it is occurring. The culmination of the program will be a series of operational demonstrations that place new technologies in the hands of user organizations so as to demonstrate real value. The full measure of the program will create/demonstrate:

a. A distributed real-time visualization and interaction of both the military and commercial transportation systems.

b. An ability to effect real-time control, planning, replanning, and rehearsal of force and sustainment movements, for both deployment and redeployment.

c. An ability for decision-makers to form policy and make investment decisions on alternative transportation infrastructure programs.

d. Total Asset Visibility environment using advanced networks, databases and communications architecture and Automated Identification Technologies (AIT).

e. Emerging technologies that enhance the performance of the transportation system by adopting better means to packaging and handling cargo, mitigation of relative motion problems and tracking assets within the system using AIT.

Clearly, the integration of IA into the overall TransTech strategy will be essential to developing the distributed real-time visualization and interaction of both the military and commercial transportation systems. Likewise, the extensive modeling of the military and commercial transportation infrastructure will greatly assist in developing a strategy for inserting IA into the system and building their knowledge base as quickly as possible.

5. Low Earth Orbit Satellite Communications

One of the most important aspects of a fully integrated transportation system is that the components must be able to communicate world wide. The combination of intelligent agents with the use of low earth orbit (LEO) satellites for communications, appears to offer great potential to accomplish this, for both the commercial and military sector. Currently, there are at least two major companies developing LEO satellite constellations and one company developing a medium-earth orbit (MEO) satellite constellation. Orbital Communications Corporation and Iridium, Inc. are developing LEO's while Odyssey is developing the MEO. Of the two LEO companies, only Orbital Communications Company (ORBCOMM) has two prototype satellites currently in orbit for early user testing. All systems, either the LEO or MEO, are expected to be operational by the year 2000. LMI has initiated action to become one of the early testers of the ORBCOMM system. We plan on conducting a limited demonstration of our IA/LEO satellite concept, under the sponsorship of several of our DoD clients.

In addition to the satellite system, communicators are required to pass data to and receive data from the LEO satellite. While there are many companies that manufacture such communicators, LMI plans to initially test the communicators made by CypherComm. The reason is that CypherComm has already established the necessary communications links with ORBCOMM and they are ready to support user testing in late Fall of 1995. The CypherComm communicators can operate in either a secure or unsecure communications mode, and appear ideal for military applications.

An added benefit resulting from the use of LEO statellites is that location positioning of the communicator can be determined without the use of the Global Positioning System (GPS). Unlike existing GPS systems, which require triangulation from at least three satellites to determine location, the ORBCOMM system uses a variation on the Doppler effect to locate communicators. In Doppler positioning, when the source of a radio signal is in motion, the frequency of the wave increases and the wave length is shortened. An example would be the rising pitch of a train whistle as a train approaches and the falling pitch as it passes. The rate of rise and fall has been used for decades in radar to calculate the speed of moving objects. But it can also be used to pinpoint a location if a couple of readings are taken from the same transmitter. ORBCOMM estimates that location accuracy within 100 meters is achievable. While this level of accuracy is sufficint for most applications, communicators can also be equipped with GPS capability for those situations where greater location accuracy is required.

6. IA Interactions and Examples of Learning Matrices

As described earlier, the location of the static IA within the transportation and distribution system is relatively straight forward. These IAs would be located at the intermodal decision points. Their function is to perform repetitive shipment processing and control within their geographic area of responsibility. In short, they assist the mobile IA in reaching its destination according to schedule and in a undamaged condition. There are however, numerous options as to the level of shipment unit (piece, container, etc.) the mobile IA(s) could be assigned. Some of the tasks the mobile IA would be expected to perform are: interface with the distribution system according to the priority established by higher authority; communicate status by LEO satellite to adjacent and higher echelons of control; function under established performance criteria, and notify appropriate control echelons when the criteria has not been met or has been exceeded (e.g. sent to the wrong port, in port too long, etc.); notify its consignee of its status. An example of how the IA could apply these rules and cooperate among themselves for a typical shipment moving from a shipping activity to an overseas destination by ocean freight, is shown in the following Tables.

6.1 IA Interactions Table 1 represents a typical sequence of events associated with a shipment entering the transportation system. The static IA would process the shipment request, and arrange movement for the shipment according to the priorities established by the shipper and its knowledge about routing to destination and carrier availability and past performance. It would then notify other static IA along the intended route to verify that its current knowledge of the state of the system and carrier schedules are correct. If the other node IA do not communicate an exception to the selected routing and carrier selection, the origin static IA will then proceed to release the shipment to the transportation system.

Static IA (origin)	Mobile IA (shipment)	other Static IA (node points)	Mobile IA (other shipments)
EVENT: 1 -Process shipment request - Assign carrier(s), route, and schedule to shipment unit		EVENT: 2 - Receive intended shipment route and schedule from origin static IA - Confirm carrier selection and schedule is feasible	
ACTION: *enter shipment into system; get clearance from other IA to proceed*		*ACTION:* *verify carrier routing and schedules; confirm no system delays; notify origin IA*	
MESSAGE: **1 container;** **shipment # 45678** **frozen foods** **from: St. Louis MO** **to: Seoul, Korea** **for: 15th Supply Company** **via: ABC rail to Oakland. CA** **vessel "Cargo King" to Pusan** **Han Jin truck to Seoul** **RDD: 20 Nov 19xx**		**MESSAGE:** **O.K. to proceed**	

LEGEND:
EVENT: conditions that the IA are likely to encounter
ACTION: what the IA are to do based on an event
MESSAGE: what the IA communicate to other IA and management concerning the event

TABLE 1

Table 2 describes the next sequence of events where the origin static IA releases the shipment unit to the transportation system. It provides shipment instructions to the mobile IA attached to the shipment unit, as well as a list of rules governed by the shipment type. In this example, because the shipment is frozen foods, the mobile IA would monitor the temperature inside the container, as well as the normal data that all mobile IA would provide, i.e. commodity information, location, destination data, etc. Other mobile IA in the transportation system would also broadcast information about the status of the transportation system as they encounter it. In Event 4, a mobile IA reports to the system that the Port of Oakland is processing shipment slower than normal.

Static IA (origin)	Mobile IA (shipment)	other Static IA (node points)	Mobile IA (other shipments)
	EVENT: 3 -Receive carrier, route and schedule instructions from static IA - Notify origin and node point static IA when movement begins and if delays occur - Report shipment condition if rules violated *Action: report status* **MESSAGE: at location XYZ; on schedule; container temperature unstable**		EVENT: 4 - Report movement status to enroute static IA *ACTION: other IA report on status of transportation system* **MESSAGE: port of Oakland taking longer than normal to process shipments**

LEGEND:
EVENT: conditions that the IA are likely to encounter
ACTION: what the IA are to do based on an event
MESSAGE: what the IA communicate to other IA and management concerning the event

TABLE 2

Event 5, in Table 3, represents the requirement for IA to communicate with each other as well as their human managers. Here, a static IA queries another static IA at the Port of Oakland based on information received from a mobile IA who reported cargo delays at that port. Likewise, the static IA informs management that information has been received from a shipment unit that there is a problem with the temperature on a shipment of frozen foods. We recognize that as the system we propose matures, the IA can communicate directly with whom ever they require.

Static IA (origin)	Mobile IA (shipment)	other Static IA (node points)	Mobile IA (other shipments)
		EVENT 5 - Receive enroute data from mobile IA - Notify management if shipment rules are violated	
		ACTION: monitor status and condition of shipments within the system	
		MESSAGES:	
		to Oakland IA are cargo delays temporary or should inbound cargo be diverted?	
		to management temperature in shipment #45678 unstable. contact carrier to have problem fixed	

LEGEND:
EVENT: conditions that the IA are likely to encounter
ACTION: what the IA are to do based on an event
MESSAGE: **what the IA communicate to other IA and management concerning the event**

TABLE 3

Table 4 characterizes the cooperation between IA that is facilitated by the ability to communicate through the LEO backbone. In Events 6 and 7, the mobile IA reports its location and intentions as it continues its journey toward destination. The static IA in Event 7 has current knowledge of the state of the system and is able to communicate new instructions to the mobile IA such that it may continue on. The static IA are able to respond dynamically to changes in the system and can act to ensure the uninterrupted flow of cargo is maintained.

Static IA (origin)	Mobile IA (shipment)	other Static IA (node points)	Mobile IA (other shipments)
	EVENT: 6. - Notify static IA when node point is reached	EVENT: 7 - Clear shipment on original route or re-route as required	
	ACTION: *report status; update instructions as required*	*ACTION:* *use information on status of the system to keep cargo moving*	
	MESSAGE: **at Oakland awaiting vessel**	**MESSAGE:** **Original vessel late. new sailing date is 1 Nov 19xx on Sea Witch**	
	ACTION: *update sailing schedule and vessel name*		

LEGEND:
EVENT: conditions that the IA are likely to encounter
ACTION: what the IA are to do based on an event
MESSAGE: what the IA communicate to other IA and management concerning the event

TABLE 4

In the final example, Table 5, the cargo reaches destination and reports its arrival and condition. This is very important to the static IA, as it uses the data to update its knowledge base concerning the selected routing and carrier performance. This data will be used repeatedly when arranging future shipments.

Static IA (origin)	Mobile IA (shipment)	other Static IA (node points)	Mobile IA (other shipments)
	EVENT: 8 -Report arrival and condition at destination		
	ACTION: notify origin static IA so database can be updated		
	MESSAGE: arrived Seoul 20 Nov 19xx; no damage		
EVENT: 9 - Update database with shipment history and carrier performance			
ACTION: maintain data on shipment history			
STORE: - all route data rail service good - ocean carrier may have unreliable vessels; monitor future performance - truck company in Seoul meets schedules			

LEGEND:
EVENT: conditions that the IA are likely to encounter
ACTION: what the IA are to do based on an event
MESSAGE: what the IA communicate to other IA and management concerning the event

TABLE 5

6.2 Learning Matrices The next series of Tables captures some examples of the learning cycle for the static IA as well as the types of data we would expect the mobile IA to capture and communicate to other IA and the human managers. Recall that we anticipate the static IA-human interface (IA learning) to evolve through the four processes of 1) seeding the IA knowledge base; 2) inductive learning from the human manager and other IA; 3) certification of the IA decision process by the human manager; and 4) the steady-state phase where the IA routinely applies decision making rules to satisfying transportation requirements.

The task of "seeding the knowledge base" involves cataloging transportation rules, regulations, and procedures applicable to shipments moving within the Defense Transportation System. This data would be extracted from various official regulations, local operating procedures, and from the transportation professionals (functional experts) in the field. The basic categories of knowledge established generally pertain to the shipment commodity and to how it is transported. Table 6 describes the type of knowledge that would be accumulated in a knowledge base.

Knowledge Category	Type of Knowledge
Shipment Commodity	- ammunition is never shipped with fuses - frozen goods are kept in the temperature range of 0 to 10 degrees Fahrenheit - main battle tanks will not fit into a shipping container
Transportation	- household goods are generally not shipped by air mode - shipments designated "high priority" must be at destination within 72 hours - shipments less than 10 pounds are eligible for mailing to destination

TABLE 6

During the inductive phase, the IA have the advantage of learning not only from the human managers, but from other IA as they broadcast information concerning the status of a shipment and the overall state of the transportation network. Table 7 portrays the type information the static IA would put into its knowledge base.

Knowledge Source	Type Information
Human Manager	- only ABC Trucking is licensed to carry ammunition from this location - it is cheaper to ship tanks by rail than by truck if the distance is over 500 miles - group passenger moves over 10 people get a discount on LMG bus lines
Other IA (real-time feedback)	- shipments carried by XYZ Trucking are damaged 50% of the time - the Port of Oakland is currently congested. Allow extra shipping time if using that port - there is a shortage of rail cars in the Ft. Swampy area. Ship by truck if possible

TABLE 7

The key to the certification phase is that the IA can not only duplicate those shipment decisions made by the human managers, but they can identify the rationale for deviating from what would be considered an appropriate response to a shipment requirement. Table 8 describes conditions that could occur where the IA would offer a shipment solution to a manager based on more precise data than would normally be available to that manager. The IA is always guided buy the basics of the shipment: meet customer requirements but do so in an efficient and cost effective manner.

Shipment Deviation	Rationale for Deviation
Schedule an ocean shipment for a later vessel	- original vessel makes two enroute stops where cargo is transferred to other vessels. Later vessel has direct service to desired overseas port and will meet customer RDD. Less handling reduces risk of loss and damage
Select a different mode of transportation	- customer requested high cost air transportation but low cost surface transportation will still meet the RDD

TABLE 8

The transition to the steady-state phase can occur incrementally, based on some predetermined shipment criteria. This is the most likely scenario, since IA learning will occur faster for shipments which occur more frequently than others. Some shipping activities only handle a few commodities, and sometimes carriers are awarded exclusive contracts to carry freight from some shipping activities. In all, the human manager can make the decision to allow the IA more responsibility based on individual circumstances. Table 9 cites some examples of routine, repetitive, or specialized shipments by type and commodity where IA could quickly be integrated into the management structure.

Shipment Type	Shipment Commodity
- group passenger movements	- household goods
- volume move (military equipment to a training exercise)	- ammunition
- high priority repair parts for weapons systems (very high value circuit boards)	- tanks (to and from a maintenance depot for overhaul)

TABLE 9

While each mobile IA would be given parameters which would govern their actions, we view their ability to communicate with the static IA, through the LEO satellite backbone, as offering the greatest benefit . This real-time feedback on status and the ability to determine location within the transportation system offers the military the flexibility and agility needed to achieve true force projection capability. Table 10 lists just a few items that can be communicated by a mobile IA that are currently within the capabilities of existing technologies.

Communication Capability
- location (with or without the Global Positioning System (GPS))
- temperature of surroundings and cargo
- acoustic data (noise)
- light information (anti-tampering mechanism)
- shock level (seismic activity; valuable for ammunition shipments)

TABLE 10

7. Areas of Further Research

There are several areas where additional research will provide valuable data that can be applied to implementing our concept of Intelligent Agents combined with a low earth orbit satellite communications backbone. The first, involves determining the appropriate programming method and architecture for the static IA Neural Network and selecting the appropriate Genetic Algorithm for the IA to learn and respond correctly to a variety of shipment requirements and conditions. The latter we feel is the most challenging since it is difficult to predict the range of operating conditions the IA will encounter in the peace to wartime military spectrum.

On balance, the concept of using intelligent agents could be applied across the military to include use for items in storage. There are currently programs exploring the use of agents for self diagnostics of equipment, to where the agents will also order the necessary repair parts based on their diagnosis. Further, the military is exploring the use of intelligent agents to accomplish routine supply transactions, such as ordering supplies when current stocks reach a predetermined level based on current and projected usage. In the field of Electronic Data Interchange (EDI), progress in the commercial and military sector is being made toward a "paperless" environment where processing shipment requirements and payment for services all occur electronically. The integration of these efforts will no doubt produce a robust environment for technology to affect the way we currently do business.

Because of the large amount of data that must be captured and maintained in a cooperative intelligent agent network as we have described it, management of the IA knowledge base will be a enormous task. How best to update the data while ensuring data integrity is an area which must be addressed before any major work is accomplished. Also, preventing the IA from learning the "wrong" procedures requires a data verification process which has yet to be devised.

Although we plan to conduct limited testing of the available LEO satellite prototypes, a larger question remains unanswered. No research has been conducted to determine the "electronic" environment that the IA will find themselves in, particularly during wartime or other crisis situations. It is known, for example that a port area is a very "hostile" electronic environment, simply because of all of the different radio transmissions with occur in a relatively small area. For example, in a recent test of some radio frequency (RF) tags within a seaport, there was only a 50% success rate for reading the tags, although the interrogator was only 50 feet from the tags. It is also known that certain military radar emit very strong signals which would make communications with a mobile IA for example, impossible. In addition, the strength of certain signals can "burn out" radio receivers. These and other related problems must be researched and solutions found before we are able to institute a comprehensive multi-agent environment for Department of Defense Distribution.

8. References

[CBD 1994] Commerce Business Daily, 24 October 1994.

[Ferguson et al. 1989] D. Ferguson, Y. Yemini, and C. Nikalson, "Microeconomic Algorithms for Load Balancing in Distributed Computer Systems," Research Report, IBM T.J. Watson Research Center, Yorktown Heights, NY, October 1989.

[Gasser 1991] Les Gasser, "Social Conceptions of Knowledge and Action: DAI Foundations and Open Systems," Artificial Intelligence, Vol. 47, pp. 107-138, 1991.

[Hahn 1982] F. Hahn, "Stability," in K. Arrow and M. Intriligator, eds., Handbook of Mathematical Economics II, Chapter 16, North Holland Publishing Co., 1982.

[Hewitt 1991] Carl Hewitt, "Open Information Systems Semantics for Distributed Artificial Intelligence," Artificial Intelligence, Vol. 47, pp. 79-106, 1991.

[Hewitt & Inman 1991] Carl Hewitt and Jeff Inman, "DAI Betwixt and Between: From 'Intelligent Agents' to Open Systems Science," IEEE Transactions on Systems, Man, and Cybernetics, Vol. 21, No. 6, pp. 1409-1419, November/December 1991.

[Hopgood 1993] Adrian Hopgood, Knowledge Based Systems, CRC Press, London, England, 1993.

[Huhns 1994] Michael N. Huhns, "Decentralized Logistics Using Autonomous Agent Technology," (unpublished white paper), Microelectronics and Computer Technology Corporation, Austin, TX, November 1994.

[Huhns & Bridgeland 1991] Michael N. Huhns and David M. Bridgeland, "Multiagent Truth Maintenance," IEEE Transactions on Systems, Man, and Cybernetics, Vol. 21, No. 6, pp. 1437--1445, November/December 1991.

[Kephart et al. 1989] J. O. Kephart, T. Hogg, and B. A. Huberman, "Dynamics of Computational Ecosystems: Implications for DAI," in Les Gasser and Michael N. Huhns, eds., Distributed Artificial Intelligence, vol. II, Morgan Kaufmann Publishers, Inc., San Mateo, CA, 1989.

[Lee & Cohen 1985] L.L. Lee and M.A. Cohen, "Multi-Agent Customer Allocation in a Stochastic Service System," Management Science, vol. 31, pp. 752-763, June 1985.

[Singh & Huhns 1994] Munindar P. Singh and Michael N. Huhns, "Automating Workflows for Service Order Processing: Integrating AI and Database Technologies," IEEE Expert, October 1994.

[USTRANSCOM 1994] United States Transportation Command, "Reengineering the Defense Transportation System: the DTS 2010 Action Plan", 1994.

[Wellman 1992] Michael P. Wellman, "A General Equilibrium Approach to Distributed Transportation Planning," Proceedings AAAI-92, San Jose, CA, July 1992, pp. 282-289.

Mutually Supervised Learning in Multiagent Systems

Claudia V. Goldman and Jeffrey S. Rosenschein
Computer Science Department
Hebrew University
Givat Ram, Jerusalem, Israel
ph: 011-972-2-658-5353
fax: 011-972-2-658-5439
email: clag@cs.huji.ac.il, jeff@cs.huji.ac.il

Abstract. Learning in a multiagent environment can help agents improve their performance. Agents, in meeting with others, can learn about the partner's knowledge and strategic behavior. Agents that operate in dynamic environments could react to unexpected events by generalizing what they have learned during a training stage.

In this paper, we propose several learning rules for agents in a multiagent environment. Each agent acts as the teacher of its partner. The agents are trained by receiving examples from a sample space; they then go through a generalization step during which they have to apply the concept they have learned from their instructor.

Agents that learn from each other can sometimes avoid repeatedly coordinating their actions from scratch for similar problems. They will sometimes be able to avoid communication at run-time, by using learned coordination concepts.

Subtopic: Learning in multiagent systems, Coordination

1 Introduction

Distributed Artificial Intelligence (DAI) is concerned with effective agent interactions, and the mechanisms by which these interactions can be achieved. One of the central issues in multiagent environments is that of appropriate coordination techniques. Much DAI research deals with this issue by giving pre-computed solutions to specific problems. For every new problem, the agents will start from scratch and derive the appropriate solution (even if it is an interaction instance identical to one they have seen before). For example, researchers have considered negotiation as a technique for deriving agreements that determine agent actions [15, 2, 7, 21]. These negotiation techniques invariably focus on a single encounter or set of encounters; agents do not (for example) improve their negotiation performance based on experience. Other DAI researchers have focused more on direct modeling of agents' beliefs and desires, as another way for an agent to decide what action to perform when dealing with others [5]. Again, learning rarely enters into this research; while the exploitation of a model of the opponent is studied, the actual derivation of the model rarely is.

Multiagent reactive systems have also been analyzed within DAI, where solutions are arrived at dynamically by reactive agents in multiagent environments. Social laws [17, 12] and cooperative state-changing rules [4] have been studied; these conventions give the agents a framework within which to act, to more harmoniously interact with the other agents participating in the same world. Learning has been investigated within this framework, particularly in [13], which investigated how conventions can evolve when the Highest Cumulative Reward update rule is used (i.e., agents choose to perform the action that has yielded the highest payoff until then).

The advantages of having agents learn within a multiagent environment are clear. In Cooperative Problem Solving systems, cooperative behavior can be made more efficient when agents adapt to information about the environment and about their partners. In competitive Multiagent Systems, agents' performance within the environment can be improved if they can learn about the strategies and preferences of their opponents.

In this paper, we present a learning algorithm for a cooperative multiagent environment. The agents in our model first go through a training step, and are then able to choose their actions by generalizing what they have learned. The agents do not need to re-coordinate their actions for every new situation or problem. The main issue in our research is how to train the agents in a way that minimizes the number of mistakes in the generalization step.

This distributed learning approach to coordination is useful whenever agents do not have enough time to negotiate, when they exist in a dynamic environment and will benefit by adapting to unpredictable situations, and when the agents face similar problems repeatedly. The actual utility of having agents use learning instead of, for example, negotiation, will depend on the tradeoff between the time it takes to train an agent (which induces an upper bound on the probability of an agent making errors) and the time it would have taken him to re-coordinate his actions from scratch (along with the communication and computation overheads involved).

Section 2 presents an overview of related research that has dealt with the topic of multiagent learning, and presents the learning models of Probably Approximately Correct Learning and P-Concept Learning. In Section 3, we describe our specific scenario, the traffic signals domain. Afterwards, in Section 4 we explain the training and generalization steps in the learning process. Finally, in Section 5, we conclude and discuss several additional points for further investigation.

2 Background on Learning

2.1 Multiagent Learning

An example of a multiagent system in which every agent has a learning module is [14]. The agents' evaluate various hypotheses while having only partial knowledge about them. The agents can know more about a specific hypothesis by receiving messages from other agents expressing their level of confidence in that hypothesis. The general aim of the system is for agents to settle on the best hypothesis they can, given the knowledge they have.

The ACE and the ACG learning algorithms were proposed for a multiagent environment in [20]. In this case, the agents can learn how to coordinate their actions by iteratively sending to one another bids for every action they can perform. These bids reflect the importance of the specific action relative to the agent's goal. The action that gets the highest bid is allowed to be executed. All incompatible actions are dropped, and the agents repeat the above steps while there exists an action with a non-zero bid proposed for it. The two algorithms differ primarily in the competition step; in the ACG algorithm, agents compete over a group of actions.

Reinforcement learning techniques have also been applied in multiagent scenarios. Agents that learn according to the Q-learning algorithm [19] and also cooperate with other agents by exchanging information (partial solutions, plans of action) can learn more quickly than agents that do not cooperate [16].

Littman proposed the use of Markov games as a framework for multiagent systems [9]. He focused on two-player games, where one agent plays the maximizer and the other the minimizer of the expected value $E\{\Sigma_{j=0}^{\infty} \gamma^j r_{i,t+j}\}$, where γ is a discount factor, and $r_{i,t+j}$ is the reinforcement value that agent i receives t steps after time j; he presented a minimax Q-learning algorithm for this problem.

Experiments using the Q-learning algorithm were also carried out in [11] and in [10]. In [11], two agents have to push a block to a goal position. Agents learned complementary policies without sharing any information with the other agent. The agents are actually not even aware of the existence of the other; they learn how to push the block by receiving reinforcement from the environment regarding the distance of the block from the optimal path. [10] covered an experimental study with the iterated prisoner's dilemma, where the players were Q-learning agents. In some experiments an agent played against the fixed TIT-FOR-TAT strategy, while in others it played against another Q-learning agent. The Q-learning algorithm has also been applied to packet routing [8]. Each node in the network is a Q-learner.

Findler [3] has investigated how expert systems can control street traffic signals. In his domain there is only one processor for each intersection. This processor, the expert system, communicates with its four adjacent neighbors. The processors exchange information about the number and the speed of cars going in each of the four possible directions, features of the traffic's flow (type and rate of change), and expert advice. Based on this information, the experts at each intersection learn about the traffic pattern and can therefore choose which rules to apply.

2.2 Probably Approximately Correct Learning

In this section we present a brief overview of Probably Approximately Correct Learning (PAC Learning), which forms the basis of the technique given below

(Section 2.3) for learning probabilistic concepts. Given the following concepts and notations [1], we can define the PAC learning algorithm.

- An *example space* $X \subseteq \Sigma^*$, where Σ is the alphabet for describing examples.
- A *concept space* C, $c \in C$ denotes a learned concept, i.e., $c : X \rightarrow \{0,1\}$
- A *sample of length* m is a sequence of m examples (i.e., $x = (x_1, x_2, \ldots, x_m) \in X$)
- A *training sample* $s = ((x_1, b_1), (x_2, b_2), \ldots, (x_m, b_m))$, $x_i \in X$ and $b_i \in \{0,1\}, b_i = c(x_i)$
- A *hypothesis space* $H \subseteq 2^X$
- The *error* of any hypothesis $h \in H$, with respect to a target concept t, is given by the probability of the event $h(x) \neq h(t)$
- μ denotes a probability distribution on X (i.e., the examples are chosen according to μ)
- $S(m,t)$ denotes the set of training samples of length m for a given target concept t, where the examples are taken from an example space X (i.e., if $x = (x_1, \ldots, x_m)$ then $s = ((x_1, t(x_1)), \ldots, (x_m, t(x_m)))$

Then, following [18, 1], we can state the following definition.

Definition 1. The algorithm L is a probably approximately correct learning algorithm for the hypothesis space H if, given

- A real number δ $(0 < \delta < 1)$;
- A real number ϵ $(0 < \epsilon < 1)$;

then there is a positive integer $m_0 = m_o(\delta, \epsilon)$ such that

- For any target concept $t \in H$, and
- For any probability distribution μ on X;

whenever $m \geq m_0$, $\mu^m \{s \in S(m,t) | er_\mu(L(s)) < \epsilon\} > 1 - \delta$.

2.3 Learning Probabilistic Concepts

Kearns and Shapire have proposed another learning model when the concept to be learned displays uncertain behavior [6]. This means that a probabilistic concept (p-concept) will be learned from examples that, although identical, will sometimes receive a positive label and sometimes a negative label. For example, if the concept to be learned is an event, which can be characterized by a parameter x, that occurs with probability $p(x)$, then the learner will receive training examples of the form $(x_i,1)$ or $(x_i,0)$, where the corresponding label is distributed according to $p(x)$. Formally, given X, the instance space, define the p-concept c to be a function, $c : X \rightarrow [0,1]$. $c(x) = \Pr[x$ is a positive example of the p-concept $c]$. An oracle, the teacher, will choose a training example $x \in X$ according to the distribution of the objects in X. Then, it will label it 1 with probability $c(x)$ and 0 with probability $1 - c(x)$.

Following [6], a p-concept class over a domain X is learnable with a model of probability, if there is an algorithm A (the learner) such that for any target p-concept c, for any distribution D over X, for any inputs $\epsilon > 0$, $\delta > 0$, the algorithm A that has access to the oracle (the teacher), halts and with probability $1 - \delta$ outputs a p-concept h that is an ϵ-good model of probability ($Pr_{x \in D}[|h(x) - c(x)| \leq \epsilon] \geq 1 - \epsilon$); for c with respect to D.

3 The Specific Scenario

In this paper, we consider how to apply learning techniques to the scenario of traffic signal controlling agents.[1] More specifically, we regard only one intersection with two agents, one responsible for the flow of traffic in each direction (no turns are allowed), as shown in Figure 1.

Fig. 1. A Simple Scenario

Let us denote the vertical road r_1 and the agent (i.e., the traffic signal) that controls the traffic of this street A_1. Similarly, we'll name the horizontal road and its agent r_2 and A_2, respectively.

We will map real, continuous time into discrete units. We sample the traffic load for each discrete time unit, in each of the two crossing roads (i.e., how many cars arrive per hour). These real values are related to the WaitingTimes of the cars in the sampled road (that is, how long cars wait at the traffic signals).[2] These numbers induce a "waiting time distribution" over the hours of the day.

Each agent can choose to perform one of two possible actions, "red" or "green." If the agent performs red then the cars in the street that he is responsible for will have to wait, and if he performs green they can move in the appropriate direction. Each agent knows the sample values from the waiting time distribution of its cars. This distribution takes into consideration the different flow in traffic during different times of the day.

---

[1] The scenario is closely related to other job scheduling and information routing activities that automated agents might be involved in, for example, packet routing in a Wide Area Network. More generally, it is a simple example of a cooperative task for two agents, which can be applied to any situation where agents have to coordinate activity to be effective.

[2] The relationship of arrival density of cars to WaitingTime depends on two other parameters, the "rate of removal" of cars from the intersection when the light is green (which might be assumed to be a constant), and the interval of time that the light is green, which is what we are trying to learn.

Although it is clearly preferable for the agents to coordinate their green/red signals so that traffic flows smoothly, it is also possible for both agents to show red (resulting in wasteful waiting) or for both agents to show green (resulting in traffic slowdown and potential collisions as cars navigate the under-regulated intersection).

Were the agents not to employ a learning algorithm, they might coordinate their actions by exchanging and comparing the current waiting times, and using some decision rule to decide which agent will be red and which will be green. The disadvantages would then be the cost of communication, the utter dependence on reliable communication to choose actions, and the fact that the decisions will be completely "local" in time, without regard for the histories of traffic flow (and while these considerations may or may not always be compelling for traffic light agents, they certainly play a role among other kinds of coordinating agents).

The agents' purpose is to learn which action they should perform, taking into account the existence of the other agent. The choice of which action to take (green or red) at any given time is based on the current information he has regarding his own stream of traffic, the sample values of his own waiting time distribution, and the information he has learned regarding the other agent's distribution.

Ideally, the two agents will choose those actions cooperatively (one is green while the other is red) so that the cars will wait as little as possible given the above intersection. The agents are inherently cooperative, and are not competing with one another. They are programmed to perform the learning step for the purpose of decreasing waiting time of cars, both for their own stream of traffic, and for the intersection as a whole (the perpendicular traffic stream). In this paper we do not explore any questions regarding the agents' motivations.

4 The Learning Algorithm

4.1 Learning in the Deterministic Case

The solution to this problem is divided into two steps. In the first step, each agent is trained by the second agent, that acts as his teacher. In the following notation, $i, j \in \{1, 2\}$. Agent A_i sends its list of sample values (i.e., a list of real values), that is a list of examples of waiting times of its cars to A_j. For each example, A_j will return to A_i a pair $(example - value, action)$. The example-value runs over all the real values in the sample list sent by A_i to A_j, and the action is the action that A_j would want A_i to perform. The action can be red or green. A_j decides which label (i.e., action) to attach to the current example value according to its own sample values. Let us denote by $example - value_i^k$ the value of the example from A_i's list at line k. Then, A_j will decide upon the label red if $example_i^k \leq example_j^k$ and green otherwise. In other words, A_j would like A_i to switch to the red light each time A_j's cars are waiting more than A_i's.

We propose a learning rule that is based on each agent remembering the waiting times when his teacher wanted him to switch between the red and green lights. The agent has to remember only the w-t_i^k and w-t_i^{k+l}'s where $a_i^k \neq a_i^{k+l}$ and $k + l$ is the first index with this characteristic.

For any new example taken from the same distribution used in the learning step, the agent is able to label it (i.e., he can decide upon which action to take). The rule for that will be as follows (see Figure 2).

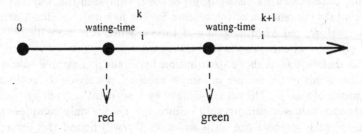

Fig. 2. The Generalization Rule

Assume the new example is given by a value v (such that $WaitingTime_i^k \leq v \leq WaitingTime_i^{k+l}$), then agent A_i will perform red if

$$WaitingTime_i^k \leq v \leq \frac{WaitingTime_i^k + WaitingTime_i^{k+l}}{2}$$

and A_i will perform green if

$$\frac{WaitingTime_i^k + WaitingTime_i^{k+l}}{2} < v \leq WaitingTime_i^{k+l}.$$

We cannot analyze this learning rule according to the PAC learning model presented above because the concept the agents are learning is not deterministic as assumed by this model. In our learning rule, we assume that values that are close enough will be labeled similarly. This assumes indirectly that both agents' distributions do not change in an extreme way. If we want the agents to learn the other's distribution of values and then according to this distribution decide which action to perform, we have to look at a model that enables the agents to learn a non-deterministic concept. In the deterministic case, if the learner gives the same example-value twice then it is assumed that he will get the same label for both of them. Since the teacher labels the learner's training values according to his own values taken from his distribution, he might attach different labels for identical training values. Therefore, we propose another learning algorithm for the agents to learn a probabilistic concept, the distribution of the teacher's values.

4.2 Learning in the Probabilistic Case

Each agent will play the role of the learner and the teacher. The training step will not be exactly as in the PAC learning model. Now, the teacher will send to the learner all its training values (denote them by t_i). Then, whenever the learner faces a new waiting-value (denote it by v), he will count how many t_is are bigger than v and how many t_is are smaller than it. The learner will decide to perform red if there are more t_is that are bigger than smaller (similarly for the green action). The aim of this algorithm is that the number of t_is given by the teacher is enough (and minimal) for the learner to approximate the real weight (according to the teacher's distribution) of the t_i values. In this way, the learner tries to imitate the reaction of the teacher for the new value v. The learner will decide to perform red when he gets v at time k, when it is more likely that the teacher will get t at time k such that $t > v$.

Let us denote the teacher's distribution by T and his sample values by t_i. The teacher sends to the learner m sample values. Let's divide the real numbers into segments of size $\frac{\epsilon}{c_1}$. The actual value of each segment is given by the weight of the teacher values according to T. Since the t_is are only samples from T, the value of each segment can have an error. We will bound this error by $\frac{\epsilon}{c_2}$. Therefore, in each one of the segments there will be between $m \times (\frac{\epsilon}{c_1} - \frac{\epsilon}{c_2})$ to $m \times (\frac{\epsilon}{c_1} + \frac{\epsilon}{c_2})$ t_is. In addition, the learner can also err when he approximates the weight of the t_is that are larger (or smaller) than a given value, because the teacher might have more samples from a less dense portion of his distribution. Hence, for each middle point of each segment t_m, we will bound the number of t_is larger than t_m by $\frac{\epsilon}{c_3}$.

We want to find the sample size m such that the learner will err at most ϵ with confidence at least $1 - \delta$. Denote a segment by s. The three following inequalities have to be true:

$$\frac{\epsilon}{c_1} + \frac{\epsilon}{c_2} + \frac{\epsilon}{c_3} \le \epsilon$$

$$\forall s_j \, Pr(\frac{|\{t_i \text{ s.t. } (t_i > v) \land (t_i \in s_j)\}|}{m} - ActualWeight(s_j) > \frac{\epsilon}{c_2}) < \frac{\delta}{2}$$

$$Pr(\frac{|\{t_i \text{ s.t. } t_i > v\}|}{m} - ActualWeight(all\ values > v\ according\ to\ T) > \frac{\epsilon}{c_3}) < \frac{\delta}{2}$$

From the first equation, we have that $c_1 = c_2 = c_3 = 3$. The left side of the second equation is bounded by $\left(2e^{-2m_1 \frac{\epsilon^2}{9}}\right) * \frac{3}{\epsilon} < \frac{\delta}{2}$. Similarly, the left side of the third equation is bounded by $\left(2e^{-2m_2 \frac{\epsilon^2}{9}}\right) * \frac{3}{\epsilon} < \frac{\delta}{2}$.

The sample size, m, that guarantees the learner to err at most ϵ with confidence $1-\delta$ has a lower bound of $max(m_1, m_2)$. For example, if we let the learner make a mistake of magnitude no greater than 1%, 95% of the time, he will need to see at least 907723 training values. If we let the learner err with magnitude at most 10%, 90% of the time, he will need to see at least 6382 training values.

4.3   Learning a P-Concept

To design autonomous agents, we'd like to let them interact with the minimal and sufficient amount of information needed for the achievement of their tasks. In the former case, each agent, acting as a teacher, needs to send to the learner agent all the values of the samples. We will show that even if the agents don't send each other these values, they can learn about the other's distribution as well. We will base our approach on the model presented in [6].

Each agent (A_i) will be trained by its teacher (A_j), as follows. Based on the model in [6], the oracle is represented by the teacher (i.e., A_j). The p-concept to be learned by both agents regards the distribution of the values of the teacher. More specifically, for our traffic problem, each agent wants to learn, for a given waiting time value v, what is the probability that the other agent will face a waiting time bigger or smaller than it. The oracle will get from the learner its sample values, x_i, and will return these values paired with a label $\in \{1, 0\}$, such that the labels have been generated according to the probability that most of the oracle's sample values, y_is, are larger than x_i. If we define the p-concept, $c(x)$, to be the number of y_is that are larger than x, then we've got that $c(x)$ is a non decreasing function. The value of $c(x)$ cannot decrease since it reflects a sum, namely how many y_is $> x$. Following [6], the p-concept class of all nondecreasing functions $c : \mathcal{R} \rightarrow [0,1]$ is polynomially learnable with a model of probability.

In our case, mutual supervised learning, both agents will act also as an oracle. So, both agents will get the other's samples anyway, and hence they can learn which action to perform according to the algorithm presented in the former section. Nevertheless, we want to find a learning algorithm for a multiagent system by which the agents will learn how the teacher would like them to behave and at the same time the teacher is not revealing all the information he has about his sample values.

One solution is the use of a mediator, that will act as intermediate teacher. Each agent will send to the mediator its sample values (i.e., the waiting times). The mediator will play the role of two teachers, depending who his learner is. For example, when he acts as the teacher of A_i, he will send him A_i's sample values paired with a label that has been generated according to the data sent by A_j (similarly when A_j is the learner). Now, we can apply the p-concept learning model as presented in [6]. First each agent will send to the mediator its own values. Then, the learning algorithm presented there for the class of all nondecreasing functions from reals to [0,1] has to be applied twice, once when the oracle is the mediator and he sends the labels to A_i, and then again when the oracle sends the labels to A_j. Given a new waiting time value, v, to any of the agents, they could evaluate what is the probability of having most of the other agent's values larger than v. If this probability is greater or equal to 1/2 then the agent will perform red, otherwise it will perform green.

5 Summary and Future work

We have presented several learning rules for a multiagent environment. The probabilistic learning cases are presented schematically. In the first case (Figure 3) both agents send to each other all their corresponding sample values. X^i stands for all the sample values of agent A_i, and Y^j for all the sample values of agent A_j.

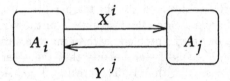

Fig. 3. All Samples Case

In the second case (Figure 4) one agent (the learner) sends to its teacher all its sample values. The teacher sends him back its sample values paired with a label, generated according to the teacher's values. When A_j is the teacher, then he knows about X^i after A_i has sent him these values (similarly when A_i is the teacher).

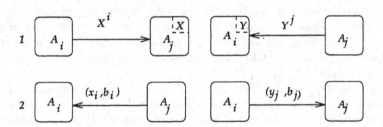

Fig. 4. Learning with Labels

In the third case (Figure 5), each agent learns how to act with the other by receiving labeled examples sent by a mediator. The mediator knows both agents' sample values. The mediator sends to each agent the agent's sample values paired with a label generated according to the other agent's values. Therefore, the agents learn about the other distribution of values by getting only a label and not the values themselves.

Each agent plays the role of the learner and the teacher. The teacher instructs the learner how he should act, in order to please him. The learner generalizes the knowledge he had acquired by testing how close a new example is to the samples that he was trained with, relative to their average, or by evaluating the

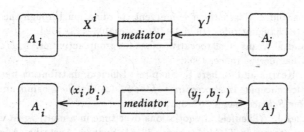

Fig. 5. Learning with the Aid of a Mediator

likelihood of how this new example would be labeled within the larger part of the sample values.

5.1 Future Work

In the traffic signal domain, we might also be interested in many agents, controllers of different roads, learning how to cooperate with one another. In this case, each agent will have many teachers, the agent's closest neighbors, who will send the agent labels for its sample values list. We can also consider another scenario, in which there are hierarchies among the streets (i.e., there are main roads, secondary roads, and so on).

In this paper we have assumed that the agents are benevolent. Alternative scenarios might involve selfish agents who could gain by lying. For example, the traffic signal domain is similar to a communication network domain, where each agent is responsible for messages flowing through the network. Agents might have an interest in delaying others' packets and letting their own flow. The agents can lie to each other by sending incorrect distributions or labels. These competitive learning issues are topics for future research, in which we hope to develop non-manipulable learning algorithms. Those algorithms will make it impossible for an agent to gain more by lying, whether as a learner or as a teacher.

Acknowledgements

We'd like to thank Dana Ron for valuable discussions on learning theory.

References

1. Martin Anthony and Norman Biggs. *Computational Learning Theory.* Cambridge University Press, 1992.
2. Edmund H. Durfee. *Coordination of Distributed Problem Solvers.* Kluwer Academic Publishers, Boston, 1988.
3. N.V. Findler. Distributed control of collaborating and learning expert systems for street traffic signals. In Lewis and Stephanon, editors, *IFAC Distributed Intelligence Systems*, pages 125—130. Pergamon Press, 1991.

4. C. Goldman and J. Rosenschein. Emergent coordination through the use of cooperative state-changing rules. In *AAAI94*, pages 408–413, 1994.

5. B. Grosz and S. Kraus. Collaborative plans for group activities. In *IJCAI93*, pages 367–373, Chambery, France, 1993.

6. Michael J. Kearns and Robert E. Shapire. Efficient distribution-free learning of probabilistic concepts. In *Proceedings of the 31st Anual Symposium on Foundations of Computer Science*, pages 382–391, 1990.

7. S. Kraus and J. Wilkenfeld. Negotiations over time in a multi agent environment: Preliminary report. In *IJCAI91*, pages 56–61, Sydney, Australia, August 1991.

8. M. Littman and J. Boyan. A distributed reinforcement learning scheme for network routing. technical report CMU-CS-93-165, Carnegie Mellon University, 1993.

9. M. L. Littman. Markov games as a framework for multi-agent reinforcement learning. In *Machine Learning 1994*, pages 157—163, 1994.

10. Tuomas W. Sandholm and Robert H. Crites. Multiagent reinforcement learning in the iterated prisoner's dilemma. *Biosystems Journal Special Issue on the Prisoner's Dilemma*, submitted.

11. S. Sen, M. Sekaran, and J. Hale. Learning to coordinate without sharing information. In *AAAI94*, pages 426–431, 1994.

12. Y. Shoham and M. Tennenholtz. Emergent conventions in multi-agent systems: initial experimental results and observations (preliminary report). In *KR92*, Cambridge, Massachusetts, October 1992.

13. Y. Shoham and M. Tennenholtz. Co-learning and the evolution of social activity. Technical Report STAN-CS-TR-94-1511, Stanford Univ., 1994.

14. S. Sian. Adaptation based cooperative learning multi-agent systems. In *Decentralized AI 2*, pages 257—272, 1991.

15. Reid G. Smith. *A Framework for Problem Solving in a Distributed Processing Environment*. PhD thesis, Stanford University, 1978.

16. M. Tan. Multi-agent reinforcement learning: Independent vs. cooperative agents. In *Machine Learning: Proceedings of the Tenth international conference*, pages 330—337, 1993.

17. M. Tennenholtz and Y. Moses. On cooperation in a multi-entity model. In *IJCAI89*, pages 918–923, Detroit, Michigan, August 1989.

18. L. G. Valiant. A theory of the learnable. *Communications of the ACM*, 27(11):1134—1142, 1984.

19. Christopher Watkins and Peter Dayan. Technical note Q-learning. *Machine Learning*, 8:279—292, 1992.

20. Gerhard Weiß. Learning to coordinate actions in multi-agent systems. In *IJCAI93*, Chambery, France, 1993.

21. G. Zlotkin and J. S. Rosenschein. A domain theory for task oriented negotiation. In *IJCAI93*, pages 416–422, Chambery, France, 1993.

A Framework for
Distributed Reinforcement Learning

Pan Gu & Anthony B. Maddox

330 Snell Center, Northeastern University,
360 Huntington Avenue, Boston, MA 02115
pan@splinter.coe.neu.edu
amaddox@gse.ucla.edu

Abstract

The paper proposes a novel learning model, called the distributed reinforcement learning model (DRLM), that allows distributed agents to learn multiple interrelated tasks in a real-time environment. DRLM consists of a hidden task model (HTM) used for dealing with incomplete perception, a composite state model (CSM) for interdependency between tasks, and a Q-learning subsystem (QLS) for updating action merit. In this paper, we also present a distributed Q-learning algorithm and an architecture that allows agents to reward their peers' actions and share their experience. DRLM is successfully implemented in a flexible manufacturing system where sensors (modeled as agents) have to learn to communicate with humans about the material handling activities using graphical actions such as displays and animation.

1 Introduction

Recently, researchers have begun to investigate the possibilities of using existing machine learning techniques in a multiagent environment. Tan (1993) has conducted three case studies of multiagent reinforcement learning involving cooperation by sharing sensations, episodic experience, (i.e., sequences of sensation, action, and reward triples), and learned decision policies. The case studies involve tasks of hunter agents seeking to capture randomly-moving prey agents in a simple grid world. Only a limited number of agents (maximum of two hunter agents and two prey agents with only hunter agents communicating to each other) are investigated. Sian (1991) has developed a distributed learning system called MALE (multi-agent learning environment) where cooperative learning is achieved via an interaction board (i.e., a blackboard paradigm). The MALE architecture is tested in the domain of commodities trading involving a maximum number of five agents. Weib (1993) has investigated distributed RL in a blocks world where agents with limited sensing and motor capabilities have to learn a sequence of actions to complete the task of transforming a starting configuration of blocks into a goal configuration. There can be only one agent and one action active at any time.

In this paper we consider scenarios where *multiple learning agents* interact with a dynamic environment and face *multiple elemental decision tasks*. The learning environment is characterized by the following:

1 Actions involved with each task can be individually rewarded or penalized. The payoffs may be immediate or delayed. An agent can perform only one task at any stage (time step). In addition, each task may require different agents to take a sequence of actions to complete it, i.e., a task may have to traverse some space of agents.

2 Each agent has its own perceptions and actions and is minimally aware of the existence of other agents. These cooperative agents may be perceptually heterogeneous because some agents have more sensing capabilities than others. For example, agents having bar code reader sensors can uniquely identify domain objects that they sense, while agents having proximity sensors can only detect the presence of objects, but are unable to determine the identities of these objects. We refer to these limited sensing capabilities as incomplete perceptions.

3 Each agent has a set of *local* actions (intraagent actions) and *transferring* actions (interagent actions that can transfer the control of a task to other agents). After an agent has completed its share of a task using its local actions, it may convey the task to other agents using transferring actions and collect additional rewards.

4 Since each agent has a limited but different view of the world, an agent may be able to sense some aspects of tasks that can not be perceived by other agents. Therefore, an agent may use its *sensations* and *experience* to provide immediate or delayed payoffs on transferring actions performed by their peers.

5 Learning solutions of these tasks are accomplished in a complex real-time system with large numbers of tasks and cooperative agents. An agent's goal is to find the best action policies that maximize the total expected rewards over the horizon of all tasks.

Due to incomplete perceptions, the multiagent system described above inherits a problem frequently encountered by a single agent system, namely, perceptual aliasing (Whitehead and Ballard, 1991). Such a problem occurs when a learning agent is unable to use its perception to distinguish two significantly different world states which need different actions (responses). In the above multiagent system, there are two potential sources for perceptual aliasing:

- *Incomplete perception.* When a set of heterogeneous agents face multiple tasks, agents with incomplete perceptions are not able to distinguish the true identity of current tasks. As a consequence, the agents are unable to deterministically map their sensations into their internal states, and the payoffs generated from such states are also non-deterministic.

- *Interdependency between tasks.* In a multiagent system facing multiple interdependent learning tasks an agent with complete perception only has a partial view of the relationships. Each agent's actions not only depend on their own internal states, but also on the internal states of other agents concurrently performing other tasks.

In the following sections, we describe the model *embedded* into *each* agent, called the *distributed reinforcement learning model* (DRLM), designed to solve the multiple learning tasks described above.

2 The DRLM

The DRLM (Figure 1) consists of a *hidden task model* (HTM), a *composite state model* (CSM), and a *Q-learning subsystem* (QLS). The HTM, adapted from the HMM in (Rabiner, 1989), is a perceptual distinction approach that tackles the problem of perceptual aliasing resulting from incomplete perceptions in the presence of multiple agents. The CSM is formulated to account for the effects of the interrelationships between tasks on action policies, in which agents have to incorporate other agents' internal states into their own internal states, forming *composite states*. The QLS is a distributed version of the *Q*-learning architecture (Watkins & Dayan, 1992) adapted here to manipulate actions and update *Q*-values of state-action pairs in a multiagent setting.

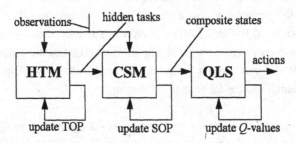

Figure 1: An Outline of DRLM for Agent e_i

The HTM makes an observation and maps it into a set of hidden tasks. The agent e_i then takes the set of hidden tasks from the HTM and forms a set of hidden composite states in CSM. The QLS finally takes an action and is expected to receive a payoff from other agents concerning the merit of the composite states obtained from the CSM.

2.1 The Hidden Task Model (HTM).

To formally state the problem, consider a set of agents that have to cooperatively learn to solve many tasks in a distributed environment. Notationally, we use {...} to represent a set and ⟨...⟩ a vector. The hidden task model is characterized by the following:

1 Let $\Psi = \{t_1, t_2, ..., t_M\}$ and $\Phi = \{e_1, e_2, ..., e_N\}$ represent the set of all tasks and the set of distributed agents in the system. Let $c_i^k(n_i) = \langle e_i, t_k \rangle$, $n_i \in I$, denote task t_k currently performed by agent e_i at stage n_i, where I is the set of all positive integers. Unless specified otherwise, superscripts denote task indices and subscripts denote agent indices. The subscript i in the term n_i is used to distinguish the stage of agent e_i from the stages of other agents. The term n_i may be simplified as n if its association with an agent is clear in an expression. For example, $c_i(n_i)$ can be simplified as $c_i(n)$ because the n is associated with the e_i by default. Let $c_i(n)$, $n \in I$, be a random variable that takes on values in

the finite set Ψ. The stochastic process $\{c_i(n), n \in I\}$, called the *task process*, is assumed to be a finite-state Markov process.

2. $\Gamma = \{v_1, v_2, ...v_K\}$ is the set of observation symbols which correspond to the physical output of the system being modeled. Let $o_i(n)$, $n \in I$ be a random variable which denotes the observation of agent e_i at stage n and the stochastic process $\{o_i(n), n \in I\}$ be the *observation process* of agent e_i at various stages.

3. $\Omega = (a_1, a_2, ..., a_L)$ is the set of possible actions available to all agents. It consists of a set of local actions Ω^l and a set of transfer actions Ω^t. In this section, we consider only transfer actions because local actions have no effect on the HTM. A stationary $M \times N$ task transition probability (TTP) matrix for agent e_i when encountering a task $t_k \in \Psi$, is denoted by $A_i^k = \{p_{ij}^k(a_p), e_j \in \Phi, a_p \in \Omega\}$, where

$$p_{ij}^k(a_p) = p[c_j(n) = t_k \mid c_i(n) = t_k, a_i(n) = a_p] \tag{1}$$

defines the probability that task t_k is transferred to agent e_j ($c_j(n) = t_k$) at stage n_j given that t_k is at agent e_i ($c_i(n) = t_k$) if action a_p is taken ($a_i(n) = a_p$) at stage n_i. Let $A_i = \{A_i^k, t_k \in \Psi\}$ denote the set of all task transition probabilities for agent e_j.

4. The observation distribution probability (ODP) for agent e_i, i.e., $B_i = \{b_i^k(v_q), t_k \in \Psi, v_q \in \Gamma\}$ in which

$$b_i^k(v_q) = p[o_i(n) = v_q \mid c_i(n) = t_k] \tag{2}$$

defines the conditional probability of observing symbol v_q given agent e_i's current task is t_k. The term $b_i^k(v_q)$ is often referred to as *a priori* probability, denoting the relationship between e_i's observation process and task process.

The HTM defined above implies the existence of two sample spaces Γ and Ψ and a many-to-one mapping from Ψ to Γ. Due to incomplete agent perceptions, the actual task at any stage is never directly observable, but only indirectly observable through Γ. The task currently encountered is now defined over all the M possible tasks in Ψ with each of them associated with a probability called the task occupation probability (TOP), denoted by ω_i^k. We refer to these tasks in Ψ with different TOPs as the set of *hidden tasks* (HTs). Agents maintain their own versions of hidden tasks whose TOPs vary as their stages progress. All tasks are assumed to be hidden by default and simply are referred to as tasks hereafter.

A Bayesian formula is used to update the TOPs:

$$\omega_j^t(n) = \eta b_j^t(v_q) \sum_{e_i \in \Phi} p_{ij}^t [a_i(n)] \omega_i^t(n) , \tag{3}$$

where η is a normalizing constant chosen to make $\sum_{t_k \in \Psi} \omega_j(n) = 1$. To improve the HTM parameters A_i, and B_i, we adopted a variant of the Baum-Welch method as follows:

$$\frac{\sum_{n \in I a_i \in \Phi} \sum p_{ij}(a_p) \omega_i(n) b_j[o_j(n)]}{} \tag{4}$$

$$b_i^t(v_q) = \frac{\sum_{n \in I} \omega_i^t(n) \delta[o_i(n), v_q]}{\sum_{n \in I} \omega_i^t(n)} , \tag{5}$$

where $\delta[o_i(n), v_q] = 1$, if $o_i(n) = v_q$
$= 0$, otherwise.

At each iteration, the following stochastic constraints $\sum_{e_i \in \Phi} p_{ij}^t(a_p) = 1$, $t_k \in \Psi, a_p \in \Omega$

and $\sum_{t_k \in \Psi} b_i^t(v_q) = 1$, $v_q \in \Gamma$ are used.

2.2 The Composite State Model (CSM)

In this section, consider the internal states and composite states of an agent. Let U be the number of states describing the conditions of a task within the territory of the agent, and $1 \leq u \leq U$ be the index into the space. An agent's internal state can be formally defined using a triple:

$$s_{i,u}^k = (e_i, t_k, u) , \tag{6}$$

where the superscript k and the subscripts i and u represent task, agent, and state indices, respectively. A more compact notation s_i is used to simplify $s_{i,u}^k$ hereafter. In this paper, we assume u in Eq. (6) can be determined with certainty. The probability of entering the internal state s_i, denoted by $\omega_{s_i}(n)$, is therefore the same as deciding the true identity of the encountering task $c_i(n)$, i.e., $\omega_{s_i}(n) = \omega_i^t(n)$.

Consider the effect of the interdependency among tasks on the action policies of agent e_i The agent selects a set of agents called the reference agents, denoted by $\Phi'_i = \{e_1, e_2, \cdots, e_{m-1}\}$. A composite state of agent e_i is a vector whose components are the internal states of agent e_i and its all reference agents:

$$\vec{s}_i = \langle s_i, s_1, s_2, \cdots, s_{m-1} \rangle \qquad (7)$$

The probability (referred to as the composite state occupation probability (SOP)) of entering such a composite state $\vec{s}_i$, denoted by $\omega_{\vec{s}_i}$, can be estimated by multiplying the corresponding internal state occupation probabilities of e_i and its reference agents:

$$\omega_{\vec{s}_i} = \omega_{s_i} \times \prod_{j=1}^{m-1} \omega_{s_j} \qquad (8)$$

2.3 The Q-Learning Subsystem (QLS)

Let $\vec{\omega}_{\vec{s}_i}(n)$ be a vector representing the agent e_i's current belief about its current composite state at stage n. The Q-value for the composite state vector is estimated by summing the Q-values of all possible states proportionally according to their state occupation probabilities. i.e.,

$$Q[\omega_{\vec{s}_i}(n), a_p] = \sum_{\vec{s}_i \in \theta_i} \omega_{\vec{s}_i}(n) Q(s_i, a_p), \qquad (9)$$

where $Q(\vec{s}_i, a_p)$ is the Q-value of state-action pair $(\vec{s}_i, a_p)$, and θ_i is the set of possible composite states entered by e_i.

After the action is taken, the next state is subsequently entered. If a local action $a_p \in \Omega^l$ is selected, the next state, denoted by $\vec{s}_i'$ resides in the same agent e_i. If a transfer action $a_p \in \Omega^t$ is chosen, the next state, denoted by $\vec{s}_j$, comes from a different agent e_j. The Q-value of state-action pair $(\vec{s}_i, a_p)$ is updated according to a modified Q-learning rule taking into account the SOP of $\vec{s}_i$:

$$Q(\vec{s}_i, a_p) = [1 - \beta \omega_{\vec{s}_i}(n)]Q(\vec{s}_i, a_p) + \beta \omega_{\vec{s}_i}(n)\hat{Q}(\vec{s}_i, a_p), \qquad (10)$$

where $0 \le \beta \le 1$ is the learning rate, and $\hat{Q}(\vec{s}_i, a_p)$ is equal to the immediate payoff r_i plus the best Q-value that can be obtained from the next state $\vec{s}_i'$ or $\vec{s}_j$, discounted by γ, i.e.,

$$\hat{Q}(\vec{s}_i, a_p) = r_i + \gamma \underset{a \in \Omega}{Max} Q(\vec{s}_i' | \vec{s}_j, a),$$ (11)

3 The Distributed Q-Leaning Architecture

The distributed Q-learning (DQL) architecture, illustrated in Figure 2*a* shows a method for constructing Q-values of composite states in a distributed setting. The computational structure of a distributed agent is modeled as three concurrent cycles: the *action, payoff,* and *episode* cycle. An agent may be in one of these three cycles at any stage. Multiple agents may be in the same cycles at the same time.

Agents have two kinds of inputs, external inputs (observations) from the world and internal inputs (messages) from their peers via a communication network. The choice of entering different cycles depends on the type of input. The payoff and episode cycles are invoked when messages are received. The action cycle is entered upon receiving observations. Figure 2*b* gives a detailed view of the action cycle.

To allow agents payoff their peers' transfer actions and share their learned experiences, a single and triple: $h_i = h(\vec{s}_i)$ and $\varepsilon_i = \varepsilon(\vec{s}_i, r_i, \vec{s}_i' | \vec{s}_j)$, called the *payoff* and the *episode,* are defined (| denotes a *or* relationship) The payoffs and episodes are communication packages that allow experiences gained for one agent to be transferred to other agents.

When an agent e_i perceives an observation o_i upon arrival of a new task, the action cycle is entered. The agent finds a set of agents, called the transfer agent set denoted by Φ_i', which accounts for the task transition. This is accomplished through interagent message *findTransferAgent*. The *mapToHT* function takes the set of transfer agents as input and maps their current hidden tasks onto e_i's own hidden tasks Ψ_i. Agent e_i then sends intraagent messages *updateTOP* and *updateODP* to update its task occupation, and observation distribution probabilities. Interagent messages *updateTTP* are sent to all agents in the transfer agent set, allowing them to update their task transition probabilities.

The *mapToHIS* function is used to map the hidden tasks Ψ_i and the observation o_i into a set of internal agent states denoted by θ_i. After the set of reference agents Φ_i' are obtained through interagent messages *findReferenceAgent*, the *mapToHCS* function is employed to construct the set of composite states $\vec{\theta}_i$ by selecting an internal state from each agent in Φ_i'.

The selection of internal states is based on a random algorithm biased toward their task occupation probabilities. That is, the higher their TOPs, the more likely they are chosen. This algorithm gives opportunities to the internal agent states with low TOPs to become more salient. Agent e_i then sends an intraagent message *updateSOP* to recompute its current state occupation probabilities. A stochastic action selector (i.e., the *select* function in the algorithm) is used to choose an action a_i based on the current composite states $\bar{\theta}_i$ and the stored Q matrix. The selection process is based on a policy such as the *Boltzmann* distribution.

If a transfer action is performed, the agent e_i constructs a payoff request H_i and broadcasts it to all agents in the system. If a local action is chosen, the *payoffLocalAction* function maps the state s_i' into a real-valued scalar r_i. The current state s_i, the payoff r_i, and the next state $\bar{s}_i'$ are then packed into an episode ε_i, which is sent to the intraagent channel so that the local action resulted in this state transition can be rewarded or penalized.

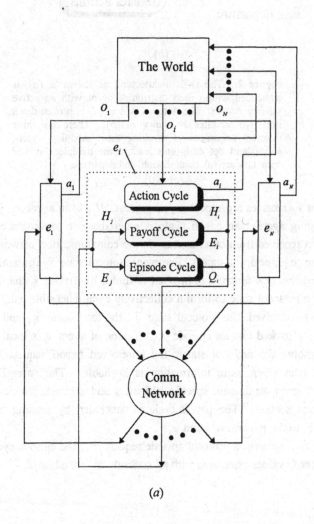

(a)

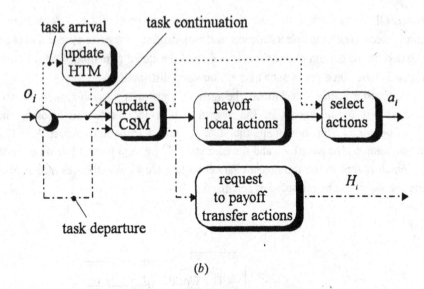

task arrival

task continuation

update HTM

O_i

update CSM

payoff local actions

select actions

a_i

request to payoff transfer actions

H_i

task departure

(b)

Figure 2: The DQL architecture, as shown in (a), is embedded within each distributed agent with an active sensory system. The Action Cycle in (a) is broken down into five modules as shown in (b). There are three different sequences of invoking these modules. Dot-, solid-, and dot dash-lines lead to the modules invoked upon task arrival, continuation, and departure.

If agent e_i receives a protocol payoff request, H_j, from agent e_j (referred to as the requesting agent), the payoff cycle is entered. For convenience, we refer to information received from other agents via the communication network as *protocol* information (e.g., protocol states). For every protocol state $\vec{s}_j$ contained in H_j, the *payoffTransferAction* function is invoked to find a local state $\vec{s}_i$ that can be paired with such a protocol state to form a collectively comprehensible pair. If these two states can be resolved, the protocol state $\vec{s}_j$, the local state $\vec{s}_i$, and the resulting payoff r_i are packed into an episode ε_i. If none of agent e_i's local states can be used to resolve the protocol states, the unresolved payoff request is stored and reinvoked later when more information is available. The *payoffTransferAction* function is based on domain specific heuristics and a realization described in the experimental section. The payoff cycle is concluded by sending out the set of episodes E_i to the requesting agent e_j.

If agent e_i receives a protocol episode request E_j, the episode cycle is entered, in which the Q values associated with all states in E_j are adjusted.

Action Cycle

update HTM

1. $\Phi_i^f \leftarrow findTransferAgent\,(o_i)$;
2. $\Psi_i \leftarrow mapToHT\,(\Phi_i^f)$;
3. send $updateTOP\,(\Psi_i, \Phi_i^f, o_i)$ to itself;
4. For every agent e_j in Φ_i^f
      send $updateTTP\,(\Psi_i, o_i)$ to e_j;
5. send $updateODP\,(\Psi_i, o_i)$ to itself.

update CSM

1. $\theta_i \leftarrow mapToHIS\,(\Psi_i, o_i)$;
2. $\Phi_i^r \leftarrow findReferenceAgent\,(o_i)$;
3. $\bar{\theta}_i \leftarrow$ the current set of composite states;
4. $\bar{\theta}_i \leftarrow mapToHCS\,(\Phi_i^r)$;
5. send $updateSOP\,(\bar{\theta}_i)$ to itself.

select action

1. $a_i \leftarrow select(\bar{\theta}_i, Q_i)$;
2. perform action a_i.

payoff local actions

1. for every state $\bar{s}_i'$ in $\bar{\theta}_i$
      $r_i \leftarrow payoffLocalAction\,(\bar{s}_i')$;
      $\varepsilon_i \leftarrow \varepsilon(\bar{s}_i, r_i, \bar{s}_i')$;
      add ε_i to episode list E_i
2. send $updateEpisode\,(E_i)$ to itself.

request to payoff transfer actions

1. for every state $\bar{s}_i$ in $\bar{\theta}_i$
      $h_i \leftarrow h(\bar{s}_i)$;
      add h_i to payoff list H_i;
2. for every agent e_j in Φ
      send $requestToPayoff(H_i)$ to e_j.

Payoff Cycle

1. $\bar{\theta}_i \leftarrow$ the set of local composite states;
   $\bar{\theta}_j \leftarrow$ the set of protocol composite states in H_j;
2. for every state $\bar{s}_i$ in $\bar{\theta}_i$ and $\bar{s}_j$ in $\bar{\theta}_j$
      $r_i \leftarrow payoffTransferAction\,(\bar{s}_i, \bar{s}_j)$;
      if r_i is a real-valued scalar
         $\varepsilon_i \leftarrow \varepsilon(\bar{s}_j, r_i, \bar{s}_i)$;
         add ε_i to episode list E_i;
      else
         add this request to the message queue;
3. send $updateEpisode\,(E_i)$ to requesting agent e_j.

Episode Cycle

1. for every episode ε_j in E_j
      $\bar{s}_i \leftarrow$ the local state; $\bar{s}_j \leftarrow$ the protocol state;
      $r_i \leftarrow$ the payoff;
      $a_i \leftarrow$ the action taken at state $\bar{s}_i$;
      apply Eq. (11);
      apply Eq. (10).

Figure 3: An outline of the steps executed in the Action, Payoff, and Episode Cycles. Messages are denoted in *italic* forms.

4   Experiments

We have successfully implemented DRLM in the domain of a flexible manufacturing system (FMS) (Luggen, 1991) to solve a sensor interpretation problem (Gu & Maddox, 1994). We restrict our attention to one important component of a FMS, a material handling system (MHS), which can be modeled as:

- A set of sensors represented by agents, and
- A set of observations sensed by these sensor agents over time.

We consider two classes of sensors, optical sensors with complete sensations (bar code readers) and binary sensors with incomplete perceptions (proximity sensors). An observation has attributes of *perceptual-status*, *-type*, *-model* and *-serial*. Perceptual status is either perceived (referred as *on*) or not perceived (referred as *off*). Perceptual type, model, and serial represent the perceptual features of an object that give rise to sensor output. For example, an object could have perceptual type as *widget*, model as *gearbox*, and serial as *A*. If such an object is perceived, a sensor creates an observation denoted by (*on, widget, gearbox, A*). An observation may also be partially defined as in (*on, nil, nil, nil*), which indicates that the other perceptual attributes are not available.

We have chosen a MHS scenario which consists of 10 sensor agents, denoted by $e_1, e_2, \cdots, e_{10}$, respectively, as shown Figure 4. These sensors are located in four stations: a load station, two CNC stations, a unload station, and two automatic guided vehicles (AGVs). In this scenario,, sensor agents e_9 and e_{10} are spatially enclosed in AGV 1 and AGV 2, respectively, and will flow along with their carriers.

Actions available to sensor agents are graphical actions for *display* and *animation* of MHS activities. For example, one action of agent e_2 is to "*move the icon of AGV 1 from the location of the load station to the location of CNC 1*".

The generation of observation sequences is dictated by the process plan and the routing algorithm assumed as follows:

gearboxes: $e_1 \rightarrow e_3 \rightarrow e_7$,
shafts: $e_1 \rightarrow e_5 \rightarrow e_3 \rightarrow e_7$.
AGV 1:   travels only to e_2, e_4, and e_6,
AVG 2:   travels only to e_4, e_6, and e_8.

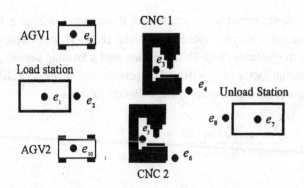

Figure 4: In the above experiment scenario, sensors e_2, e_4, e_6, and e_8 are used to position AGVs, and e_1, e_3, e_5, e_7, e_9, and e_{10} to buffer widgets.

The agent e_1 in the load station alternatively generates gearboxes and shafts with a mean period of 30 seconds. If an AGV is idle, it will be sent to pick up the widget and deposit it to another station based on the process plan. Sensor agents, however, do not have this knowledge. In fact, one of the objectives of these agents is to determine what graphical actions to take depending upon observations.

There are 4 learning tasks identified as: *"predict the activities of gearboxes, shafts, AGV 1, and AGV 2"*. These learning tasks are dynamically interrelated. For example, when a gearbox is transferred from the load station to AGV 1, the current learning task of agent e_2 (i.e., *"predict the activities of AGV 1"*) becomes dependent on the current learning task of agent e_9 (i.e., *"predict the activities of the gearbox"*). That is, AGV 1 will move to CNC1 according to the process plan.

The *payoffTransferAction* (s_i, s_j) function in Figure 3 is used to payoff agents' animating actions based on the following three heuristics.

- the *temporal* constraint - the absolute difference between the perception times of states $\vec{s}_i$ and $\vec{s}_j$ satisfy prespecified lower and upper bounds,
- the *perceptual* constraint - states $\vec{s}_i$ and $\vec{s}_j$ are describing the same domain objects, and
- the *spatial* constraint - the perceptual status' of $\vec{s}_i$ and $\vec{s}_j$ must be opposite (i.e., one is *on*, and the other is *off*, or vice versa).

The state pair $\vec{s}_i$ and $\vec{s}_j$ that satisfy the conditions are rewarded.

We have experimented with variations of the scenario in Figure 4, altering the number of agents with incomplete perceptions (Exp. 1) and employing different sensation sharing policies (Exp. 2). All agents used a learning rate of $\beta = 0.5$, and a temporal discount factor of $\gamma = 0.6$. The performance measure, called the correct action percentage (CAP), is given by the following formula.

$$CAP = \frac{no.\ of\ correct\ actions\ taken}{total\ no.\ of\ actions\ taken} \qquad (12)$$

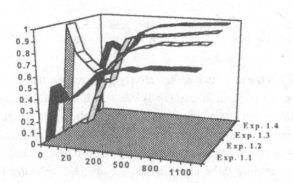

Figure 5: A plot of the number of total observations perceived by all the agents in the system as a function of the correct action percentage (CAP).

In Exp. 1, there are 10, 6, 4, and 0 sensor agents with incomplete perceptions, referred to as Exp. 1.1, 1.2, 1.3, and 1.4, respectively. The results in Figure 5 show that, as the number of agents with incomplete perceptions increases, it takes longer to converge to lower CAPs.

Because the composite state space is increasing exponentially with respect to the number of sensations shared, in a distributed system with a large number of agents, constructing composite states must be selective. In Exp. 1, we employed dynamic sensation sharing accomplished through interagent communications (i.e., the *findReferenceAgent* function in Figure 3). The dynamic sensation sharing is based on a spatial relationship indicating enclosure of one sensed observation inside another. For example, a sensor may perceive an AGV that encloses another sensor that senses a gearbox. Once such a relationship is found, the sensations involved are incorporated into composite states. We are currently developing a generalization technique to group relevant composite states together and form more abstract states.

In Exp. 2, we used the same experimental parameters as in Exp. 1.3 (there are 4 agents with incomplete perceptions) while varied the sensation sharing policies as follows:

- no sharing,
- sharing with all sensors within the same station,
- sharing with all sensors for the same purpose, and
- the dynamic sensation sharing.

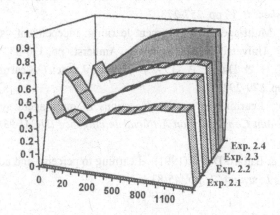

Figure 6: A plot of number of total observations as a function of CAP for 4 different sensation sharing policies.

The results of employing these 4 sensation sharing strategies are depicted in Figure 6. As we expected, there is no reasonably good performance when sensations are not shared (Exp. 2.1). The performance improves to a certain extent when fixed sensation sharing policies (Exp. 2.2 and Exp. 2.3) are used. The dynamic sensation sharing (Exp. 2.4) converges quickly to steady state performance and achieves satisfactory CAP.

Acknowledgments

This research was supported in part by the National Aeronautics and Space Administration through the Jet Propulsion Laboratory under contract 959946. We thank Kimberly Ringer for her valuable review on this work.

References

Luggen, W. W. (1991). Flexible manufacturing cells and systems. *Printice Hall*, Englewood Cliffs, NJ.

Gu, P. & Maddox, A. B. (1994). A protocol for mutisensor interpretation. *Technical report*. Department of IE/IS, Northeastern University, Boston, MA.

Rabiner, L. R.. (1989). A Tutorial on hidden Markov models and selected applications in speech recognition. *Proceedings of IEEE*, 77(2), pp. 257-286.

Sian, S. S. (1991). Adaptation based on cooperative learning in multi-agent systems. *Decentralized A.I. - 2, In Yves Demazeau & Jean-Pierre Muller (eds.). Elsevier Science Publishers B. V.* pp. 257-273.

Tan, M. (1993). Multi-agent reinforcement learning: independent vs. cooperative agents. *ML-93*. University of Massachusetts, Amherst. pp. 330-337.

Watkins, C. J. C. H. & Dayan, P. (1992.) Technical note: Q-Learning. *Machine Learning*, 8, pp. 279-292.

Weib, G. (1993). Learning to coordinate actions in multi-agent systems. *13th International Joint Conference on Artificial Intelligence (IJCAI-93)*, France, pp. 311-316.

Whitehead S. D. & Ballard D. H. (1991). Learning to perceive and act by trial and error. *Machine Learning*, 7. pp. 45-83,.

Evolving Behavioral Strategies
in Predators and Prey

Thomas Haynes and Sandip Sen

Department of Mathematical & Computer Sciences
The University of Tulsa
e–mail: [haynes,sandip]@euler.mcs.utulsa.edu

Abstract. The predator/prey domain is utilized to conduct research in Distributed Artificial Intelligence. Genetic Programming is used to evolve behavioral strategies for the predator agents. To further the utility of the predator strategies, the prey population is allowed to evolve at the same time. The expected competitive learning cycle did not surface. This failing is investigated, and a simple prey algorithm surfaces, which is consistently able to evade capture from the predator algorithms.

1   Introduction

Our goal is to generate programs for both the cooperation of autonomous agents and for handling adversity in the face of such cooperation. These two types of strategies are referred to as behavioral strategies in that they guide the actions of agents in a domain. The identification, design, and implementation of strategies for coordination is a central research issue in the field of Distributed Artificial Intelligence (DAI) [2]. Current research techniques in developing coordination strategies are mostly off–line mechanisms that use extensive domain knowledge to design from scratch the most appropriate cooperation strategy. It is nearly impossible to identify or even prove the existence of the best coordination strategy. In most cases a coordination strategy is chosen if it is reasonably good.

In [5], we presented a new approach to developing coordination strategies for multi–agent problem solving situations. Our approach is different from most of the existing techniques for constructing coordination strategies in two ways:

- Strategies for coordination are incrementally constructed by repeatedly solving problems in the domain, i.e., on–line.
- We rely on an automated method of strategy formulation and modification, that depends very little on domain details and human expertise, and more on problem solving performance on randomly generated problems in the domain.

The approach proposed in [5] for developing coordination strategies for multi–agent problems is completely domain independent, and uses the strongly typed genetic programming (STGP) paradigm [13], which is an extension of genetic programming (GP) [10]. To use the STGP approach for evolving coordination strategies, it is necessary to find an encoding of strategies depicted as symbolic expressions (S–expressions) and choose an evaluation criterion for a strategy corresponding to an arbitrary S–expression. Populations of these structures are evaluated by a domain–specific evaluation criterion to develop, through repeated problem solving, increasingly efficient coordination strategies. The mapping of various strategies to S–expressions and vice versa can be accomplished by a set of functions and terminals representing the fundamental actions in the domain of the application. Evaluations of the strategies represented by the structures can be accomplished by allowing the agents to execute the particular strategies in the application domain. We can then measure their efficiency and effectiveness by some criteria relevant to the domain.

We have used the predator–prey pursuit game [1] to test our hypothesis that useful coordination strategies can be evolved using the STGP paradigm for non-trivial problems. This domain involves multiple predator agents trying to capture a prey agent in a grid world by surrounding it. The predator–prey problem has been widely used to test new coordination schemes [4, 9, 12, 15, 16]. The problem is easy to describe, but extremely difficult to solve; the performances of even the best manually generated coordination strategies are less than satisfactory. We showed that STGP evolved coordination strategies perform competitively with the best available manually generated strategies.

In our initial experiments on evolving coordination strategies for predator agents in the predator–prey domain, the STGP paradigm was able to evolve a program which had a better strategy than all but one of four manually derived greedy algorithms [5, 6]. In the belief that the static program of the prey was limiting the search for a better program, we decided to explore coevolving cooperation strategies in a predator population and avoidance strategies in a prey population. The basic premise of coevolution is that if one population devises a good ploy then the other population will construct a counter to that ploy. We expect that the populations will see-saw between being better on the average. This has been shown in Reynold's work on coevolution in the game of tag [14]. In his work, the two opposing agents, from the same population, take turns being the predator and the prey. Whereas in our work, there are separate populations and the predator population has to manage cooperation between multiple agents.

What this research is going to show is that a prey strategy can be evolved which can evade capture against the manually designed algorithms, and the best programs that STGP has been able to generate. It will also show the reasons why the current predator strategies are not successful against this prey algorithm. The lesson is that evolution can provide opportunities that are not obvious to human designers.

2 The Pursuit Problem

The original version of the predator–prey pursuit problem was introduced by Benda, *et al.* [1] and consisted of four blue (predator) agents trying to capture a red (prey) agent by surrounding it from four directions on a grid–world. Agent movements were limited to either a horizontal or a vertical step per time unit.

The movement of the prey agent was random. No two agents were allowed to occupy the same location. The goal of this problem was to show the effectiveness of nine organizational structures, with varying degrees of agent cooperation and control, on the efficiency with which the predator agents could capture the prey.

Korf [9] claims in his research that a discretization of the continuous world that allows only horizontal and vertical movements is a poor approximation. He calls this the orthogonal game. Korf developed several greedy solutions to problems where eight predators are allowed to move orthogonally as well as diagonally. He calls this the diagonal game. In Korf's solutions, each agent chooses a step that brings it nearest to the predator. A *max norm* distance metric (maximum of x and y distance between two locations) is used by agents to chose their steps. The predator was captured in each of a thousand random configurations in these games. But the *max norm* metric does not produce stable captures in the orthogonal game; the predators circle the prey, allowing it to escape. Korf replaces the traditional randomly moving prey with a prey that chooses a move that places it at the maximum distance from the nearest predator. Any ties are broken randomly. He claims this addition to the prey movements makes the problem considerably more difficult. It is our conjecture that the real difficulty is because in his experiments the predators and prey take turns moving. In all of our experiments the prey and predator agents move simultaneously.

3 Genetic Programming

Holland's work on adaptive systems [7] produced a class of biologically inspired algorithms known as genetic algorithms (GAs) that can manipulate and develop solutions to optimization, learning, and other types of problems. In order for GAs to be effective, the solution should be represented as n-ary strings (though some recent work has shown that GAs can be adapted to manipulate real-valued features as well). Though GAs are not guaranteed to find optimal solutions (unlike Simulated Annealing algorithms), they still possess some nice provable properties (optimal allocation of trials to substrings, evaluating exponential number of schemas with linear number of string evaluations, etc.), and have been found to be useful in a number of practical applications [3].

Koza's work on Genetic Programming [10] was motivated by the representational constraint, i.e. fixed length encodings, in traditional GAs. He claims that a large number of apparently dissimilar problems in artificial intelligence, symbolic processing, optimal control, automatic programming, empirical discovery, machine learning, etc. can be reformulated as the search for a computer program that produces the correct input–output mapping in any of these domains. To facilitate this search, he uses the traditional GA operators for selection and recombination of individuals from a population of structures, and applies the operators on structures represented in a more expressive language than used in traditional GAs. The representation language used in GPs are computer programs represented as Lisp S–expressions. GPs have attracted a large number of researchers because of the wide range of applicability of this paradigm, and the easily interpretable form of the solutions that are produced by these algorithms [8, 11].

In GP, the user needs to specify all of the functions, variables and constants that can be used as nodes in the S–expression or parse tree. Functions, variables and constants which require no arguments become the leaves of the parse trees and thus are called *terminals*. Functions which require arguments form the branches of the parse trees, and are called *non–terminals*. The set of all terminals is called the *terminal set*, and the set of all non–terminals is called the *non–terminal set*. In traditional GP, all of the terminal and non–terminal set members must be of the same type. Montana [13] introduced strongly typed genetic programming, in which the variables, constants, arguments, and returned values can be of any type. The only restriction is that the data type for each element be specified beforehand.

A STGP algorithm can be described as follows:

1. Randomly generate a population of N programs made up of functions and terminals in the problem with the constraint that the programs are syntactically correct, i.e. they honor the typing.
2. Repeat the following step until the termination condition is satisfied:
   (a) Assign fitnesses to each of the programs in the population by executing them on domain problems and evaluating their performance in solving those problems.
   (b) Create a new generation of programs by applying fitness proportionate selection operation followed by genetic recombination operators as follows:
      – Select N programs with replacement from the current population using a probability distribution over their fitnesses.
      – Create new population of N programs by pairing up these selected individuals and swapping random substructures of the programs. Again, the programs must honor the type constraints.
3. The best program over all generations (for static domains) or the best program at the end of the run (for dynamic domains) is used as the solution produced by the algorithm.

4 Cooperation Strategies

For our experiments, a STGP algorithm was put to the task of evolving both a program that is used by a predator to choose its moves and a program that is used by a prey to choose its moves. The same program was used by all four of the predators in a simulation. Each program in the population, therefore, represented a strategy for implicit cooperation to capture the prey. Likewise, the program used by the prey represented a strategy to avoid capture in an adverse situation. We postpone the discussion of evolution of these programs to Section 5.

In our experiments, the initial configuration consisted of the prey in the center of the grid, which was 30 by 30, and the predators placed in random non–overlapping positions. All agents choose their action simultaneously. The environment is accordingly updated and the agents choose their next action based on the updated environment state. Conflict resolution is necessary since we do not allow two agents to co–occupy a position. If two agents try to move into the same location simultaneously, they are "bumped back" to their prior positions. One predator, however, can push another predator (but not the prey) if the latter decided not to move. The prey does not move 10% of the time; this effectively makes the predators travel faster than the prey. The grid is toroidal in nature, and the orthogonal form of the game is used. A predator can see the prey, and the prey can see all the predators. In the early set of experiments, the predators can not see each other. We relax this restriction when we begin to consider coevolution. Furthermore, the predators do not possess any explicit communication skills; two predators cannot communicate to resolve conflicts or negotiate a capture strategy.

Korf's basic claim is that predators need not jointly decide on a strategy, but can choose locally optimal moves and still be able to capture the prey. We used this philosophy as the basis for our research in this domain. Like Korf, our predators choose their moves individually. Our research shows that the algorithm generated by the STGP system captures the prey more often than Korf's original algorithms.

4.1 Encoding of behavioral strategies

Behavioral strategies are encoded as S–expressions. Terminal and function sets in the pursuit problem are presented in Tables 1 and 2. The same sets are used for both prey and predator program evolution. In our domain, the root node of all parse trees is enforced to be of type *Tack*, which returns the number corresponding to one of the five choices the prey and predators can make (*Here*, *North*, *East*, *West*, and *South*). Notice the required types for each of the terminals, and the required arguments and return types for each function in the function set.

Our choice of sets reflect the simplicity of the solution proposed by Korf. Our goal is to have a language in which the algorithms employed by Korf can be represented.

4.2 Evaluation of cooperation strategies for predators

To evolve cooperation strategies for the predators using STGP we need to rate the effectiveness of the cooperation strategies represented as programs or S–expressions. We chose to evaluate such strategies by putting them to task on k randomly generated pursuit scenarios. For each scenario, a program is run for 100 time steps (moves made by each agent), which comprises one simulation. The percentage of capture is used as a measure of fitness when we are comparing several strategies over the same scenario. Since the initial population of strategies are randomly generated, it is very unlikely that any of these strategies will produce a capture. Thus we need additional terms in the fitness function to

Terminal	Type	Purpose
B	Boolean	TRUE or FALSE
Bi	Agent	The current predator.
Pred1	Agent	The first predator.
Pred2	Agent	The second predator.
Pred3	Agent	The third predator.
Pred4	Agent	The fourth predator.
Prey	Agent	The prey.
T	Tack	Random Tack in the range of Here to North to West.

Table 1. Terminal Set

Function	Return	Arguments	Purpose/Return
CellOf	Cell	Agent A and Tack B	Get the cell coord of A in B.
IfThenElse	Type of B and C	Boolean A, Generic B and C	If A then do B else do C. (B and C must have the same type.)
<	Boolean	Length A and Length B	If A < B, then TRUE else FALSE.
MD	Length	Cell A and Cell B	Manhattan distance between A and B.

Table 2. Function Set

differentially evaluate these non–capture strategies. The key aspect of STGPs or GAs is that even though a particular structure is not effective, it may contain useful substructures which when combined with other useful substructures, will produce a highly effective structure. The evaluation (fitness) function should be designed such that useful sub–structures are assigned due credit.

With the above analysis in mind, we designed our evaluation function of the programs controlling the predators to contain the following terms:

– After each move is made according to the strategy, the fitness of the program representing the strategy is incremented by (Grid width) / (Distance of predator from prey), for each predator. Thus higher fitness values result from strategies that bring the predators closer to the prey, and keep them near the prey. This term favors programs which produce capture in the least number of moves.

- When a simulation ends, for each predator occupying a location adjacent to the prey, a number equal to (# of moves allowed * grid width) is added to the fitness of the program. This term is used to favor situations where one or more predators surround the prey.
- Finally, if a simulation ends in a capture position, an additional reward of (4 * # of moves allowed * grid width) is added to the fitness of the program. This term strongly biases the evolutionary search toward programs that enable predators to maintain their positions when they succeed in capturing a prey.

In our experiments with the STGP scheme, the distance between agents is measured by the Manhattan distance (sum of x and y offsets) between their locations. Also, the simulations are carried out for two hundred time steps. The capture rate will increase as the simulation time steps increases.

In order to generate general solutions, (i.e., solutions that are not dependent on initial predator–prey configuration), the same k training cases were run for each member of the population per generation. The fitness measure becomes an average of the training cases. Note these training cases can be either the same throughout all generations or randomly generated for each generation. In our experiments, we used random training cases per generation.

4.3 Evaluation of cooperation strategies for prey

In each simulation there is a maximum number of fitness points that the predator program can be awarded. When the prey is more successful at avoiding capture, the predators fare poorly. Therefore the prey's fitness is the maximum allowed fitness minus that attained by the predators.

5 Experimental Results

Figures 1 and 2 compare some predator algorithms versus prey algorithms. The initial predator locations were taken from 30 test cases from Stephens [15] which are used as a base for comparison to previous work in this domain. Each test case was run with one of twentysix different random seeds. The averaged results of these matchups are shown in Figures 1 and 2, along with the performance of the STGP program generated in [6]. Furthermore, four human derived algorithms are also shown: *max norm* (MN), *Manhattan distance* (MD), Korf's original *max norm* (MNO), and Korf's original *Manhattan distance* (MDO). The *max norm* algorithms determine the best move to make based on the diagonal distance between a predator and the prey. The *Manhattan distance* algorithms determine the best move to make based on the sum of the differences of the x and y coordinates of a predator and the prey. The predators in the original algorithms take turns moving, and thus have no conflict for cells. The predators in the modified algorithms all follow the rules outlined in Section 2. These algorithms are discussed in detail in [5].

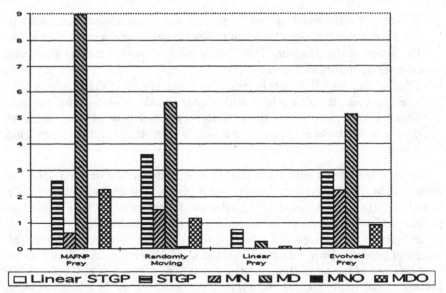

Fig. 1. Average number of captures for prey moving first. (Stephen's 30 test cases)

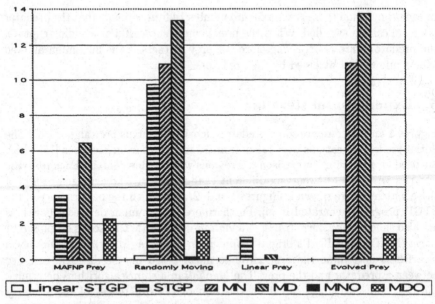

Fig. 2. Average number of captures for prey moving in sync with predators. (Stephen's 30 test cases)

In our initial experiments, we examine the utility of predator agents controlled by an STGP algorithm versus prey controlled via either a Move Away From Nearest Predator (MAFNP) strategy or by an algorithm that chooses moves randomly (Randomly). The predators can not see each other in these experiments. From Figures 1 and 2 we can see that while one manually derived greedy algorithm, MD, consistently outperforms the STGP program, the STGP program is able to outperform all of the other greedy algorithms in most cases. The behavioral strategies utilized by the STGP program, MN, and MD can be seen in Figure 3. The STGP program is deterministic in its movements, while the MN and MD algorithms are non–deterministic in that ties can occur. Thus the arrow heads in Figure 3(a) denote the direction a predator *will* take in the current time step, and in Figures 3(b) and 3(c) the arrow head denotes the first direction, in the order *N, E, S,* and *W,* the agent *might* take in the current time step.

Believing that we we could exploit competitive coevolution to evolve an even better strategy, we conducted some further experiments. This system was to produce predator and prey programs which were better than both our previous results and manually derived greedy algorithms. This was to be accomplished by the two populations competing against each other to develop increasingly efficient strategies. In short, we expected an arms race.

During the course of the execution of the program, we did not see the results that we were expecting. The predators seemed incapable of even moving towards the prey. This corresponded to a high fitness level for the prey. There were two main differences from our previous efforts to generate cooperation strategies: the predators could see each other, and the prey was learning to escape the predators.

We had enhanced the language of the predators, to allow them to see each other, for two reasons: the predators and prey would share the same languages, and the predators would be capable of more cooperation. We investigated the predators being able to see each other by evolving strategies in a given prey environment. We found the evolved strategies still ignored other predator locations.

In order to test the second hypothesis, i.e. that the prey was learning to escape the predators, we decided to conduct some experiments where the prey was pitted against our version of *Manhattan distance* (MD) algorithm [5]. The prey was very successful in evading the predators. We were surprised that the algorithm developed by the prey was simple: pick a random direction and move in a straight line in that direction. This prey algorithm, which we will refer to as the linear prey, produced less capture than that found in all the previously examined prey algorithms.

Now we thought that if we forced the prey to look at the predators, then an even better program would evolve. We forced the prey to be initially placed such that it must look at the predators in order to successively evade them. From Figures 1 and 2, it is apparent that the evolved prey is not very much better than, if not equal to, the random prey. The most surprising result is that all the predator algorithms perform poorly against the linear prey.

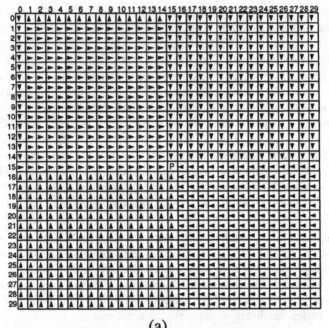

(a)

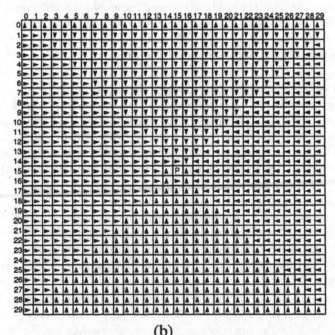

(b)

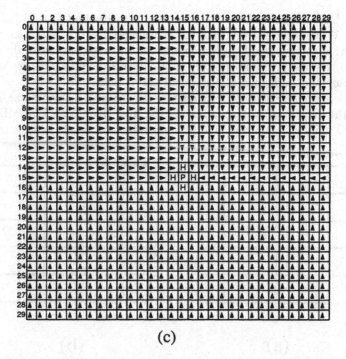

(c)

Fig. 3. Example pursuit paths found by (a) STGP, (b) Korf's algorithm with *max norm* and (c) Korf's algorithm with Manhattan distance.

The initial results from the prey learning experiment also prompted us to conduct an experiment in which predators were trained against a prey which moves in a straight line. From Figures 1 and 2 , it is evident that the Linear STGP predator is not very general, and only has significant performance in the prey scenario in which it was developed.

6 Analysis

Some compelling questions arose from our experiments:

1. Why is the linear prey so effective?
2. Is the encoding of domain responsible for our failure to capture the prey?

The linear prey is so effective because it avoids locality of movement. The greedy strategies [9, 5] rely on the prey staying in a small neighborhood of cells. Locality allows the predators both to surround the prey and to escape any deadlock situations, such as that in Figure 4(a). In this situation, predator #2 can get out of deadlock with predators #1 and #4 while the prey "tends" to stay in the neighborhood of where it currently is located. Since the linear prey avoids locality, the predators tend to "fall" behind the prey.

The MAFNP prey can be captured due to a situation as depicted in Figure 4(b). While moving away from the nearest predator, it allows itself to become surrounded by the other predators. Since the linear prey stays ahead of the predators, and the predators greedily move towards the prey, the prey is able to avoid being stopped by a predator directly in its path.

Our choice of function and terminal sets may be responsible for *our* failure to capture the prey. It is *not* responsible for the Korf algorithms, MN, MD, MNO, and MDO, failure. Again, the failure is a result of the agents being greedy.

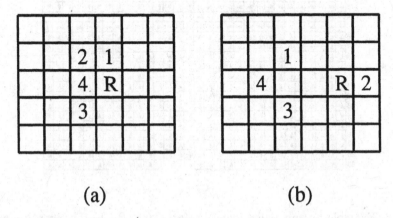

(a)　　　　　　　　(b)

Fig. 4. Scenarios showing weaknesses of some prey strategies. (a) Deadlock situation for the predators. (b) MAFNP can lead to capture.

7 Conclusions

Using strongly typed genetic programming, we were able to evolve apparently complex cooperation strategies for predators to capture a prey moving in a grid world. This is possible without providing any deep domain knowledge to the STGP. The evolved strategies fared extremely well compared to some of the best manually constructed strategies. We believe this approach to developing coordination schemes holds further promise for domains in which a human designer has much less understanding of what a good coordination strategy would be.

In trying to further the utility of the evolved cooperation strategies we ran some experiments in competitive coevolution. We encountered two obstacles, which have far-reaching consequences: the competitive coevolution did not work in the domain, and a simple algorithm for controlling the prey agent was able to successfully evade even the best human derived algorithm for the predator agents. These two obstacles are actually related in that the first is brought about as a result of the second. We believe the reason that competitive coevolution failed in our domain is due to the fact that one population, the prey, quickly found one of the two algorithms capable of confounding the language we had selected for our agents. The cooperation strategies for the predator agents need one of two abilities in order to have a chance of capturing the prey agents; either a means to detect when the local greedy algorithm should yield to the global cooperative algorithm or a history mechanism which would enable the predators to not only predict where the prey will move to in the next time step, but also where it will be in k time steps.

Of particular interest is the fact that a simple linearly moving prey is able to successfully evade capture from all evolved or greedy heuristic predator strategies. In particular, this invalidates Korf's claim [9] that a simple greedy solution exists for the predator–prey domain. Furthermore, this result illustrates that the predator–prey domain is not a "solved" case; it still provides interesting challenges to experiment, with new multiagent coordination techniques.

8 Acknowledgments

This research was partially supported by OCAST Grant AR2-004, NSF Research Initiative Award IRI-9410180 and Sun Microsystems, Inc. We would also like to thank Larry Stevens for providing the test cases he and Matthias Merx used in their research.

References

1. M. Benda, V. Jagannathan, and R. Dodhiawalla. On optimal cooperation of knowledge sources. Technical Report BCS-G2010-28, Boeing AI Center, Boeing Computer Services, Bellevue, WA, August 1985.
2. Alan H. Bond and Les Gasser. *Readings in Distributed Artificial Intelligence.* Morgan Kaufmann Publishers, San Mateo, CA, 1988.
3. Lawrence Davis, editor. *Handbook of genetic algorithms.* Van Nostrand Reinhold, New York, NY, 1991.
4. Les Gasser, Nicolas Rouquette, Randall W. Hill, and John Lieb. Representing and using organizational knowledge in DAI systems. In Les Gasser and Michael N. Huhns, editors, *Distributed Artificial Intelligence*, volume 2 of *Research Notes in Artificial Intelligence*, pages 55–78. Pitman, 1989.
5. Thomas Haynes, Roger Wainwright, and Sandip Sen. Evolving cooperation strategies. Technical Report UTULSA-MCS-94-10, The University of Tulsa, December 16, 1994.
6. Thomas Haynes, Roger Wainwright, Sandip Sen, and Dale Schoenefeld. Strongly typed genetic programming in evolving cooperation strategies. In *Proceedings of the Sixth International Conference on Genetic Algorithms*, pages 271–278, 1995.
7. John H. Holland. *Adpatation in Natural and Artificial Systems.* University of Michigan Press, Ann Arbor, MI, 1975.
8. Kenneth E. Kinnear, Jr., editor. *Advances in Genetic Programming.* MIT Press, Cambridge, MA, 1994.

9. Richard E. Korf. A simple solution to pursuit games. In *Working Papers of the 11th International Workshop on Distributed Artificial Intelligence*, pages 183–194, February 1992.

10. John R. Koza. *Genetic Programming: On the Programming of Computers by Means of Natural Selection*. MIT Press, 1992.

11. John R. Koza. *Genetic Programming II, Automatic Discovery of Reusable Programs*. MIT Press, 1994.

12. Ran Levy and Jeffrey S. Rosenschein. A game theoretic approach to the pursuit problem. In *Working Papers of the 11th International Workshop on Distributed Artificial Intelligence*, pages 195–213, February 1992.

13. David J. Montana. Strongly typed genetic programming. Technical Report 7866, Bolt Beranek and Newman, Inc., March 25, 1994.

14. Craig W. Reynolds. Competition, coevolution and the game of tag. In *Artificial Life IV*. MIT Press, 1994.

15. Larry M. Stephens and Matthias B. Merx. Agent organization as an effector of DAI system performance. In *Working Papers of the 9th International Workshop on Distributed Artificial Intelligence*, September 1989.

16. Larry M. Stephens and Matthias B. Merx. The effect of agent control strategy on the performance of a DAI pursuit problem. In *Proceedings of the 1990 Distributed AI Workshop*, October 1990.

To Learn or Not to Learn* ......

Anupam Joshi

Department of Computer Sciences
Purdue University
West Lafayette, IN 47907–1398 USA

Abstract. Multiagent systems in which agents interact with each other are now being proposed as a solution to many problems which can be grouped together under the "distributed problem solving" umbrella. For such systems to work properly, it is necessary that agents learn from their environment and adapt their behaviour accordingly. In this paper we present a system which uses a combination of neuro–fuzzy learning and static adaptation to coordinate the activity of multiple agents. An epistemic utility based formulation is used to automatically generate the exemplars for learning, making the process unsupervised. The system has been developed in the context of a scientific computing scenario.

1 Introduction

Systems whose behaviour emerges from the interaction of multiple autonomous agents are becoming increasingly important in computer science. There is a need to study the modalities and mechanisms used by individual agents in interacting with each other, and reacting to their environment. Since the environment is affected by the activities of multiple autonomous agents, it seems evident that an interaction strategy that adapts to the changing circumstances would be better than a static, non adaptive one. It also seems intuitive that the adaptive behaviour would occur as a product of *learning*. The intuitive, however, is not always correct, and it is our thesis that such is the case here. Specifically, we will argue that multiple strategies are needed for efficient coordination. Some of these react by learning, others react following predetermined formats. We thus propose a combination of nativist and empiricist approaches to the problem.

Rather than argue the thesis *in vacuo*, we will marshal our arguments in the context of a concrete and complex computational system. We limit our analysis here to cooperative agents. Our interest in multi agent systems arises out of work we are doing in the domain of scientific and ubiquitous computing[1].

In the scientific research environment, computational simulation of experimental processes is now an essential component of scientific experimentation. An important goal in the area of Computational Science & Engineering (CS&E) is to develop a unified environment where the experimental and computational

* This work was supported in part by NSF awards ASC 9404859 and CCR 9202536, AFOSR award F49620-92-J-0069 and ARPA ARO award DAAH04-94-G-0010

models can interact with and complement each other in the problem–solving process. Such an environment has been described as a Problem Solving Environment (PSE)[2]. It supports the construction of mathematical models for the experimental process, the definition of the geometry and associated conditions, the specification of the solution strategy, and finally, the generation and validation of results. It also speaks to physical experimentation – allowing the specification of experimental input, process, data acquisition and data analysis in such a way that the information could be used to control the physical equipment in the laboratory. Another important characteristic of this environment is its ability to access information. Information of all kinds, including that which was traditionally published in archival journals or conference proceedings, is increasingly available on line. Besides being concentrated in traditional repositories such as libraries, such information is also increasingly distributed, residing in workstations and computers belonging to individual researchers or research groups, and linked together to form an infosphere. The World Wide Web (WWW, Web) is an example of such a scenario. A PSE is thus a system that provides all the computational facilities necessary to solve a target class of problems. These features include advanced solution methods, automatic or semiautomatic selection of solution methods, and ways to easily incorporate novel solution methods. Moreover, PSEs use the language of the target class of problems, so users can run them without specialised knowledge of the underlying computer hardware or software.

Scientific computing systems will also become increasingly *ubiquitous*[3]. While one component of ubiquity involves computers that are mobile and connected over wireless links, another equally important aspect is computers that can be used by everyone. In other words, ubiquity aims to bring computers everywhere, and for everyone. This requires that the systems be easy to use, and that interaction with such systems follow an indirect management, rather than a direct manipulation, approach. In order to develop systems that are truly easy to use, PSEs need to provide the user with a high level abstraction of the complexity of the underlying computational facilities[4]. The user can not, and should not, be expected to be well versed in selecting appropriate numerical, symbolic and parallel systems, along with their associated parameters, that are needed to solve a problem. The goal of these PSEs is to assist the user to carry out the numerical solution of mathematical models and analyze their solutions. Depending on the mathematical characteristics of the models, there are "thousands" of numerical methods to apply, since very often there are several choices of parameters or methods at each of the several phases of the solution. On the other hand, the numerical solution chosen must satisfy several objectives, primarily involving error and hardware resource requirements.

1.1 PYTHIA

In the PYTHIA[5] project, our aim is to develop a system that will accept a description of a problem from the user, and then automatically select the appropriate numerical solver and computing platform, along with values for the various associated parameters. While the theoretical framework underlying PYTHIA is being developed in the generic context of scientific computing, our specific implementation deals with Partial Differential Equation (PDE) based systems. Currently, it automatically selects only the solution method.

PYTHIA was originally conceived as a stand alone system, a single agent in this context. Its input would be a description of a PDE in a special format that we have developed[2]. In response, PYTHIA produced a recommendation regarding a solution method, and its confidence in ranking this method as the best. This recommendation was based on the information contained in its knowledge base regarding similar problems, and what methods had worked best for them. Clearly, in order to recommend a good method for a given problem, PYTHIA must have seen a similar problem before.

Recently, we have begun to move towards making PYTHIA a collaborative multiagent system. This is, as we shall illustrate, a more natural implementation. PDEs can be widely varying. Most application scientists tend to solve only a limited kind, and hence any PYTHIA agent they are running is likely to be able to answer questions effectively only about a limited range of problems. If there were mechanisms that allowed PYTHIA agents of various application scientists to collaborate, then each agent could share knowledge and potentially answer a broader range of questions – call upon the collective wisdom of all agents, as it were.

2 When to learn, ...

The question that PYTHIA is trying to answer is the following. Given a problem, and user imposed constraints on it (like error bounds, max time allowable), which method should be used to solve the problem, and on which hardware platform. Each individual agent is therefore learning a mapping from *(problem, constraints)* to *(method, platform, parameters)*. The parameters term here refers to things like how long the solution is expected to take, what error can be expected, besides the "numerical" parameters associated with the method. Clearly, some parameters of the solutions will reflect the effort by the PYTHIA agent to conform to the user's constraints. Other parameters will reflect confidence measures of the agent in proposing the method and hardware. Our recent work has concentrated on applying various learning techniques to this single agent problem. Specifically, we have used Bayesian belief nets[6], neural networks[7] and fuzzy systems[8]. We are now working on applying learning to the multiagent scenario. Specifically, what happens if the agent discovers that it does not have "enough" confidence in the prediction it is making ? We propose that the agent initially use some broker/agent name server to find out which other PYTHIA agents are available to answer queries, and send them all the query. Presumably, it will get a set of answers from its peer agents, and will need to decide which one is "correct". As remarked upon earlier, it is likely that some given PYTHIA agent will know a

---

[2] The format is a characteristic vector, whose elements denote various PDE properties.

great deal about a certain type of problem. Thus from the answers received by an agent, it should be able to "learn" a mapping from the type of the problem to the (peer) agent which is most likely to have a correct answer. In future thus, it could direct queries more effectively, rather than using a flooding like technique to seek answers.

We are using a neuro-fuzzy method of learning to this end. The reason to use a fuzzy system is that in the PYTHIA scenario, classification of problems is not crisp. For instance, the solution of a given PDE could have a singularity, and also show some oscillatory behaviour on the boundaries. Thus the given PDE would have membership (to different extent) in the classes representing "solution–singular" and "solution–oscillatory". A conventional, binary membership function would not model this situation accurately. We feel that such fuzziness will be inherent in the learning task whenever agents model complex, real world problems.

The basic idea of the method we use was proposed by Simpson[9, 10], and is a variation of the leader cluster algorithm, enhanced with the notion of fuzziness. Similar methods have been proposed by Newton[11] and Grossberg et. al.[12]. Simpson describes a supervised learning neural network classifier that uses fuzzy sets to describe pattern classes. Each fuzzy set is the fuzzy union of several n-dimensional hyperboxes. Such hyperboxes define a region in n-dimensional pattern space that have patterns with full-class membership. A hyperbox is completely defined by it's min-point and max-point and also has associated with it a fuzzy membership function (with respect to these min-max points). This membership function helps to view the hyperbox as a fuzzy set and such "hyperbox fuzzy sets" can be aggregated to form a single fuzzy set class. This provides degree–of–membership information that can be used in decision making. Thus each pattern class in the given space is represented by an aggregate of several fuzzy sets and the resulting structure fits neatly into a neural network assembly. Learning in the fuzzy min-max network proceeds by placing & adjusting the hyperboxes in pattern space. Recall in the network consists of calculating the fuzzy union of the membership function values produced from each of the fuzzy set hyperboxes. The fuzzy min-max network provides good accuracy, facilitates *single pass learning*, has few parameters to tune & most importantly, provides on-line adaptation.

However, the method as proposed by Simpson does not allow for classes that are mutually non exclusive. It would thus fail to account for a situation where more than one agent might be expected to provide a correct answer. We have enhanced the method to allow it operate under this situation. Initial results from this approach [8] have been very promising. This method clearly outperforms most "backpropagation" like methods[13], with the exception of Resilient Propagation[14]. In Figure 1, we show the results obtained in learning a mapping from problem class to the agent which provides the best advice on solution technique. In this experiment, there were five different problem classes. The number of agents in the world was varied, so that in some cases each agent specialised in a particular class, whereas in others each agent knew about multiple classes.

Results are presnted for our neuro-fuzzy technique, as well as for the Resilient Propagation method. The results indicate that learning techniques are very successful in this environment. Also, our method which has advantages like single pass learning does as well as, or outperforms, Resilient Propagation.

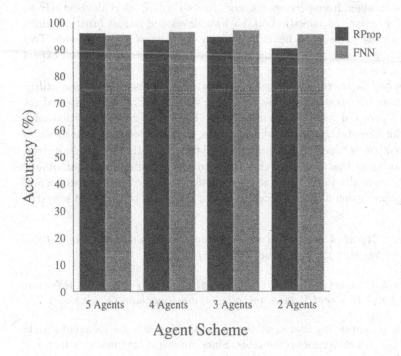

Fig. 1. Results of Learning

We are also studying other improvements to this method using techniques from computational geometry. The method as it stands tries to form classes by using isothetic hyperboxes. Clearly, this approach is extremely naive, since it would cover regions of space that did not belong to a class. We are trying to study improvements that can be obtained by allowing the boxes to have arbitrary orientation, as well as by using hyperspheres/hyperellipsoids as our space covering primitives.

3 ..... what to do while learning, ...

Once an agent has learned a mapping from problem types to (other) agents which are likely to know the answer, it can direct queries to other agents appropriately. However, learning in this instance would require some known exemplars. Since the PYTHIA agent is assumed to be a *tabula rasa* at start, it does not have any such exemplars. The straightforward approach would be to provide the system with a list of agents to query for each problem type. While this would allow the system to direct its queries, it would still not provide labeled exemplars of the type "agent a provides the correct/best answer for problem type p." Another option would be to involve the user in the process. PYTHIA would present all the answers obtained from peer agents, and the user would select the best. Given this kind of a scenario, Lashkari *et. al.*[15] have developed a trust function which each agent uses to measure its belief that a peer agent has a correct answer. This is self defeating in our case since the aim of the system is to allow a non expert (in HPC) to use it.

We propose an alternate approach formulated in terms of *epistemic utility*. We summarize the ideas here following Lehrer's[16] presentation of internal coherence and personal justification in humans. The basic idea here is that each agent has an *acceptance system*, which it uses to accept certain hypothesis as true. This system is based on two principles, obtaining truth and avoiding error. It informs an agent that it is more reasonable to accept some things than others. It enables the agent to judge which sources of information to trust and which not. Adapting Lehrer's definitions of acceptance and coherence to the agent scenario, we define

Definition 1 *Agent A is justified in accepting proposition P at time t if and only if P coheres with the acceptance system of A at t.*

Definition 2 *P coheres with the acceptance system of A if and only if it is more reasonable for A to accept P than any other competing claim Q.*

In effect, we are saying that of all the competing hypotheses, an agent should accept the one which is more reasonable. Since we introduce time as a factor in the definitions, we leave open the possibility that an agents acceptance system, and hence its notion of what is reasonable, will evolve over time. Note that reasonableness is not the same as he probability of being true. Consider, for instance, the following statements

It looks like there is snow on the ground.

There is snow on the ground.

Now, it could appear that there is snow on the ground for a whole bunch of reasons (white confetti, TP-ing by a fraternity party, hallucination ....) other than there actually being snow on the ground. Accepting the first statement therefore is less likely to make us err. On the other hand, it doesn't really tell us quite as much as the second statement, so we don't gain in the area of obtaining truth. To obtain a quantitative measure of *reasonable*-ness, we need to combine two factors, one which denotes the probability of a proposition q being true, and the other which denotes its utility. Specifically, let $U_t(q)$ denote the positive utility of accepting q if it is true, $U_f(q)$ denote the negative utility of accepting

q if it is false. Further, let $p(q)$ be the probability that q is true. Then, the reasonableness of accepting q can be defined as [16]

$$r(q) = p(q)U_t(q) + p(not(q))U_f(q).$$

Such formulations of reasonableness derive from the work of Issac Levi [17], and from the work by Neyman & Pearson on rational decisionmaking [18, 19]. The work of Neyman & Pearson deals with decision making when prior probabilities of the truth of hypothesis are not available. Consider a binary decision problem, with H_0 and H_1 as the two competing hypotheses. They suggested that in such a case, the objective of the decision making process should be to maximize the power probability (the probability of deciding in favour of H_1 when it is active) , subject to some constraint on the false alarm rate (the probability of deciding in favour of H_1 when H_0 is active). The complement of power probability, and the false alarm rate are also referred to as errors of type I and type II, respectively.

Levi's work[17, 20] is a philosophical treatise, dealing with the process of human decision making in general, and scientific enquiry in particular. He has developed a theory of epistemic utility which deals with decisionmaking by a single rational agent. It provides ideas on how an agent interacts with the environment to acquire "error free" knowledge, and how it revises its beliefs. His work provides mechanisms which enable one to develop measures of reasonableness. Reasonableness quantifies a combination of the two aims of an agent, to acquire new knowledge and to avoid error. Like much of decision theory, it is based on the notion of maximizing utility, but differs in as much as its formulation of what utility is. Based on his work, Stirling & Morrow have recently proposed schemes that are used for coordinated intelligent control [21, 22].

In the case of PYTHIA, each agent produces a number denoting confidence in its recommendation being correct, so $p(q)$ is trivially defined, and $p(not(q))$ is simply $1 - p(q)$. The utility is a more tricky measure. We have earlier posited that the more problems of a type that an agent has seen, the more likely it is to recommend an appropriate method etc. for a new problem of the same type. Moreover, the reason for the epistemic module is to provide exemplars for learning. Thus the utility of accepting an agent's recommendation (and using it as an exemplar for learning) should reflect the number of problems of the present type that it has seen. In this instance, we chose to make the positive and negative utilities the same in value, but opposite in sign. This is done since the value of utility is measuring the amount of knowledge that an agent appears to have.Thus $U_t(q) = -U_f(q) = f(N_e)$, where f is some squashing function mapping the domain of $(0, \infty)$ to a range of $(0, 1]$, and N_e is the number of exemplars of a given type(that of the problem being considered) that the agent has seen. We chose $f(x) = \frac{2}{1+e^{-x}} - 1$. Note however that this is just one possible formulation of the utility measure. In fact, such a formulation suffers from a problem if it is asked to chose between two alternative hypotheses with low probabilities of being correct. Specifically, assume that the probabilities of hypothesis h_1 and h_2 being true are both p, and their utilities are u_1 and $u_2, u_1 \geq u_2$ respectively.

When $p \leq 0.5$, the second hypothesis will be assigned a greater *reasonableness* measure, even though the first hypothesis has a greater utility. An alternative which does not suffer from this problem is to use $\frac{1}{f(N_e)}$ as the measure of utility of accepting a recommendation in the formulation for r whenever the probability of being true is less that half, and use $f(N_e)$ otherwise. This however tends to bias reasonableness towards truth, and away from utility.

4   ..... and when not to learn

An important component of scientific computation is the optimal use of the available, heterogeneous High Performance Computing (HPC) hardware. We view each hardware platform as an agent, with bounded (computational) capability. Part of this capability is inherent in the hardware. The other part is a function of the amount of load on it. We have outlined in the previous section a mechanism using which PYTHIA can decide which method would best solve a problem, and propose a hardware platform as well. However, this problem is actually more complicated, since the hardware platforms in question are mostly parallel, or networked workstation clusters. Thus their configurations (for instance, the number of processors devoted to a problem) can be changed. So the mapping to be learned is from *(problem, method, hardware, config)* to *time*. Even if one were to restrict the notion of configuration to merely the number of processors, it would still be a computationally intense task to learn the time taken by a given hardware with a given number of processors to solve a given problem by a given method. The naive approach here, in our opinion, would be to throw a learning mechanism at this problem. We believe that direct learning is not required in this case, and the system can be adaptable without it.

The adaptability can be achieved by a combination of learning and modeling. We have illustrated in a previous section how PYTHIA will recommend a hardware platform, and give an estimate of the time required to solve the problem. This time estimate would be with respect to some standard configuration of the hardware in question. The appropriate configuration of the system can be obtained by providing the PYTHIA agent the capability to model the configuration to speedup characteristics of various hardware agents. Since a heterogeneous system would not have more than a few tens of different computing platforms, this would not be a burden. Analytic models predicting speedups in parallel platforms are notoriously difficult to obtain. However, seminal work in this direction has been done by colleagues in our group [23]. The system proposed by them parameterizes scalability of computation using three quantities that are in turn functions of the number of processors. These are:

1. $E(P)$, the number of communication events
2. $f(p)$, the fraction of time spent in sequential and duplicated work
3. $I(P)$, the instruction execution rate

Using such an approach, the PYTHIA agent can model the behaviour of hardware agents to predict what number of processors would be optimal for a given problem on a given platform.

The speedup scheme has been expounded in the context of a single program executing on a given platform at a time. However, it provides the requisite framework for extension to the case where each hardware agent is actually a multiprocessing system. In such cases, the (computational) capability of the hardware agents will dynamically vary. Each agent will be aware of the load on it at any given time, and can query other agents for their loads as well. Our multiagent system will be responsive to this dynamic behaviour, and will adapt by moving computations around. This will be achieved by systems similar to those proposed in [24] by Rego *et. al.* . Such systems use threads of control to efficiently migrate tasks across processing systems, and have been shown to be extremely effective in simulations [25].

5 Architecture and Implementation

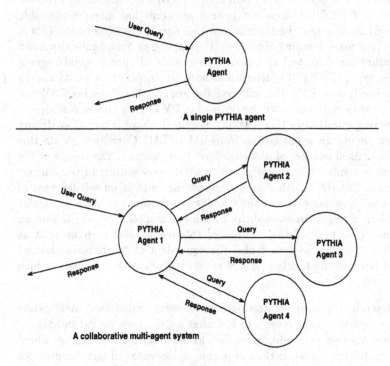

Fig. 2. The architecture of multiagent PYTHIA

We have developed a preliminary implementation of the ideas outlined in the preceding sections. The overall system architecture is illustrated in Figure 2. We modified the original PYTHIA agent to have a "memory" of agents it knows about, the problems each agent has seen, and statistical information about the performance of each agent in regard to each type of problem the agent has been queried about. An agent can be in either a "learning mode" (LM) or a "stable mode" (SM). During the LM, a PYTHIA agent asks all other known agents for solutions about a particular type of problem. It collects all the answers, including its own, and then chooses the best result as the solution. In effect, each agent is using what has been described in [15] as "desperation based" communication. While in this mode, each agent is also "learning" the mapping from problem class to the agent which gave the best solution. The best solution in LM is computed by the epistemic utility formulation described earlier. After the "learning period", each agent has learned a mapping describing which agent is best for a particular type of problem. From this point on, PYTHIA is in the SM. It now switches to what we label as stable communication. In other words, it will only ask itself and the best agent to answer a particular question. It evaluates the answers received according to the reasonableness criterion defined earlier. If none is "reasonable" then we switch to an "exploratory" communication mode [15]. Figure 3 illustrates the layered systems of each PYTHIA agent that are involved in this process. If PYTHIA does not believe an agent has given a plausible solution, it will ask the next best agent, until all agents are exhausted. This is facilitated by our fuzzy learning algorithm. By varying an acceptance threshold in the defuzzification step, we can get an enumeration of "not so good" agents for a problem type. If PYTHIA determines no plausible solution exists among its agents or itself, then PYTHIA will give the answer that "was best". When giving such an answer, the user will be notified of PYTHIA's lack of confidence.

An interesting question in this scenario described above is one of switching modes. When should an agent switch from LM to SM? Currently, we do this after an *a priori* fixed number of problems have been learned. The timing of the reverse switch is a more tricky matter which we do not address in the current implementation. Clearly, as other agents are adding to their knowledge base of "previously seen" problems, their ability to answer questions about a particular type of problem changes. In essence, by learning a mapping, we are taking an instantaneous "snapshot" of the abilities of the agents, and then using it as a "cache". We therefore need to evolve the equivalent of "cache invalidation" strategies for our learning function. There are several potential candidates which we describe next.

- **Time based:** The simplest approach is to use a time based invalidation scheme, where the agent reverts to LM after a fixed time period in SM.
- **Reactive:** Another possibility is for each agent to send out a message whenever its confidence for some class of problems has changed significantly. An agent can then chose to revert to LM when it next receives a query about that type of problem.
- **Time based Reactive:** A combination of the two approaches outlined above would send out a "has anyone's abilities changed significantly" message at fixed time intervals, and switch to LM if it received a positive response.
- **Proactive:** In this approach, the agent would use the fact that switching into the exploratory mode meant that the agent it thought would best solve

Fig. 3. System Layers of each PYTHIA agent

a problem could not. It would then switch into a learning mode by itself, without waiting for any other agent to explicitly indicate a change in its capabilities.

The backbone of any agent based system is the ability to communicate effectively among agents. In recent years the Knowledge Query and Manipulation Language, (KQML) [26] has been proposed as a medium of interagent communication. KQML was developed by the DARPA Knowledge Sharing Initiative External Interfaces Working Group especially for agent based communication. KQML based communications is based on a protocol defining performatives. Performatives are universal, in the sense that they are understood by all KQML compliant agents. The content of the performative can be in a special language that only some of the agents know. For the collaborative PYTHIA case, we use a private language (*PYTHIA-talk*) that all PYTHIA agents understand.

6 Conclusion

That Multiagent systems have to be adaptable and involve learning is, in our opinion, evident. In this paper, we have presented a multiagent system operating in a complex, scientific computing environment. We have argued that learning is not the panacea that will make the difficulties of coordination in multiagent systems disappear. Specifically, we have shown scenarios from our research where learning is used, and where the system adapts based on *a priori* known models of other agents. We have also shown how *epistemic utility* theory can be used to facilitate learning in an unsupervised manner. Of course, where supervised learning is available, it can be (and is) trivially incorporated into the system.

References

1. T. Drashansky, A. Joshi, and J.R. Rice. SciAgents – An Agent Based Environment for Distributed, Cooperative Scientific Computing. Technical Report TR-95-029, Dept. Comp. Sci., Purdue University, 1995. (submitted to Tools with AI '95).
2. E. Gallopoulos, E. Houstis, and J.R. Rice. Computer as Thinker/Doer: Problem-Solving Environments for Computational Science. *IEEE Computational Science and Enginerring*, 1(2):11–23, 1994.
3. A. Joshi, T. Drashansky, E. Houstis, and S. Weerawarana. SciencePad: An Intelligent Electronic Notepad for Ubiquitous Scientific Computing. In *International Conference on Inteligent Information Management Systems*, June 1995. (to appear).
4. S. Weerawarana et al. Using NCSA Mosaic to build notebook interfaces for CS&E applications. Technical Report CSD-TR-95-006, Department of Computer Sciences, Purdue University, 1995. (submitted to IFIP WG2.7 EHCI '95).
5. E. Houstis et al. The PYTHIA projet. In *Proc. First Intl. Conf. on Neural, Parallel and Scientific Computing*, 1995. (to appear).
6. S. Weerawarana. *Problem Solving Environments for Partial Differential Equation Based Systems*. PhD thesis, Dept. Comp. Sci., Purdue University, 1994.
7. A. Joshi et al. The Use of Neural Networks to Support Intelligent Scientific Computing. In *Proc. IEEE Intl. Conf. Neural Networks*. IEEE, IEEE Press, July 1995.
8. N. Ramakrishnan et al. Neuro-Fuzzy Systems for Intelligent Scientific Computing. Technical Report TR-95-026, Dept. Comp. Sci., Purdue University, 1995.
9. P.K. Simpson. Fuzzy min-max neural networks-part I: Classification. *IEEE Trans. Neural Networks*, 3:776–786, Sept 1992.
10. P.K. Simpson. Fuzzy min-max neural networks-part II: Clustering. *IEEE Trans. Fuzzy Systems*, 1(1):32–45, Feb 1993.
11. S. Newton and S. Mitra. Self organizing leader clustering in a neural network using a fuzzy learning rule. In *SPIE Proc. 1565: adaptive signal processing*. SPIE, 1991.
12. G. Carpenter, S. Grossberg, and S. Rosen. Fuzzy ART: Fast stable learning and categorization of analog patterns by an adaptive resonance system. *Neural Networks*, 4:759–771, 1991.
13. A. Joshi, S. Weerawarana, N. Ramakrishnan, E.N. Houstis, and J.R. Rice. Neural and Neuro-Fuzzy Approaches to Support "Intelligent" Scientific Problem Solving. Technical Report TR-95-039, Dept. Comp. Sci., Purdue University, 1995.

14. H. Braun and M. Riedmiller. Rprop : A Fast and Robust Backpropagation Learning Strategy. In *Proceedings of the ACNN*, 1993.

15. Y. Lashkari, M. Metral, and P. Maes. Collaborative Interface Agents. In *Proceedings AAAI '94*. AAAI, 1994.

16. K. Lehrer. *Theory of Knowledge*. Westview Press, Boulder, CO, USA, 1990.

17. I. Levi. *Decisions and Revisions*. Cambridge University Press, Cambridge, U.K., 1984.

18. J. Neyman and E.S. Pearson. The Testing of Statistical Hypotheses in Relations to Probabilities a priori. *Proc. Cambridge Phil. Soc.*, 29:492–510, 1932.

19. J. Neyman. Basic Ideas and Some Recent Results of the Thoery of Testing Statistical Hypotheses. *J. Royal Stat. Soc.*, 105:292–327, 1942.

20. I. Levi. *The Enterprise of Knowledge*. The MIT Press, CAmbridge, MA, USA, 1980.

21. W.C. Stirling. Coordinated Intelligent Control via Epistemic Utiliyu Theory. *IEEE Control Systems*, pages 21–29, October 1993.

22. W.C. Stirling and D.R. Morrell. Convex Bayes Decision Theory. *IEEE Trans. System, Man and Cybernetics*, 21:173–183, 1991.

23. D. Marinescu and J.R. Rice. On the scalability of Asynchronous Parallel Computations. *J. Parallel and Distributed Computing*, 22, 1994.

24. E. Mascarenhas and V. Rego. Ariadne: Architecture of a Portable Threads System Supporting Mobile Processes. Technical Report CSD-TR-95-017, Dept. Comp. Sci., Purdue University, 1995.

25. V. Rego et al. Process Mobility in Distributed Memory Simulation Systems. In *Proc. Winter Simulation Conference*, pages 722–730, 1993.

26. R. Fritzson et. al. KQML- A Language and Protocol for Knowledge and Information Exchange. In *Proc. 13th Intl. Distributed Artificial Intelligence Workshop*, July 1994.

A User-Adaptive Interface Agency for Interaction with a Virtual Environment

Britta Lenzmann and Ipke Wachsmuth

University of Bielefeld
Faculty of Technology
AG Knowledge-Based Systems
D-33501 Bielefeld, Germany
{britta,ipke}@techfak.uni-bielefeld.de

Abstract. This paper describes an approach to user adaptation realized in a multiagent interface system for interaction with a virtual environment. The interface agency adapts to users' individual preferences by learning from direct feedback. The core idea is that agents that were successful in meeting the user's expectations are given credit while unsuccessful agents are "discredited." Communicating credit values, agents organize themselves so that the overall behavior of the interface agency gradually adapts to the individual user as the session is proceeding.

1 Introduction

Agent systems have proven especially useful in the design of more intelligent user interfaces. By allowing more human-like communication forms, they can add comfort in human-computer interaction [Laurel, 1990]. Beyond this, agent systems may act as mediator between the user and the application system [Maes, 1994]; [Wachsmuth & Cao, 1995]. The user can instruct the application system by way of abstract commands (virtual interaction), and the interface agency interprets them (intuitive communication) and transmits the results to the application system via technical communication (see figure 1).

While communication between humans is situated naturally, the interface system must be able to meet varying conditions to enable an effective human-computer interaction. Thus, incorporating adaptation facilities in the agent system becomes essential. In our work, we distinguish two aspects of adaptation: adaptation in respect to individual differences across users and adaptation to varying situation circumstances. In this paper we focus on the first aspect, i.e., user adaptation.

A prominent approach is to build user-adaptive interface agents by applying machine learning techniques. For example, [Maes & Kozierok, 1993] use techniques such as learning by observing the user, learning from direct or indirect user feedback, or learning from examples given by the user. Applying these techniques, [Maes, 1994] describes learning personal assistants, e.g., for electronic mail handling and electronic news filtering which accumulate knowledge about tasks and habits of their users to act on their behalf. Similarly,

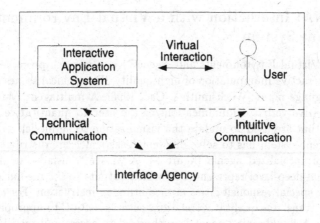

Fig. 1. Agent-mediated interaction: Software interface agents free the user from the burden of knowing and communicating technical detail.

[Mitchell et al., 1994] have built learning apprentices for calendar management, electronic newsgroup filtering, and email negotiation which automatically customize to individual users by learning through experience. In these applications, a visual agent gives advice to the user by expressing facial emotions or by prompting suggestions. Common to these approaches is that a solitary interface agent is used which adapts to individual preferences of its user by aquiring user data and changing its internal functionality accordingly.

In our approach, we consider a system of *multiple* interface agents which adapts to user preferences by learning from direct feedback without explicit acquisition of user data. The user gives an implicit feedback by way of correcting solutions offered by the agency until the agent generating the preferred solution becomes dominant in the system-user interaction. Thus, internal functionalities of agents can remain unchanged but individual agents are preferred from among a variety of heterogeneous interface agents. The core idea is that agents which were successful in meeting the user's expectations are given credit while unsuccessful agents are "discredited." By this, the overall behavior of the interface agency gradually adapts to the individual user as the session is proceeding.

Our approach is realized in a multiagent interface system for interaction with a virtual environment, and is carried out in the VIENA project. We start with explaining the VIENA system, describe then our approach to user adaptation by a multiagent system and, in concluding, discuss our results and sketch future work.

2 VIENA: Interaction with a Virtual Environment by a Multiagent System

VIENA[1] ("Virtual Environments and Agents") is a research project concerned with the interactive manipulation of high-quality 3D graphical scenes by way of natural language input [Wachsmuth & Cao, 1995]. A multiagent system translates qualitative verbal communications of the user to quantitative, technical commands that are used to update the visualization scene model. To this end, the multiagent system has to solve different tasks which are distributed among a number of specialized agents (figure 2). A parser translates an instruction to an internal deep-level representation which outputs to the mediating agents. Agents take special responsibilities in mediating an instruction. For example, a space agent translates qualitative relations such as 'left of' to appropriate scene coordinates. A bookkeeping agent is authorized to access and modify the augmented data base to supply current situation information to agents on request. Some of these agents are actually agencies, that is, they incorporate agents of the same type but slightly different functionality. For instance, this is the case for the space agent discussed in section 3. Typically, such agents compete in the allocation of sub-tasks.

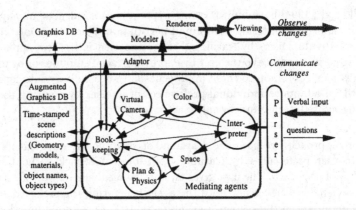

Fig. 2. The architecture of the VIENA system (after [Wachsmuth & Cao, 1995])

For computing the entire solution of a user's instruction agents have to communicate and cooperate with each other. Defining agents as autonomous, heavy-weight processes which can be installed on different computers in the network, communication is realized by message exchange. A Client-Server concept

[1] The VIENA project is part of the "Artificial Intelligence and Computer Graphics" research program at the University of Bielefeld and is partly supported by the Ministry of Science and Research of the Federal State North-Rhine-Westphalia under grant no. IVA3-107 007 93.

was designed which formally defines the agents as clients, and a communication subsystem as server to handle the messages. The cooperation method is basically characterized by a negotiation process similar to the contract-net approach [Davis & Smith, 1983]. Each agent can take on the role of a contractor as well as the role of a bidder. In detail, the process consists of a sequence of message passing operations which are: the posting of tasks, the generation of bids, the allocation of tasks or the rejection of bids, resp., and the return of computed results. In addition, a master-slave and a blackboard type of behavior can be modeled by allocating tasks directly, or, resp., by addressing tasks to groups of agents simultaneously. A more detailed description of the VIENA multiagent system is given in [Lenzmann et al., 1995].

The multiagent system is used in a prototype scenario with various items of furniture as well as color and light impressions of a virtual office room. A sequence of possible interactions with the VIENA system is shown in figure 3. The inputs shown allow interactive modification of the visible scene. Furthermore, changes of the viewpoint and the processing of simple deictic instructions are possible[2].

1. move the chair to the left .
2. a bit less .
3. turn the chair left .
4. put the desk behind the chair .
5. put the palmtree on the desk .
6. move the palmtree to the left .
7. put the bowl on the desk .
8. put the chair on the table .
9. move the chair to the window .
10. turn the desk right .

Fig. 3. Sample sequence of interactions with the VIENA system

Since the computed solutions do not always meet the expectations of the user, the VIENA system accepts corrections such as 'a bit less' which modify the previous solution accordingly by inspection of the current and the previous scene models which are stacked for this purpose. In this way, the semantics of instructions can be negotiated in the system-user discourse; we refer to this as "negotiated semantics."

However, frequent corrections are uncomfortable for the user. Moreover, the practical experience with the system has shown that variations of individual

---

[2] Such example interactions are part of a demo video presented in the IJCAI-95 videotape program [Cao et al., 1995].

preferences exist across users which call for expanded internal functionalities of the interface agents. This gave rise to the idea of incorporating adaptation facilities in the interface agency. In section 3, we explore this idea in more detail and describe an approach where user adaptation is achieved by learning from direct feedback.

3 User-Adaptation in a Multiagent Interface System

Our aim is that user adaptation be achieved without the need to acquire knowledge about tasks and habits of the user or to accumulate explicit user models. Avoiding explicit user modeling seems a desirable goal in several respects. Explicitly acquired information is less likely to change on the short term whereas implicit information is more dynamic as it is usually acquired incrementally during the course of a session, and dynamic models are more useful as they adapt to changing characteristics of users [McTear, 1993]. Moreover, there are social and legal issues with explicit user models since they will contain a great deal of personal information; for this reason, explicit user models have found critique with respect to privacy of user data [McTear, 1993]; [Norman, 1994].

The core idea of our approach to *implicit user adaptation* is that agents of the same type but slightly different functionality — corresponding to possible variations of users' preferences — organize themselves to meet the preferences of the individual user. Getting positive or negative feedback from the user, agents increase or decrease their amount of selfconfidence, so that successful agents become dominant in the ongoing session. In detail we present the learning technique in section 3.2. Before that, we describe the problematics of using different spatial reference frames when transforming objects in the virtual scene as an example application of our approach to user adaptation.

3.1 Users' Preferences for Different Spatial Reference Frames

In VIENA spatial transformations of scene objects are communicated by way of qualitative verbal instructions, as in 'move the palmtree to the left' (cp. instruction 6 in figure 3). The semantics of such spatial instructions may depend on different perspectives [Retz-Schmidt, 1988]: from the user's point of view (deictic perspective) or from the point of view of an object which has a prominent front (intrinsic perspective). In addition, users' preferences for spatial reference frames may depend on the orientation of the desk given in the actual situation. This 'situated' aspect of preferring one spatial reference frame over the other is a further research subjective but not the focus of this paper. Figure 4 illustrates the two alternative solutions when an object located on a desk is to be moved to the left.

The first VIENA prototype system just offered the possibility of transforming objects from the deictic perspective. When we demonstrated the system to a number of test users, some of them mentioned that they expected the palmtree to be moved to the left from the intrinsic perspective. We then assumed that,

Fig. 4. Example scene from the VIENA test application: The palmtree located on the desk can be moved to the left from an intrinsic perspective (1) or from a deictic perspective (2).

depending on their individual preferences, users may choose one of either perspective. For verification of this assumption, we carried out an empirical study. A total of 64 probands were asked to perform the instruction 'move the object to the left' in a simplified setting of the one presented in figure 4. The results showed that 36% of the probands used the intrinsic perspective (solution 1), whereas 64% used the deictic perspective (solution 2). Hence, we could substantiate that designing space agents able to adapt to users' preferences for different spatial reference frames is a useful goal.

Consequently, we conceptualized two instances of a space agent that are similar in the way they compute spatial transformations, and different with respect to the reference scheme they take on. More concrete, we have implemented one space agent embodying the user's egocentric reference frame (deictic reference) and one space agent embodying an externally anchored reference frame (intrinsic reference).

Instructing the system with a spatial transformation, the space agent which is currently dominant, e.g., the deictic agent, offers a possible solution. In case the visualized solution does not meet the user's expectation, the user can correct the system by stating 'wrong'. The negative user feedback leads the agents to reorganize themselves in a way that the intrinsic space agent can now generate an offer which modifies the previous solution. By this, adaptation to a user's preferred reference scheme is achieved by direct user feedback.

3.2 Learning from direct feedback

Extrapolating from this example application of spatial transformations, the interface agency as a whole, including the space agency, adapts to users' preferences by learning from direct feedback. In more detail, direct feedback is derived from implicit positive or explicit negative feedback. Implicit positive feedback is given when a user's instruction is followed by any instruction which does not decline the previous one. Explicit negative feedback is given when the user corrects the visualized solution computed by the interface agency. Consider the following sequence of example instructions:

> 1. *put the palmtree on the desk.*
> 2. *move the palmtree to the left.*
> 3. *wrong.*
> 4. *turn the desk right.*

Since the second instruction does not directly refer to the first one it can be interpreted as positive feedback regarding the previous instruction. The correction within instruction 3, on the other hand, indicates a negative feedback in reference to the second one. While user feedback regarded from the point of view of the entire interface agency happens more or less directly, single agents learn by indirect feedback since users' instructions are decomposed in subtasks and distributed among the agents.

From the system internal point of view, the adaptation process is achieved by a form of *reinforcement learning* [Kaelbling, 1993]. Learning is realized in a way that the system will take actions that maximize the reinforcement signals received from the environment. In our approach, this means that users' instructions (or corrections, resp.) represent reinforcement signals which are interpreted and encoded by the interface agency in the form of *credit values*. Each agent stores a credit value corresponding to its quality ("strength") at discrete periods of time. Learning is achieved by adjusting agents' credits in correspondence to the users' feedback and assigning those agents which are eligible for the task in question and have maximal credits.

In more detail, the process consists of several steps. When the user gives an instruction, the interpreter agent (cp. figure 2) determines which agents (subagency) are eligible to solve the task and informs the corresponding ones by sending a task posting. Depending on the task description, each of these agents generates a bid which includes its actual credit value and sends it to the contractor. All received bids are pooled and evaluated by comparing their associated credit values. The agent offering the best bid, that is, the bid with the highest credit, gets the task whereas the bids of the other agents are rejected. Figure 5 illustrates a detail of the VIENA coordination structure where two agents compete with each other to compute a solution regarding the user's instruction.

For adapting to users' preferences, agents have to adjust their credit values dynamically while the session is going on. Adjustment takes place if a user corrects the system (cp. the example instructions above). A correction can come

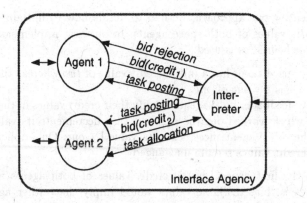

Fig. 5. A detail of the VIENA coordination strategy: both agents make offers qualified by their current credit values; agent 2 generating the better bid gets the task, whereas the bid of agent 1 is rejected.

about because a different user now works with the system, or the same user undergoes short-term change of his/her preferences. In this case, the interpreter informs the corresponding agents about the correction by generating a task posting which includes a label indicating a unsatisfactory solution. Receiving this message, each potential bidder checks to see if it has worked out the previous task and because of that has caused the unsatisfactory solution. The agent which has worked out the task then makes the bookkeeping agent reset the database and reduces its own credit value whereas the other agents increase their credits (cf. section 4). Having modified their credit values, each of these agents generates a bid with changed credit value. Again, the agent with the currently best bid gets the task whereas the bids of the other agents are rejected (cp. figure 5). In this way, adaptation to user preferences, even those dynamically changing, can be realized.

Speaking metaphorically, increasing or reducing credit values induced by being successful/nonsuccessful in meeting the user's expectations corresponds to agents being more or less selfconfident. Based on their selfconfidence, agents are able to organize themselves in the way individual users' preferences call for without the need to accumulate explicit user models.

4 First Results

A prototype version of the adaptation method described above has been implemented and tested for the case of users' preferences for different spatial reference frames. As described in section 3.1, we have implemented two space agents, the deictic and the intrinsic space agent, which correspond to the possible variations of users' preferences regarding spatial reference frames.

In implementing our approach, we had to decide how to initialize and how to modify credit values of both space agents. In our first implementation, the following simple heuristics is used:

1. The deictic space agent has a initial credit value of *two* whereas the intrinsic space agent has a value of *one*.
2. On negative feedback, both agents modify their credit values in the way that the agent which worked out the previous task decrements its value by *one* whereas the other agent increments its value by *one*. On implicit positive feedback, credit values remain unchanged.

Regarding the first aspect, initial credit values of both agents are chosen differently, that is, biased. Same values would imply that either agent could be elected at random (depending on network communication speed) whenever various interactions without negative feedback are given in the preceding session. The decision on initializing the credit value of the deictic space agent higher than the one of the intrinsic agent is based on results of the empirical study (cp. section 3.1) where probands used the deictic perspective more frequently than they used the intrinsic perspective.

Credits are modified as explained in the second aspect because the interface agency can, in this way, immediately alter its bias for reference frames. The modifications of credit values can be illustrated by considering the second and third instruction of the example interactions presented in section 3.2. Assuming the deictic space agent is the dominant one in this situation, both space agents generate the bids illustrated in figure 6 when receiving the task posting induced by instruction 2.

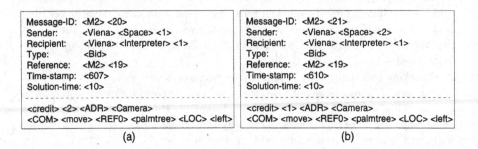

(a) (b)

Fig. 6. Each space agent sends a bid message comprising its current credit value and the task description. Whereas the deictic agent (a) offers a task solving qualified by a credit of *two* <2>, the intrinsic agent (b) makes an offer with a credit of *one* <1>. Note that the interpretation of <left> will be different depending on which agent is allocated the task.

Indicating a difference between the solution produced and the user's preference, instruction 3 induces a modification of credit values. Figure 7 shows the bid messages sent by each space agent to the contractor after updating its credit value.

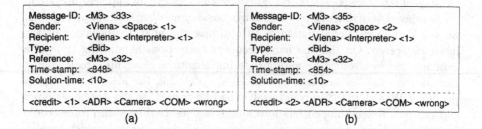

Fig. 7. Having received negative user feedback, both space agents generate bids including modified credit values and a label indicating an unsatisfactory solution. Whereas the deictic agent (a) has decreased its credit value to *one* <1>, the intrinsic agent (b) has increased it to *two* <2>.

By this simple procedure, adaptation to varying users' preferences for different spatial reference frames can be achieved. An alternative approach to be investigated and implemented next is to increase credit values incrementally whenever the user gives a positive feedback. This corresponds to agents becoming more selfconfident by having solved tasks in the expected manner. Furthermore, a more complex relationship between agents and subagencies could be taken into account. However, alterations of users' preferences have to be realized in a slightly different way: agents decrease their credit values, on the one hand, but, inform their contractor of working out a task corrected by the user in the preceding interaction, on the other hand.

5 Discussion and Future Work

In this paper we presented an approach to user adaptation by a multiagent system for interacting with a virtual environment. Learning from direct feedback is used to adapt the interface agency to users' individual preferences. While the session is continuing, more successful individual agents within the agency are preferred. Agents organize themselves by communicating credit values which represent their amount of selfconfidence. Depending on their success in the preceding session, agents adjust their credit values dynamically to meet the user's expectations. The system's knowledge of user preferences is expressed in credit adjustments of agents and is distributed across agents. Thus, user adaptation is achieved without accumulating explicit user models.

We illustrated our approach by focusing on users' preferences for different spatial reference frames. As further preferences which the agent system could adapt to, differences in color perception as well as differences in strength regarding transforming or scaling objects will be investigated. Furthermore, we have considered the interaction with a virtual environment as an example application but, in our view, the approach seems also applicable in other scenarios where a multiagent interface is used to mediate between users and an application system.

Besides of verifying our techniques by considering other kinds of preferences, we think of more global measures to optimize the adaptive behavior of the interface agency. On the one hand, frequent corrections at starting time of a session could be avoided by appropriate initializations of agents' credit values. Our idea is that "anonymous user profiles" (replacing the idea of stereotypes [Kobsa & Wahlster, 1989]) could evolve, and be pooled, as the system becomes experienced. Resembling correlations among agents' credits, such profiles could be used to enhance adaptation speed by more global adjustments which, implicitly, follow stereotype preferences of groups of users.

On the other hand, we plan to investigate in which form users' individual preferences depend on actual situation circumstances. As mentioned in section 3, users' preferences for spatial reference frames may depend on the orientation or position of objects given in the actual situation. Therefore, actual scene data would have to be integrated in the adaptation process. By this, we envisage adaptation to users' preferences as well as adaptation to varying situation parameters to be realized by multiagent systems.

References

[Cao et al., 1995] Y. Cao, B. Jung, I. Wachsmuth. Situated verbal interaction in virtual design and assembly. IJCAI-95 Videotape Program. Abstract in *Proceedings of IJCAI-95.*

[Davis & Smith, 1983] R. Davis and G. Smith. Negotiation as a Metaphor for Distributed Problem Solving. In A.H. Bond and L. Gasser, editors, *Readings in Distributed Artificial Intelligence*, pages 333–356. Morgan Kaufmann, 1983.

[Kaelbling, 1993] L.P. Kaelbling. *Learning in Embedded Systems.* The MIT Press, 1993.

[Kobsa & Wahlster, 1989] A. Kobsa and W. Wahlster (eds.). *User Models in Dialog Systems.* Springer Verlag, London, 1989.

[Laurel, 1990] B. Laurel. Interface agents: Metaphors with character. In B. Laurel, editor, *The art of human-computer interface design*, pages 355–365. Addison-Wesley, 1990.

[Lenzmann et al., 1995] B. Lenzmann, I. Wachsmuth, and Y. Cao. An intelligent interface for a virtual environment. KI-NRW (Applications of Artificial Intelligence in North-Rine Westphalia) Report 95-01.

[Maes, 1994] P. Maes. Agents that reduce work and information overload. *Communications of the ACM*, 37(7):31–40, 1994.

[Maes & Kozierok, 1993] P. Maes and R. Kozierok. Learning interface agents. In *Proceedings of the Eleventh National Conference on Artificial Intelligence (AAAI-93*, pages 459–465. AAAI Press/The MIT Press, 1993.

[McTear, 1993] M.F. McTear. User modelling for adaptive computer systems: a survey of recent developments. *Artificial Intelligence Review*, 7:157–184, 1993.

[Mitchell et al., 1994] T. Mitchell, R. Caruana, D. Freitag, J. McDermott, and D. Zabowski. Experiences with a learning personal assistent. *Communications of the ACM*, 37(7):80–91, 1994.

[Norman, 1994] D.A. Norman. How might people interact with agents. *Communications of the ACM*, 37(7):68–71, 1994.

[Retz-Schmidt, 1988] G. Retz-Schmidt. Various views on spatial prepositions. em AI magazine, 9(2):95–105, 1988.

[Wachsmuth & Cao, 1995] I. Wachsmuth and Y. Cao. Interactive graphics design with situated agents. In W. Strasser and F. Wahl, editors, *Graphics and Robotics*, pages 73–85. Springer, 1995.

Learning in Multi–Robot Systems

Maja J Matarić
Volen Center for Complex Systems
Computer Science Department
Brandeis University
Waltham, MA 02254
maja@cs.brandeis.edu

Abstract. This paper discusses why traditional reinforcement learning methods often result in poor performance in dynamic, situated multi–agent domains characterized by multiple goals, noisy perception and action, and inconsistent reinforcement. We propose a methodology for designing the representation and the forcement functions that take advantage of implicit domain knowledge in order to accelerate learning in such domains, and demonstrate it experimentally in two different mobile robot domains.

1 Introduction

Successful applications of RL methodologies to well–behaved domains (Sutton 1988, Watkins 1989, Kaelbling 1990) have encouraged researchers to hypothesize about their value in learning on situated agents such as mobile robots. However, while simulation results are encouraging, work on physical robots has not yet repeated that success. We discuss why traditional methods typically perform poorly in situated domains with multiple goals, noisy state, and inconsistent reinforcement. We then propose an approach to representing the learning space and shaping the reinforcement so as to take advantage of implicit domain knowledge in order to both enable and accelerate learning.

2 Learning in Situated Domains

One of the fundamental causes for the inapplicability of theoretical RL paradigms to real–time robotic systems lies in the assumption that the interaction between the agent and the environment can be modeled as a Markov Decision Process (MDP). To explain why this assumption does not hold in situated domains, we address each of the key aspects of the MDP assumption in turn.

2.1 States vs. Descriptors

The state of a situated agent consists of a collection of discrete and continuous properties based on discrete and continuous sensor and effector values. A monolithic descriptor of all of those properties, even for the simplest of agents, is very large, and thus results in a combinatorial explosion in standard RL. Much of simulation work attempts to hide continuous state, such as the inputs from complex sensors, by presuming higher–level filters which, while effective in simulations, have been shown to be unrealistic in physical systems (Agre & Chapman 1990). In general, in situated domains, which are dynamic and noisy, the agent cannot sense world state or even its own state correctly or completely.

2.2 Transitions vs. Events

Traditional deterministic state transition models are largely inappropriate for situated domains where world and agent states change asynchronously, in response to various events of different duration, only some of which are caused by and in control of the agent. Furthermore, noise and uncertainty have specific usually complex properties that cannot be usefully modeled with simple probability distributions. Nondeterministic and stochastic models with probabilistic state transitions are truer to situated domains, but the information for constructing such models is not usually readily available. In general, it can take as long to experimentally acquire a model as to learn an implicit policy with the same effect. The properties that make modeling difficult make learning world models even more challenging (Whitehead 1992).

2.3 Learning Trials

Traditional RL models allow for proving convergence properties of various forms of certain well–understood algorithms such as temporal differencing (TD) applied to deterministic MDP environments. However, the provable convergence properties require infinite trials (Jaakkola & Jordan 1993). Thus, even in ideal Markovian worlds the required number of trials is prohibitive for all but the smallest state spaces. Furthermore, properties required for provable convergence typically cannot be achieved or guaranteed in situated domains. In those, the agent cannot choose what states it will transition to, it cannot visit all states with equal frequency, and it cannot afford large number of repeated trials. Thus, convergence of situated learning depends on focusing only on the relevant parts of state and maximizing the amount of information learned from each trial. The smaller the state space, the better the problem is formulated and the fewer learning trials are required.

2.4 Reinforcement vs. Feedback

Design of reinforcement functions is not often discussed, although it is perhaps the most difficult aspect of setting up an RL system. Immediate reinforcement, when available, is the most effective (Maes & Brooks 1990). More delayed reinforcement requires the introduction of subgoals in order to make the task learnable under realistic time constraints (Mahadevan & Connell 1991). Situated domains tend to fall in between the two popular reinforcement extremes, providing some immediate rewards, plenty of intermittent delayed ones, and only few very delayed ones. Although impulse reward only at the goal avoids biasing the learner, it fails to model most situated scenarios. These scenarios usually offer some estimate of progress which, even if intermittent, internally biased, and inconsistent, can provide an informative learning signal.

2.5 Multiple Goals

In situated domains agents typically pursues multiple goals not all of which can be sequenced. In traditional RL, learning a multi–goal policy requires that the goals must be formulated as sequential and consistent subgoals of a monolithic reward function (Singh 1991), or that separate state spaces and reinforcement functions are used for each of the goals (Whitehead, Karlsson & Tenenberg 1993). The former requires further expansion of the learning space, while the latter involves some hand crafting by the designer, and is more along the lines of what we propose.

3 . Designing Reward Functions

Rather than encode knowledge explicitly, RL methods hide it in the reinforcement function which often employs some *ad hoc* embedding of the doman semantics. One more direct way to utilize implicit domain knowledge is to convert reward functions into error signals, akin to those used in learning control (Atkeson 1990). Immediate reinforcement in RL is a weak version of error signals, using only the sign of the error but not the magnitude. Intermittent reinforcement can be used similarly, by weighting the reward according to the accomplished progress.

We suggest that such reinforcement can be introduced 1) by reinforcing multiple goals, and 2) by using progress estimators. Since situated agents have multiple goals, it is straightforward to reinforce each one individually, with a *heterogeneous reinforcement function*, rather than to attempt to collapse them into a monolithic goal function. However, multiple goals are not sufficient for speeding up situated learning if each of them involves a complex sequence of actions. Such time–delayed goals are aided by progress metrics along the way, in addition to reinforcement upon achievement. We propose *progress estimators*, functions which provide positive or negative reinforcement based on immediate measurable progress relative to specific goals. These "partial internal critics" serve a number of important functions in noisy worlds: they decrease the learner's sensitivity to intermittent errors, they encourage exploration and minimize thrashing, and they decrease the probability of fortuitous rewards for inappropriate behavior that happened, by chance, to achieve the desired goal. For a detailed discussion please see Matarić (1994).

Fig. 1. Up to four robots were used in the learning experiments, each consisting of a differentially steerable wheeled base and a gripper for grasping and lifting objects. The robots' sensory capabilities include piezo–electric bump and gripper sensors, infra–red sensors for collision avoidance, internal sensors of motor current, voltage, and position, and a radio transmitter for positioning.

4 Experimental Design

Our learning experiments were conducted on a group of four fully autonomous R2 mobile robots with on–board power, sensing (consisting of bump and infra–red sensors for detecting collisions and contacts), and radio transceivers (used for positioning, communication, and data gathering), situated on a differentially steerable wheeled base equipped with a gripper (Figure 1). The robots are programmed in the Behavior Language (Brooks 1990) and are controlled by collections of parallel, concurrently active behaviors that gather sensory information, drive effectors, monitor progress, and contribute reinforcement.

4.1 The Learning Task

The learning task consisted of finding a mapping of all conditions and behaviors into the most efficient policy for group foraging. Individually, each robot learns to select the best behavior for each condition, in order to find and take home the most pucks. Foraging was chosen because it is a nontrivial and biologically inspired task, and because our previous group behavior work (Matarić 1992) provided the basis behavior repertoire from which to learn behavior selection, consisting of *avoiding*, *dispersing*, *searching*, *homing*, and *resting*. Utility behaviors for grasping and dropping were hard–wired as were their conditions. By considering only the space of conditions necessary and sufficient for triggering the above behaviors, the agents' learning space was reduced to the power set of the following state variables: *have-puck?*, *at-home?*, *near-intruder?*, and *night-time?*.

As described, the foraging task may appear trivial, since its state space has been appropriately minimized. In theory, an agent should be able to quickly explore and learn the optimal policy. In practice, however, such quick and uniform exploration is not possible. Even the relatively small state space presents a challenge to the learner situated in a nondeterministic, noisy and uncertain world. Even in its current reformulated version, our data shows that this problem poses a challenge for the traditional RL methodologies.

4.2 The Learning Algorithm

The learning algorithm produces and maintains a total order on the appropriateness of behaviors (b) associated with every condition (c), expressed as a matrix $A(c, b)$. The values in the matrix fluctuate over time based on received reinforcement, and are updated asynchronously, with any received reinforcement. Particular events produce immediate positive reinforcement: grasped-puck (p), dropped-puck-at-home (gd), and woke-up-at-home (gw), while others result in immediate negative reinforcement: dropped-puck-away-from-home (bd) and woke-up-away-from-home (bw). All are combined into a heterogeneous reinforcement function $E(c)$.

Two progress estimating functions are used. I is associated with minimizing interference and is triggered whenever an agent is very close to another agent. If the behavior being executed has the effect of increasing the physical distance to the other agent, the agent receives positive reinforcement. Conversely, lack of progress away from the other agent is punished, and after a fixed time period of no progress, the current behavior is terminated.

Formally, I is the intruder avoiding progress function s.t.:

$$I(c, t) = \begin{cases} m \text{ distance to intruder decreased} \\ n \text{ otherwise} \end{cases}$$

$$near - intruder \in c, \quad m > 0, \quad n < 0$$

The other progress estimator, H, is associated with *homing*, and is initiated whenever a puck is grasped. If the distance to home is decreased while H is active, the agent receives positive reinforcement, *status quo* delivers no reinforcement, and movement away from home is punished.

Formally, H is the homing progress function s.t.:

$$H(c, t) = \begin{cases} i \text{ closer to home} \\ j \text{ farther from home} \\ 0 \text{ otherwise} \end{cases}$$

$$have - puck \in c, \quad i > 0, \quad j < 0$$

For the sake of a bottom–up methodology, we implemented and tested the simplest learning algorithm that uses the above reinforcement functions. The algorithm sums the reinforcement over time, weighting the values of the feedback constants appropriately.

$$A(c, b) = \sum_{t=1}^{T} R(c, t)$$

$$R(c, t) = uE(c, t) + vI(c, t) + wH(c, t)$$

$$u, v, w \geq 0, \quad (u + v + w) = 1$$

Binary–valued and real–valued E, H, and I functions were tested, but differentially weighted reinforcement did not result in faster or more stable learning. This is not surprising, since the subgoals in the foraging task are independent and thus their learning speed is uncorrelated.

Behavior selection is induced by events, each of which can be triggered externally, internally, and by progress estimators. Whenever an event is detected, appropriate reinforcement is delivered to the current condition–behavior pair, the current behavior is terminated, and another behavior is selected, choosing an untried behavior first, otherwise trying the best behavior.

Learning is continuous and incremental over the lifetime of the agent, thus ensuring that the agent remains responsive to changes in the environment (e.g., no more pucks are left at a particular location) and internal changes in function (e.g., drained batteries result in lower speeds, broken sensor affect the perception of conditions).

5   Experimental Results

In order to evaluate the effectiveness of the proposed heterogeneous reinforcement functions and progress estimators, we compared their performance against two alternative learning strategies:

1. a monolithic single–goal (puck delivery to the home region) reward function using Q-learning, $R(t) = P(t)$,

2. a heterogeneous reinforcement function using multiple goals: $R(t) = E(t)$,

3. a heterogeneous reinforcement function using multiple goals and two progress estimator functions: $R(t) = E(t) + I(t) + H(t)$.

Data from twenty trials of each of the three strategies were collected and averaged. The experiments were run on four different robots, and no significant machine–specific differences were found. Data from runs in which persistent sensor failures occurred were discarded. The set of conditions c consisted of the power set of *have-puck?*, *at-home?*, *near-intruder?*, *night-time?* while the set of behaviors was *safe-wandering*, *dispersion*, *resting*, and *homing* based on the basis behavior set developed in Matarić (1994).

Values of $A(c, b)$ were collected twice per minute during each learning experiment and the final learning values after each 15 minute run were collated. The

15 minute threshold was chosen empirically, since the majority of the learning trials reached a steady state after about 10 minutes, except for a small number of rare conditions, as discussed below.

Evaluating performance of situated systems is notoriously difficult (Matarić 1995). Standard evaluation metrics, such as time–to–convergence, do not directly apply since the time required for a robot to discover the correct policy depends on the frequency of external events that trigger different states in its learning space. Additionally, noise and error make certain parts of the policy fluctuate. We defined convergence as a relative ordering of condition–behavior pairs using an empirically derived optimal policy.

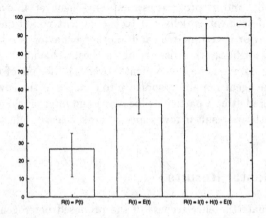

Fig. 2. The performance of the three reinforcement strategies on learning to forage. The x-axis shows the three reinforcement strategies. The y-axis maps the percent of the correct policy the agents learned, averaged over twenty trials.

5.1 Evaluation

The performance of the three approaches is compared in Figure 2. The Q-learning algorithm was tested on the reduced state space, and is functionally equivalent to a simplified version of the second algorithm, using only positive reinforcement for the single goal of dropping a puck in the home region. Given the nondeterminism of the world, and the uncertainty in sensing and state transitions, the single goal provides insufficient feedback for learning all aspects of foraging, in particular those that rely on accurate delayed credit assignment. The performance of Q-learning was very vulnerable to interference from other robots, and declined most rapidly of the three approaches when tested on increased group sizes. Q does not perform better than chance but discovers a partial policy that is consistent over all trials and consists of the few condition–behavior pairings that receive immediate and reliable reinforcement.

The second learning strategy, utilizing reinforcement from multiple goals, outperforms Q because it detects the achievement of the subgoals on the way of the top–level goal of depositing pucks at home. However, it also suffers from the credit assignment problem in the cases of very delayed reinforcement, since the nondeterministic environment with other other agents does not guarantee consistency of rewards over time. This strategy does not prevent thrashing, so certain behaviors are active unnecessarily long, such as *searching* and grasping which are pursued persistently, at the expense of *homing*. With 60% average performance, heterogeneous reinforcement demonstrates that additional structure is necessary to aid the learner.

The complete heterogeneous reinforcement and progress estimator approach outperforms the other two approaches because it maximizes the use of all available information for every condition and behavior. As predicted, thrashing is eliminated in learning the conditions for both *dispersing* and *homing*, because the progress estimator functions enforce better exploration and fortuitous rewards have less impact than in the alternative algorithms. The implicit domain knowledge shapes the reinforcement in order to guide and accelerate the learning process.

In addition to averaging the performance of each algorithm on learning the complete policy, we also evaluated each part of the policy separately to capture the dynamics of the learning process. Each condition–behavior pair was evaluated according to 1) the number of trials required, 2) correctness, and 3) stability. The number of trials was measured relative to a stable solution, whether the solution was optimal or not. The second criterion sought out any tendencies toward incorrect solutions. Finally, the third criterion focused on unstable policies, looking for those in which the behavior orderings tended to fluctuate. For details, please see Matarić (1994).

6   Extensions and Continuing Work

We have applied to described learning approach to another multi–agent problem, consisting of two six–legged robots jointly learning the best strategy for cooperatively moving an oversized elongated box to a specified goal, as shown in Figure 3. Unlike the foraging task described above, the box–pushing task requires careful coordination between the agents, in turn requiring either accurate sensing, or communication, or both. The task is designed so that a single–agent solution, due to the size and shape of the box, is much less efficient than an effective two–agent solution, but the two–agent solution requires intricate cooperation or the box is pushed in the wrong direction or out of reach of one of the robots.

As in the foraging case, the box–pushing task was decomposed into appropriate behaviors, including pushing, pausing, and turning in different directions. The cooperative nature of the task required that each agent learn not only its own strategy for keeping the box within reach and moving toward the goal (indicated with a light) but also the right behaviors in response to the other agent,

Fig. 3. Two Genghis-II six–legged robots were used in the experiments. The robots are 30 cm long and 15 cm high. The sensory suite of each robot consists of two frontal contact whiskers and five pyroelectric sensors for detecting moving IR sources. The robots are powered by rechargeable batteries and controlled by five 68HC11 microprocessors.

as sensed through the state of the box and as communicated between the agents. We successfully applied the above–described learning paradigm to this task and explored different communication and turn–taking strategies. The details of the experiments and the data are described in Simsarian & Matarić (1995).

7 Related Work

Numerous simulations of multi–agent systems have been developed in the Artificial Intelligence, Distributed Artificial Intelligence, and Artificial Life communities. However, they typically rely on simplistic models of sensors, effectors, communication, and interaction dynamics compared to those employed on physical robots, resulting in conclusions that do not generalize to physical systems and environments. More recently, several groups have experimented with physical multi–robot systems. Fukuda, Nadagawa, Kawauchi & Buss (1989) and subsequent work describe an approach to coordinating multiple homogeneous and heterogeneous mobile robotic units, and demonstrate it on a docking task. Arkin, Balch & Nitz (1993) describes a schema–based approach to designing simple navigation behaviors for multiple agents working on a retrieval task. Noreils (1993) applies a traditional planner–based control architecture to a box–moving task implemented with two robots in a master–slave configuration. Parker (1994) describes a behavior–based task–sharing architecture for controlling groups of heterogeneous robots, and demonstrates it on a group of four physical robots performing puck manipulation and box–pushing. Donald, Jennings & Rus (1993) report on an implementation of a cooperative sofa–pushing task with two mobile robots. Altenburg (1994) describes a variant of the foraging task using a group of LEGO robots controlled in reactive, distributed style. Beckers, Holland & Deneubourg (1994) demonstrate a group of four robots clustering initially randomly distributed pucks.

Work in learning in the physical multi–robot domain is even more rare, and that related to the approaches introduced here has been discussed throughout the paper. To summarize, the heterogeneous reward functions we presented are related to subgoals used by Mahadevan & Connell (1991) as well as subtasks used by Whitehead et al. (1993). However, unlike previous work, which has focused on learning action sequences, we use a higher level of description. The proposed subgoals are directly tied to behaviors which are used as the basis of learning. Similarly, progress estimators are also mapped to one or more behaviors, and expedite learning of the associated goals, unlike a single complete external critic used with a monolithic reinforcement function (Whitehead 1992).

Multi–agent learning has been largely treated in simulation. For example, Tan (1993) has successfully applied RL to a simulated multi–agent domain whose simplicity allows for retaining the MDP assumption that fails to hold for physical robots. This and other work that uses communication between agents relies on the assumption that agents can correctly exchange learned information. This often does not hold true on physical systems whose noise and uncertainty properties extend to the communication channels. We used the box–pushing learning task to evaluate the effectiveness of different communication strategies in the physical robot domain.

8 Summary

The goal of this paper has been to bring to light some of the important properties of situated domains, and their impact on the existing reinforcement learning strategies. We have discussed why modeling agent–world interactions as Markov Decision Processes is unrealistic, and how the traditional notions of state, state transitions, goals, and reward functions fail to transfer to the physical world.

We have argued that the noisy and inconsistent properties of complex worlds require the use of domain knowledge. We proposed a principled approach to embedding such knowledge into the reinforcement based on utilizing heterogeneous reward functions and goal–specific progress estimators. We believe that these strategies take advantage of the information readily available to situated agents, make learning possible in complex dynamic worlds, and accelerate it in any domain.

9 Acknowledgements

The research reported here involving wheeled robots was done at the MIT Artificial Intelligence Laboratory, supported in part by the Jet Propulsion Laboratory and in part by the Advanced Research Projects Agency under the Office of Naval Research. The work is being continued in the Interaction Laboratory, at the Brandeis University Volen Center for Complex Systems. The research with two six–legged robots was performed at the Swedish Institute of Computer Science.

References

Agre, P. E. & Chapman, D. (1990), What Are Plans for?, in P. Maes, ed., 'Designing Autonomous Agents: Theory and Practice from Biology to Engineering and Back', MIT Press, pp. 17–34.

Altenburg, K. (1994), Adaptive Resource Allocation for a Multiple Mobile Robot System using Communication, Technical Report NDSU–CSOR–TR–9404, North Dakota State Univeristy.

Arkin, R. C., Balch, T. & Nitz, E. (1993), Communication of Behavioral State in Multi-agent Retrieval Tasks, in 'IEEE International Conference on Robotics and Automation', pp. 588–594.

Atkeson, C. G. (1990), Memory-Based Approaches to Approximating Continuous Functions, in 'Proceedings, Sixth Yale Workshop on Adaptive and Learning Systems'.

Beckers, R., Holland, O. E. & Deneubourg, J. L. (1994), From Local Actions to Global Tasks: Stigmergy and Collective Robotics, in R. Brooks & P. Maes, eds, 'Artificial Life IV, Proceedings of the Fourth International Workshop on the Synthesis and Simulation of Living Systems', MIT Press.

Brooks, R. A. (1990), The Behavior Language; User's Guide, Technical Report AIM-1127, MIT Artificial Intelligence Lab.

Donald, B. R., Jennings, J. & Rus, D. (1993), Information Invariants for Cooperating Autonomous Mobile Robots, in 'Proc. International Symposium on Robotics Research', Hidden Valley, PA.

Fukuda, T., Nadagawa, S., Kawauchi, Y. & Buss, M. (1989), Structure Decision for Self Organizing Robots Based on Cell Structures - CEBOT, in 'IEEE International Conference on Robotics and Automation', Scottsdale, Arizona, pp. 695–700.

Jaakkola, T. & Jordan, M. I. (1993), 'On the Convergence of Stochastic Iterative Dynamic Programming Algorithms', Submitted to Neural Computation.

Kaelbling, L. P. (1990), Learning in Embedded Systems, PhD thesis, Stanford University.

Maes, P. & Brooks, R. A. (1990), Learning to Coordinate Behaviors, in 'Proceedings, AAAI-91', Boston, MA, pp. 796–802.

Mahadevan, S. & Connell, J. (1991), Automatic Programming of Behavior-based Robots using Reinforcement Learning, in 'Proceedings, AAAI-91', Pittsburgh, PA, pp. 8–14.

Matarić, M. J. (1992), Designing Emergent Behaviors: From Local Interactions to Collective Intelligence, in J.-A. Meyer, H. Roitblat & S. Wilson, eds, 'From Animals to Animats: International Conference on Simulation of Adaptive Behavior'.

Matarić, M. J. (1994), Interaction and Intelligent Behavior, Technical Report AI-TR-1495, MIT Artificial Intelligence Lab.

Matarić, M. J. (1995), Evaluation of Learning Performance of Situated Embodied Agents, in 'Proceedings, Advances in Artificial Life, Third European Conference on Artificial Life (ECAL)', pp. 579–589.

Noreils, F. R. (1993), 'Toward a Robot Architecture Integrating Cooperation between Mobile Robots: Application to Indoor Environment', The International Journal of Robotics Research 12(1), 79–98.

Parker, L. E. (1994), Heterogeneous Multi–Robot Cooperation, PhD thesis, MIT.

Simsarian, K. T. & Matarić, M. J. (1995), Learning to Cooperate Using Two Six-Legged Mobile Robots, *in* 'Proceedings, Third European Workshop of Learning Robots', Heraklion, Crete, Greece.

Singh, S. P. (1991), Transfer of Learning Across Compositions of Sequential Tasks, *in* 'Proceedings, Eighth International Conference on Machine Learning', Morgan Kaufmann, Evanston, Illinois, pp. 348–352.

Sutton, R. (1988), 'Learning to Predict by Method of Temporal Differences', *Machine Learning* 3(1), 9–44.

Tan, M. (1993), Multi-Agent Reinforcement Learning: Independent vs. Cooperative Agents, *in* 'Proceedings, Tenth International Conference on Machine Learning', Amherst, MA, pp. 330–337.

Watkins, C. J. C. H. (1989), Learning from Delayed Rewards, PhD thesis, King's College, Cambridge.

Whitehead, S. D. (1992), Reinforcement Learning for the Adaptive Control of Perception and Action, PhD thesis, University of Rochester.

Whitehead, S. D., Karlsson, J. & Tenenberg, J. (1993), Learning Multiple Goal Behavior via Task Decomposition and Dynamic Policy Merging, *in* J. H. Connell & S. Mahadevan, eds, 'Robot Learning', Kluwer Academic Publishers, pp. 45–78.

Learn Your Opponent's Strategy (in Polynomial Time)!

Yishay Mor and Claudia V. Goldman and Jeffrey S. Rosenschein
Computer Science Department
Hebrew University
Givat Ram, Jerusalem, Israel
ph: 011-972-2-658-5353 fax: 011-972-2-658-5439
email: yish@cs.huji.ac.il, clag@cs.huji.ac.il, jeff@cs.huji.ac.il

Abstract. Agents that interact in a distributed environment might increase their utility by behaving optimally given the strategies of the other agents. To do so, agents need to learn about those with whom they share the same world.

This paper examines interactions among agents from a game theoretic perspective. In this context, learning has been assumed as a means to reach equilibrium. We analyze the complexity of this learning process. We start with a restricted two-agent model, in which agents are represented by finite automata, and one of the agents plays a fixed strategy. We show that even with this restrictions, the learning process may be exponential in time.

We then suggest a criterion of simplicity, that induces a class of automata that are learnable in polynomial time.

Keywords: Distributed Artificial Intelligence, Learning, repeated games, automata

1 Introduction

Standard notions of equilibria in game theory involve a set of players holding strategies, such that no player can gain by deviating from his current strategy while the others' strategies stay fixed. This idea implicitly assumes some degree of knowledge about the players' strategies [1]. An obvious question is how this knowledge came to be. One possible answer is to have the players negotiate over their strategies. This solution cannot hold in the absence of communication.

We are interested in the case in which the players don't communicate with each other, apart from observing each other's move. Thus the problem we pose in this work is the problem of learning: how the players model their opponent and compute their best response at the same time? We are also interested in the complexity issue of the learning process.

When a player is engaged in a repeated interaction, he is in fact doing three things at the same time: first, he is playing the game defined by the payoff structure of the interaction, according to some strategy. If we attribute the players some degree of rationality, this strategy should be what the player believes is a best response to his opponent's strategy. Secondly, he is trying to learn what his opponent's strategy is. Note that the player's incentive to learn is limited to information that is relevant for his own choice of strategy. The third behavior the player might be involved in is what can be called "training". If the player assumes his opponent is also trying to learn his strategy, he might try to influence the opponent's beliefs, so as to push him towards a preferable strategy. For instance, in the repeated *Battle of the Sexes* game (Figure 1) player I might consistently play D, even at the cost of receiving a payoff of 0 for a period, in order to "teach" player II to play R.

II

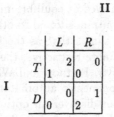

Fig. 1. The Battle of the Sexes game matrix

Much is yet to be done before a model allowing for these three simultaneous behaviors is available. We examine a restricted setting: player A chooses a strategy and plays by it. Player B tries to learn A's strategy and design her strategy as a best response to it. We require that B learn A's strategy in polynomial time. We assume A restricts herself to strategies realizable by *Deterministic Finite State Automata* (DFS). We do so for two reasons: on one hand, DFS strategies have been accepted widely as a model of *bounded rationality*. On the other hand, learning the structure of an automaton has been shown to be a very hard problem [5].

We focused, as an example, on the repeated game of *The Prisoner's Dilemma* (Fig. 2). However, most, if not all, of our results can easily be generalized to a wider class of two-person non-zero-sum games.

1.1 Related Work

Finite automata players were suggested as a model of bounded rationality, and as a means of resolving the prisoner's dilemma paradox, by Rubinstein [12] and by Neyman [8]. An extensive survey of the relevant literature appears in [4]. The basic concept underlying this trend is that the players are rational, but are constrained to submit automata of limited size as their agents in the game. The number of states in the automata is accepted as a measure of their complexity.

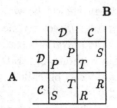

Fig. 2. The Prisoner's dilemma game

A series of "folk theorems" have shown that if the players are restricted to automata of size sub-exponential in the game length (i.e. the number of rounds) then cooperative behavior can be achieved at equilibrium.

This line of work is, in a sense, contrapositional to other common measures of complexity. Papadimitriou [9] has shown that as the bound on the number of states of the automaton becomes more restrictive, the problem of designing the optimal automaton becomes harder. Fortnow and Whang [2] were the first to assume total ignorance of the opponent's automaton. They show that in zero-sum games, a rational player can discover an optimal strategy w.r.t. the opponent's automaton in polynomial time, but in non-zero-sum games this is not the general case.

The apparent dissent is perhaps made clear by the following observation: Let K_A be the limit on the number of states in player A's automaton. If player B is allowed to use an automaton of size super-exponential in K_A, she can construct an automaton that will be optimal against any strategy of A. All B has to do, is to construct a 2^{K_A} deep tree, that will enable her to identify A's automaton, then compute the best-reply automaton to every K_A size automaton, and attach it to the relevant branch of the tree. This idea has two pitfalls from the point of view of traditional complexity theory. First, it is obvious that the time needed to construct such an automaton is unacceptable. Second, allowing automata of such size undermines the essence of computational learning theory: this automaton is an "instant learning machine". In fact, it serves as a table of all possible states of the world, replacing the desired decision process.

1.2 Outline of this paper

Section 2 unfolds the theoretical framework used in this paper. A central concept introduced in this section is that of automata *supporting* certain payoffs. The idea is to restrict the automata to those displaying some level of rational behavior, ensuring they cannot be exploited.

Section 3 addresses the issue of designing an automaton tuned towards a specific equilibrium payoff. The novelty of the work presented is not in the existence of the equilibrium, but in the constructive proof, presenting a polynomial time algorithm. The reason we bring this proof, is that we do not see any point in polynomial time learning of strategies that cannot be designed in polynomial time.

Section 4 is the focal point of this paper. In this section we show that even restricting the set of automata to those supporting rational payoffs is not sufficient to make them learnable. A further criterion of simplicity is needed. This criterion goes beyond the standard number-of-states criterion.

2   Preliminaries

This paper examines the role of learning in two-person, non-zero-sum repeated games. In this section we define the concepts of games and game equilibrium.

Definition 1. [Games]
A Game is a 3-tuple $\mathcal{G} = \{N, \alpha, \Pi\}$ Where:

- N is the number of players,
- $\alpha = \{\alpha^i\}_{i=1...N}$, $\alpha^i = \{\alpha^i_1 \ldots \alpha^i_{M_i}\}$ is the set of *actions* available to player i, and
- $\Pi : \times_i \alpha_i \to \mathcal{R}^N$ is the *Payoff* function, i.e. Π assigns each player a real number payoff for any combination of all players actions.

We will use π_i to denote the payoff to player i.

Definition 2. [Equilibrium]
A **(Nash) equilibrium** in an n-player game is a set of strategies, $\Sigma = \{\sigma^1, ..\sigma^n\}$, such that, given that for all i player i plays σ^i, no player j can get a higher payoff by playing a strategy other then σ^j.

Consider two players, A, and B, playing this game. Each player's strategy, σ_i, $i \in \{A, B\}$, is a sequence of actions taken by player i. Strategy i can be represented by a deterministic finite (DFS) automaton where i's actions are given in every state of the automaton and the transitions are determined by the actions taken by i's opponent. For example if the automaton in Fig. 3 represents A's strategy then, both players will stay in the initial state if both perform *cooperate*. A will move to the other state if he performs *cooperate* and B performs *defect* (TIT-FOR-TAT).

Fig. 3. A's strategy - example

When one or more players are restricted to playing strategies realized by DFSs, the set of equilibria change. We will always interpret the notion of equilibrium with respect to the set of strategies available to each player. For instance, in the repeated PD game, if all players are rational, the only equilibrium is mutual defection throughout the game. However Neyman [8], Rubinstein [12] and others have shown that even if only one player is restricted to an Automaton with a limited number of states, any payoff pair in the *Individually Rational Region* (Fig. 4) can be accomplished as an equilibrium payoff.

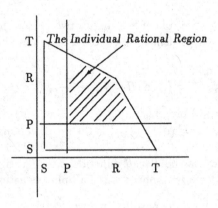

Fig. 4. Payoffs of the PD game

We will denote the automaton that represents i's strategy ($i \in \{A, B\}$), and have Q states by A_i^Q. In this work, we are concerned with connected automata. In this we follow other researchers [3, 2] who used this restriction to avoid "infinitly vengeful" strategies. Connected automata are such that have no disjoint states, i.e. for any states i, j there is an input sequence that leads from i to j. Another way to avoid unrevertable actions is to allow players to *opt out* (see [7, 6]).

When playing against an automaton, the game history is eventually cyclic. If player A is an automaton, and B is indeed trying to maximize her payoff, it is enough for her to consider only simple cycles in A (i.e. cycles in which every state is passed only once). Thus, when considering the possible payoffs induced by an automaton, it is sufficient to examine it's simple cycles.

Definition 3. A cycle C in A_i^Q *implements* $< \alpha, \beta >$ if $\overline{\Pi}_A(C) = \alpha$ and $\overline{\Pi}_B(C) = \beta$

Definition 4. A cycle C in A_i^Q *supports* $< \alpha, \beta >$[1] if .

1. C implements $< \alpha, \beta >$
2. $\forall$ C' s.t. C' implements $< \alpha', \beta' >$, if $\alpha' < \alpha$ then $\beta' < \beta$

---

[1] Notice that if $< \alpha, \beta >$ is not a Nash equilibrium point then it cannot be supported

Definition 5. A cycle C in A_i^Q *ε-supports* $< \alpha, \beta >$ if it supports $< \alpha', \beta' >$ s.t. $\| < \alpha', \beta' > - < \alpha, \beta > \| \leq \epsilon$

Definition 6. An automaton A_i^Q *ε-supports* $< \alpha, \beta >$ if $\exists C \in A_i^Q$ s.t. C *ε-supports* $< \alpha, \beta >$.

3 Polynomial Time Design of an Automaton Strategy

Theorem 7. $\exists A_i^Q$, A_i^Q *ε-supports* $< \alpha, \beta >$.(where $\epsilon = c \times Q^{-1}$)
Furthermore, there exists an algorithm that constructs the appropiate automaton for any $< \alpha, \beta >$ in polynomial time in Q.

Proof. For any given $< \alpha, \beta >$, we have the equalities:

$$\alpha = K_T \cdot T + K_S \cdot S + K_R \cdot R + K_P \cdot P \tag{1}$$

$$\beta = K_S \cdot T + K_T \cdot S + K_R \cdot R + K_P \cdot P \tag{2}$$

where K_π denotes the number of states in A_i^Q in which player A gets the payoff π. To be precise, this is the payoff the player gets in this state when playing his optimal strategy at that point. We will refer to the payoff that B gets as the *type* of this state. The payoff is defined by the actions of both players, while the state defines only the action of the automaton player. However, the optimal or best response strategy is unique for any state, even if the state under question would not have been reached by an optimal strategy.

Without loss of generality, we will assume P=0. In general we have, $K_T + K_S + K_R + K_P = K$. We will first normalize these values, getting $K_T + K_S + K_R = 1 - K_P$. Putting the above equations in a matrix form we have the equation:

$$\begin{pmatrix} T & S & R \\ S & T & R \\ 1 & 1 & 1 \end{pmatrix} \cdot \begin{pmatrix} K_T \\ K_S \\ K_R \end{pmatrix} = \begin{pmatrix} \alpha \\ \beta \\ 1 - K_P \end{pmatrix}$$

Denote by M the above matrix, and by δ its determinant.

$$\delta = T^2 - S^2 - 2 \cdot R \cdot (T - S)$$

$$M^{-1} = \frac{1}{\delta} \cdot \begin{pmatrix} (T-R) & -(S-R) & R(S-T) \\ -(S-R) & (T-R) & -R(T-S) \\ S-T & -(T-S) & T^2 - S^2 \end{pmatrix}$$

Now, we can deduce the coefficients of Equation 1 and Equation 2 by fixing a value for K_P.

$$K_T = \frac{1}{\delta}(\alpha(T-R) - \beta(S-R) + (1-K_P)R(S-T)) \tag{3}$$

$$K_S = \frac{1}{\delta}(-\alpha(S-R) + \beta(T-R) - (1-K_P)R(T-S)) \tag{4}$$

$$K_R = \frac{1}{\delta}(\alpha(S-T) - \beta(T-S) + (1-K_P)(T^2 - S^2)) \tag{5}$$

We have normalized the coefficients values to 1, but the sum of the coefficients should be the number of states of the automaton A_i^Q, that is Q. Hence, the final values of the coefficients are given by :

$$K'_T = K_T \cdot Q, \ K'_S = K_S \cdot Q, \ K'_R = K_R \cdot Q, \ K'_P = K_P \cdot Q \qquad (6)$$

We can now construct the desired automaton. The construction consists of three stages:

- Construct a cycle C_{imp} with $\frac{Q}{2}$ states that ϵ-implements $< \alpha, \beta >$, using the coefficients computed above to determine the number of states of each type.
- Construct a "punishment" chain C_{pun}: $\frac{Q}{2}$ states in which A plays D. The chain is linked so that B can only escape from it by playing C for $\frac{Q}{2}$ successive rounds.
- link C_{imp} to C_{pun} so that any deviation from the cycle will lead to the first state in C_{pun}, and the last punishing state is linked back to the first state of the cycle.

This automaton ϵ-supports $< \alpha, \beta >$ because this is the way we built it.

Notice that after we have computed the coefficients from equations 4 to 6 (in $O(1)$ time), we can build the automaton by determining the action and the transitions among the states in one pass over all states. □

4 Learnable and Unlearnable Strategies

4.1 An Unlearnable Automaton Strategy

Denote by $\overline{TL_B}(A_A^Q)$ the expected time that will take player B to learn A's automaton whose number of states is bounded by Q.

Theorem 8. $\exists A_A^Q$ s.t. $A_A^Q \epsilon$-supports $< \alpha, \beta > \wedge \overline{TL_B}(A_A^Q) = \Omega(2^Q)$ [2]

Proof.

For any $< \alpha, \beta >$, we construct an automaton that ϵ-supports $< \alpha, \beta >$ as follows:

- Build a cycle, C_{imp} that implements $< \alpha, \beta >$ as in Theorem 7. Denote it the consensus cycle.
- Build the punishing chain, C_{pun} that is based on the automaton presented in [2]. The idea is to choose a random binary string of Cs and Ds and to construct the punishing chain so that B can escape from it only by following this string.

---

[2] Exponential time might not disturb some researchers. Many of the strategies discussed in the context of PD are two or three state automata strategies. However, note that the number of states defines the granularity of the grid of possible payoff vectors. Thus, for instance, the class of two-state automata allows for 10 distinct payoff vectors, only 3 or 5 of which are in the rational region (depending or the relation between S, P, and R).

It was shown in [2] that C_{pun} cannot be learnt in polynomial time. Therefore if B enters C_{pun} then $\overline{TL_B}(A_A^Q) = \Omega(2^Q)$.

Lemma 9. *B enters C_{pun} with probability $(1 - (\frac{1}{2})^{\frac{Q}{2}})$.*

Proof. When B visits a state in the consensus cycle for the first time, he has no information regarding which action he should choose in order to stay in this cycle. Hence with probability $\frac{1}{2}$, B stays in the consensus cycle and with probability $\frac{1}{2}$, he enters C_{pun}. There are $\frac{Q}{2}$ states in the consensus cycle, therefore the probability of B following the whole consensus cycle is given by $(\frac{1}{2})^{\frac{Q}{2}}$ and the probability of B entering C_{pun} is $(1 - (\frac{1}{2})^{\frac{Q}{2}})$. □

Figure 5 is an example of such an automaton for

$$\alpha = \beta = \frac{3P + 2R}{5}$$

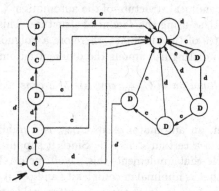

Fig. 5. An Example of an Unlearnable Automaton strategy

4.2 Learnable Automata Strategies

Our objective is to categorize a class of game-playing automata that are learnable in polynomial time. The categorization we propose is based on a criterion of simplicity. Indeed, one motivation for studying automata-based strategies was their relative simplicity. Although the standard measure of complexity used for automata is the number of states, it obviously does not capture the intuitive notion of complexity. Consider the automaton we used as an example for unlearnability. Clearly, it is more complex than an automaton with the same number of states, which are all identical.

Definition 10. $[C_{simp}]$ In the course of theorem 7 we defined four types of states in an automaton for the PD game. We will group the states of the automaton into chunks of connected (in the automaton graph) states of the same type. Let $\#(A)$ be the number of states in an automaton A, and $\#C(A)$ be the number of chunks of equi-type states. We denote by $<_c$ the complexity relation between two automata:

$A <_c \tilde{A}$ if:

1. $\#(A) < \#(\tilde{A}) \lor$
2. $\#(A) = \#(\tilde{A}) \land \#C(A) < \#C(\tilde{A})$

The class of simple automata is:

$$C_{simp} \equiv A : \exists < \alpha, \beta > \ s.t. \ A \ supports \ < \alpha, \beta > \land$$
$$\forall \tilde{A} : \tilde{A} \ supports \ < \alpha, \beta > \Rightarrow A <_c \tilde{A}$$

Theorem 11. *The class C_{simp} is learnable in polynomial time, i.e.* $\overline{TL_B}(A_A^Q) = O(Q)$

Proof. The proof consists of the following stages:

First, we show a canonical structure of the automata in C_{simp}, then we compute the size of this class using the canonical structure. This size is polynomial in the number of states of the automata, therefore a polynomial number of examples is sufficient to distinguish among the different automata in the class.

Lemma 12. *Any automaton in C_{simp} consists of a consensus cycle and a punishment chain.*

Proof. By definition, an automaton A in C_{simp} is a minimal-complexity automaton that supports a certain $< \alpha, \beta >$. Since it supports $< \alpha, \beta >$ it must have at least one cycle that implements this payoff vector. Among all these cycles, choose the one that is minimal in complexity and call it the consensus cycle (i.e. C_{imp}). The transition table of the automaton holds two entries for each state in the consensus cycle. One entry is part of this cycle and the other is not, leading to another chain which eventually will have a connection back to the consensus cycle. We are left to prove that there is at most one such chain.

Assume the contrary. Choose the chain, $\tilde{C}$, s.t. $\overline{\pi}_B(\tilde{C})$ is minimal. Denote by $s_{\tilde{C}}$ a state in $\tilde{C}$ that is accessed from the consensus cycle. Redirect all the transitions out of the consensus cycle to $s_{\tilde{C}}$. Since all the other chains different from $\tilde{C}$ and the consensus cycle are no longer accessible, remove them. We have constructed an automaton that still supports $< \alpha, \beta >$ but has less states than A in contradiction to A being in C_{simp}. Denote $\tilde{C}$ the punishment chain. □

Lemma 13. *All the states in the punishment chain are of type S.*

Proof. From Lemma 12, we know that there exists at most one punishment chain in automaton A. Replace this chain, C_{pun}, by another one, C'_{pun}, with the same number of states which are all of type S. Denote by A' the modified automaton.

$\overline{\pi}_B(C'_{pun}) \le \overline{\pi}_B(C_{pun})$ so if A supported $< \alpha, \beta >$ so does A'. However, $A' \le_c A$ $(A' =_c A$ when the states in C_{pun} are equi-type). therefore $A \in C_{simp}$ iff all the states in C_{pun} were equi-type.

By contradiction, assume all the states in C_{pun} are of type different from S. W.lo.g. assume this type is P. Every chain $\tilde{C} \ne C_{imp}$ in A can be decomposed into two parts: a prefix of C_{imp} that will be denoted by h, and C_{pun}. The average payoff of B in $\tilde{C}$ is given by

$$\overline{\pi}_B(\tilde{C}) = \frac{K_h \cdot \overline{\pi}_h + K_{pun} \cdot P}{K_h + K_{pun}}$$

where K_h is the number of states in h, K_{pun} is the number of states in C_{pun} and $\overline{\pi}_h$ is the average payoff that B receives in h.

Let K'_{pun} be the number of states in C_{pun} when they are all of type S and $\overline{\pi}_B(\tilde{C})$ remains unchanged.

$$\frac{K_h \cdot \overline{\pi}_h + K_{pun} \cdot P}{K_h + K_{pun}} = \frac{K_h \cdot \overline{\pi}_h + K'_{pun} \cdot S}{K_h + K'_{pun}}$$

$$K'_{pun} \le K_{pun} \cdot \frac{K_h \cdot (\overline{\pi}_h - P)}{K_h \cdot (\overline{\pi}_h - P) + \epsilon}, \epsilon > 0$$

Therefore $K'_{pun} < K_{pun}$ in contradiction to the assumption that A is in C_{simp}. □

Lemma 14. *For each automaton $A \in C_{simp}$, and for each type of state t, there is at most one chunk of states of type t in A.*

Proof. By contradiction: assume that $\exists A \in C_{simp} \exists t$ s.t. there is more than one chunk of states of type t in A. We construct an automaton $\tilde{A}$ that supports the same payoff vector, and $\tilde{A} <_c A$. This contradicts A being in C_{simp}: all we have to do is to group all the states of type t together. □

Lemma 15. $|C_{simp}| < 4!Q^3$

Proof. There are four possible types of states, therefore by Lemma 14 there could be at most four chunks. Hence there are 4! possible ways to arrange them. Each chunk has at most Q states, but the number of states in one of the chunks is determined by the size of the others. Therefore there are less than Q^3 possible combinations of chunks' sizes for each of the 4! arrangements. □

We have shown that for every Q, the number of automata with $O(Q)$ states in C_{simp} is polynomial in Q. Therefore, player B could enumerate all the possible automata and he could learn which automaton is A's in time polynomial in A's automaton's size. This completes the proof of Theorem 11. □

4.3 An example of a learning algorithm

So far, we dealt with all payoff vectors in the individually rational region. However, the range of possible payoffs requires a more detailed inspection in our context.

In the setting we studied, player A designs an automaton that is "tuned" towards a certain payoff vector, and player B tries to learn that automaton and play accordingly. It is reasonable that A will choose an automaton that gives B a payoff of P (or $P + \epsilon$), so as to maximize his own payoff. However, we might want to allow more complex situations, emerging from various possible beliefs of the players. Consider, for instance a setting in which B can opt out of the game, and be matched with a different partner. If both players believe B can receive an expected payoff of θ if he opts out, then A will construct his automaton so as to award B at least θ in equilibrium. [3] Let us assume that A restricts himself to strategies that grant B a payoff of at least β at equilibrium. Still, among all these strategies, A will choose that which maximizes his own payoff. Consider again the graph in Figure 4. Given that A maximizes his payoff for a certain minimal payoff he attributes to B, the only possible payoffs to be received by both players can be represented in the upper and rightmost boundaries. The first line is defined by $K_R + K_T = 1$ and the second is defined by $K_R + K_S = 1$.

Assuming player B knows that A's automaton is simple, i.e., A's automaton is in C_{simp}, we construct the following learning algorithm for B (see Figure 6). Notice that B doesn't know how many states there are in A's automaton (Q). In the algorithm LearnSR(Q), B could have played C all the time in order to play according to A's automaton (a chunk of S type states connected to a chunk of T type states). But, if B would have played so, A could have taken advantage of that and play D forever. Hence we have added in B's learning algorithm, a step where B will play D to prevent A from abusing him. B will discover the size of Q in polynomial time since he will know it after log_2 steps.

5 Conclusions and Future Work

When players do not communicate about their actions, it might take each of them exponential time to find the best response to his opponent's strategy. We have shown that this holds even if one of the players is playing a fixed, Nash–equilibrium strategy.

We have first defined the notion of an automaton that supports a payoff vector $< \alpha, \beta >$. We have also presented an algorithm to design an automaton that supports a certain payoff vector to be received by the players if they play according to it. We have shown that the complexity of this algorithm is polynomial in the number of states of the automaton. The reason for deriving this proof is that we do not see any point in polynomial time learning of strategies that cannot be designed in polynomial time.

---

[3] This observation coincides with empirical data on human behavior [11].

```
Learn(Q):
K_S, K_P, K_R, K_T ← 0
Play C
If payoff = S then
  LearnSR(Q)
else
  LearnRT(Q)
Repeat {
  Play C for K_S + K_R times
  Play D for K_T times
}

LearnSR(Q):
  i=1 to ∞ {
    For j=1 to 2^i {
      Play C
      if payoff=S and PreviosPayoff=R then
        Break;
      if payoff=S then
        K_S ← K_S + 1
      else       K_R ← K_R + 1
    }
    Play D for 4^i times
  }
}
```

```
LearnRT(Q):
{
  Play C for K_R times
  Play D
  Play D
  If payoff = P then
    K_R ← K_R + 1
  else break
}
While (payoff = T) {
  Play D
  K_S ← K_S + 1
}
}
```

Fig. 6. The Learning algorithm

We have defined the class of automata C_{simp} that can be learned in polynomial time and we have also given an example sub-class for which we have specified the learning algorithm.

Other issues that need to be further investigated regard extensions of the results presented in this paper: In the Prisoner's dilemma, a player can punish his opponent without harming himself. An interesting question is which payoffs can be supported when this doesn't hold.

In some games, equilibria in pure strategies do not exist, players must randomize their actions. It might be possible to use unlearnable automata in order to create pseudo-random strategies.

In this work we have confined ourselves to a scenario in which one player remains static and the other is adaptive. A more general model will need to account for mutual learning. In such a model, players have to learn non-fixed strategies. Furthermore, players may attempt to manipulate each other's learning process.

We have shown the existence of a learning algorithm for the class of simple automata, but have not constructed an algorithm. The automata learning literature [10, 5] shows how to construct such algorithms, when "homing sequences" are available - input sequences that guarantee a certain state is reached. A side-effect of Lemma 13 is to identify such a sequence: Once the learning player is thrown out of the consensus cycle, she can return to its first state by playing C for a known number of rounds.

References

1. R. Aumann and A. Brandenburger. Epistemic conditions for Nash equilibrium. Working Paper 91-042, Harvard Business School, 1991.
2. L. Fortnow and D. Whang. Optimality and domination in repeated games with bounded players. Technical report, Department of Computer Science University of Chicago, Chicago, 1994.
3. I. Gilboa and D. Samet. Bounded vs. unbounded rationality: The tyranny of the weak. *Games and Economic Behavior*, 1:213–221, 1989.
4. Ehud Kalai. Bounded rationality and strategic complexity in repeated games. In T. Ichiishi, A. Neyman, and Y. Tauman, editors, *Game Theory and Aplications*, pages 131–157. Academic Press, San Diego, 1990.
5. Michael J. Kearns and Umesh V. Vazirani. *An Introduction to Computational Learning Theory*. MIT press, Cambridge, Massachusetts, 1994.
6. Yishay Mor. Computational approaches to rational choice. Master's thesis, Hebrew University, 1995. In preparation.
7. Yishay Mor and Jeffrey S. Rosenschein. Time and the prisoner's dilemma, 1995. International Conference on Multiagent Systems.(to appear).
8. A. Neyman. Bounded complexity justifies cooperation in finitely repeated prisoner's dilemma. *Economic Letters*, pages 227–229, 1985.
9. Christos H. Papadimitriou. On players with a bounded ,number of states. *Games and Economic Behavior*, 4:122–131, 1992.
10. R. Rivest and R. Schapire. Inference of finite automata using homing sequences. *Information and Computation*, 103:299–347, 1993.
11. Alvin E. Roth, Vesna Prasnikar, Mashiro Okuno-Fujiwara, and Shmuel Zamir. Bargining and market behavior in jerusalem, ljubljana, pittsburg, and tokyo: an experimantal study. *American Economic Review*, 81(5):1068–1095, 1991.
12. A. Rubinstein. Finite automata play the repeated prisoner's dilemma. ST/ICERD Discussion Paper 85/109, London School of Economics, 1985.

Learning to Reduce Communication Cost on Task Negotiation among Multiple Autonomous Mobile Robots

Takuya Ohko[1], Kazuo Hiraki[2] and Yuichiro Anzai[1]

[1] Anzai Laboratory, Department of Computer Science, Keio University, 3-14-1,
Hiyoshi, Kohoku, Yokohama 223, Japan
E-mail: {ohko, anzai}@aa.cs.keio.ac.jp
[2] Electrotechnical Laboratory, MITI, 1-1-4, Umezono, Tsukuba 305, Japan
E-mail: khiraki@etl.go.jp

Abstract. This paper describes LEMMING, a learning system for task negotiation in multi-robot environments. LEMMING focuses on the problem of communication costs on Contract Net Protocol. Contract Net Protocol has been recognized as an attractive way for task negotiation. However, it is difficult for multi-robot systems to use wide-band communication lines enough to utilize standard Contract Net Protocol. It has been observed that the main communication cost on Contract Net Protocol is caused by broadcasting task announcements. In order to reduce this cost LEMMING uses Case-Based Reasoning(CBR). By using CBR, LEMMING can derive useful knowledge from messages in Contract Net Protocol and can find a suitable robot that should receive task announcements. We evaluate the idea of LEMMING in a simulated multi-robot environment. The result shows the advantage of LEMMING over standard contract net systems.

1 Introduction

Reduction of communication cost is an important issue for cooperation among multiple autonomous mobile robots, and it is worth spending much computation cost, since it is difficult for multi-robot systems to use high-speed and wide-band communication lines, compared with desktop-computer systems.

This paper describes LEMMING[4], a learning system for reducing communication cost for task negotiation using the Contract Net Protocol[5] with Case-Based Reasoning(CBR)[1].

In general, messages handled by the Contract Net Protocol include Task Announcement messages, Bid messages, Award messages, and Report messages. It is observed that a high proportion of the communication cost comes from Task Announcement broadcasting. To reduce this cost, Smith proposes *focused addressing*[5]. But the knowledge for the focused addressing must be provided by human experts in advance. Thus, we proposes a technique to let robots acquire such knowledge by Case-Based Learning.

In previous approaches, the information gathered from a contract is not fully utilized and is disposed after each negotiation. Thus, this paper presents an

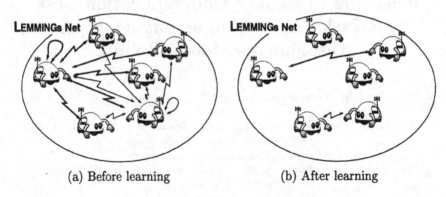

(a) Before learning   (b) After learning

Fig. 1. Addressee Learning

attempt to extract useful knowledge from the messages in order to reduce the total number of message exchanges. CBR is employed to infer the most suitable robot to carry out the task specified in a particular Task Announcement message. This technique of learning with CBR is called *Addressee Learning*. LEMMING, a control system residing in each robot, is developed to facilitate task negotiation with Contract Net Protocol and Addressee Learning. LEMMING learns to reduce communication as shown in Fig. 1.

The performance of LEMMING is evaluated in a simulated multi-robot environment, where requests on robots consist of handling or carrying various objects from one place to another. Each robot has different capabilities, and some objects may only be handled by some particular robots. Thus, on receiving a request for service, a robot is required to negotiate a task with its peer robots if it cannot manage it by itself. In this paper, communication cost is assumed as the number of the robots which receive message. The focus of evaluation is on the reduction of the communication cost.

2 LEMMING

Fig. 2 overviews the architecture of LEMMING.

- Each LEMMING controls a robot for negotiating tasks with Contract Net Protocol.
- Such robots with LEMMING composes LEMMINGs Net.
- LEMMING consists of *Negotiator, Reasoner, Knowledge Extractor*, and *Case Base*. The Negotiator is a contract net protocol handler, and communicates with other Negotiators. The other modules, the Reasoner, the Knowledge Extractor, and the Case Base are the handlers for Addressee Learning by CBR.

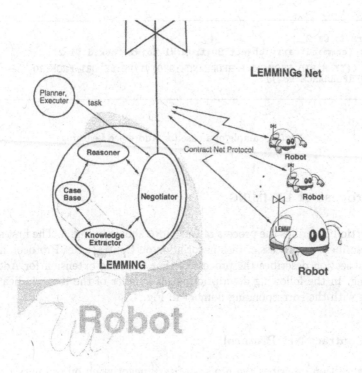

Fig. 2. Architecture of LEMMING

- The Negotiator handles the messages of contract net protocol for negotiating a task. To reduce communication cost, the Negotiator calls the modules for Addressee Learning.
- The Reasoner determines a suitable robot for an addressee of a task announcement.
- The Knowledge Extractor generates and modifies cases(Fig. 3).
- The Case Base stores the cases. Essentially, the case consists of a contract identifier, a task, Bid messages, and a Report message.
    * A contract identifier(in the **contract** slot of Fig. 3) is used for recognizing which contract generates this case.
    * A task(**task** slot) is a list of attribute-value pairs.
    * Bid messages and a Report message are memorized in **BR** slot(Fig. 3). Each Bid message and Report message contains a message type(the value of TYPE:), the sender of the message(the value of FROM:), and a *performance*(the value of PERFORMANCE:).

Concrete examples of a task and some messages are detailed at section 4.

```
contract: C1-2
task: (command:carry object:00 from:W1 to:W2 taskid:T1-2)
BR: ((TYPE:BID FROM:RO PERFORMANCE:980)(TYPE:REPORT FROM:RO
     PERFORMANCE:982))
```

Fig. 3. Sample of a case for Addressee Learning

3   Process of LEMMING

This section describes the process of LEMMING shown in Fig. 4. The first subsection describes the process of task negotiation on Contract Net Protocol, and the next subsection describes the process of that with the extension for Addressee Learning. In the following description, each number of the items indicates the process with the corresponding number in Fig. 4.

3.1   Contract Net Protocol

This subsection describes the process of task negotiation on ordinary Contract Net System which always broadcasts Task Announcement message.

A1 When a new task is input to Contract Net handler, the handler(manager-Negotiator) broadcasts Task Announcement message for the input task to all the system(receiver-Negotiator), and waits for Bid messages for a while.

A2 The receiver-Negotiator of the Task Announcement message examines the task in the message whether the receiver-robot can execute the task or not.

A3 If the receiver-robot can execute the task, the receiver-Negotiator calculates the *estimated performance* for the task. The estimated performance is a task-dependent scalar value. Then the receiver-Negotiator returns a Bid message with the estimated performance for the task.

A4 If the manager-Negotiator cannot get any consistent Bid message, the manager-Negotiator broadcasts the next Task Announcement message of the task and waits for Bid message as in step A1.

A5 Else if the manager-Negotiator can get consistent Bid messages, the manager-Negotiator selects the Bid message that contains the best performance. And the manager-Negotiator authorizes the bidder of the best Bid message as a contractor for the task.

A6 The manager-Negotiator sends an Award message to the contractor-Negotiator so as to let the contractor execute the task.

A7 When the contractor finished the task, the contractor-Negotiator returns a Report message with the result of the task.

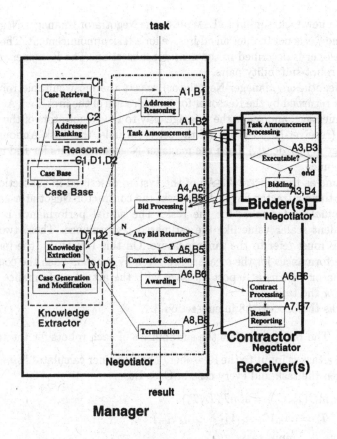

Fig. 4. Process of LEMMING

Each number in this figure indicates the enumerated number in this section.

A8 When the manager-Negotiator receives the Report message, the manager-Negotiator outputs the result of the input task and terminates the negotiation.

3.2 Addressee Learning

This subsection describes the process of task negotiation with the extension for Addressee Learning. The first paragraph describes the process of Negotiator module, the second one describes that of Reasoner, and the last one describes those of Knowledge Extractor and Case Base.

Negotiator: The Negotiator handles Contract Net Protocol. The process of Negotiator likes the process described in the former subsection.

B1 When a new task is input to LEMMING, the Negotiator (manager-Negotiator) calls the Reasoner to infer an addressee for a task announcement. The process of Reasoner is described in the next subsubsection. The Reasoner returns a list of robot-suitability pairs.

B2 The Negotiator (manager-Negotiator) selects the most suitable robot from the list returned by the Reasoner for an addressee of the first Task Announcement message, and sends the message only to the Negotiators of the selected robot (receiver-Negotiator). (If the selection fails, the Task Announcement message is broadcast.) Then the manager-Negotiator waits for Bid messages for a while.

B3-B6 Same as the process A3-A6 of the system described in subsection 3.1.

B7 When the contractor finished the task, the contractor-Negotiator calculates the *actual performance* for the task. The actual performance is a task-dependent scalar value like the estimated performance. These two performances must refer to the same measure. On this LEMMING, the formula of the performances for the measure are given by human. Then the contractor-Negotiator returns a Report message with the actual performance and the result of the task.

B8 Same as the process A8 in subsection 3.1.

Reasoner: The Reasoner infers the suitabilities of each robots for the task.

C1 When a task is input to the Reasoner, The Reasoner calculates "*similarities*" between the task and every case in Case Base:

$$simC(T_t, C_c) = simT(T_t, T_c)$$
$$T_t = (A_{t0}V_{t0}\ A_{t1}V_{t1} \cdots A_{tm}V_{tm})$$
$$: \text{input task}$$
$$T_c = (A_{c0}V_{c0}\ A_{c1}V_{c1} \cdots A_{cn}V_{cn})$$
$$: \text{task in case } C_c$$
$$simT(T_t, T_c) = \sum_{i=0}^{m} \sum_{j=0}^{n} W(A_{ti}, A_{cj}) E(V_{ti}, V_{cj})$$
$$W(A_{ti}, A_{cj}) = W(A_{cj}, A_{ti}) : \text{constant}$$
$$E(V_{ti}, V_{cj}) = \begin{cases} 1 & \text{if } V_{ti} = V_{cj} \\ 0 & \text{otherwise} \end{cases}$$

$SimC(T_t, C_c)$ is the similarity between the input task T_t and a case C_c. The similarity $simC(T_t, C_c)$ equals to $simT(T_t, C_c)$ which is a similarity between T_t and T_c, the task in C_c. The tasks, T_t and T_c are expressed as lists of attribute-value pairs. The similarity $simT(T_t, Tc)$ is a weighted sum of the equalities between each attribute-value pair of T_t and T_c. The weight ($W()$) is given by human experts appropriately.

Then, the complexity of searching similar cases in LEMMING is $O(CM^2)$, where C is the number of the cases in Case Base; M is the maximum number of attribute-value pairs in a task.

C2 According to the similarities, the Reasoner sorts the cases, and selects certain similar cases. And the Reasoner calculates *"suitabilities"* of the robots from the similar cases:

$$suit(r) = \max_{i,j} perf(m_r(Sc_i, j))$$

$$perf(m_r(Sc_i, j))$$

: performance value of $m_r(Sc_i, j)$

$$m_r(Sc_i, j)$$

: jth bid/report message from robot r in Sc_i

Sc_i : ith similar case

$Suit(r)$ is the suitability of robot r. The suitability is a maximum *"performance"* (described later) of robot r extracted from the bid and report messages in the similar cases. Then the Reasoner returns a list of the robot-suitability pairs to the Negotiator.

Knowledge Extractor and Case Base: The Knowledge Extractor extracts the knowledge for the inference from the messages, generates and modifies the case, and stores the case in the Case Base.

D1 The Knowledge Extractor makes the cases from the information handled by the Negotiator like tasks and messages. When Negotiator generates Task Announcement message for a task; the Knowledge Extractor generated a frame work of a case for the task from the Task Announcement message, and stores the case in the Case Base.

D2 When Negotiator receives Bid message or Report message; the Knowledge Extractor searches the case by the value of **contract** of the message, and modifies the case to add the list of important factors of the message to the **BR** slot of the case. The important factors are the attribute-value pairs of message-type, message-sender, and performance(Fig. 3).

4 Evaluation

In this section, we evaluates the LEMMING in a simulated multi-robot environment.

4.1 Conditions

Simulated Environment and Task: Fig. 5 shows the simulated environment.

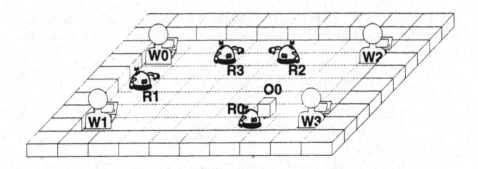

Fig. 5. Simulated environment

There are four mobile-robots(R0,R1,R2,R3) and four sitting-workers(W0,W1, W2,W3) in the world. Each robot can carry an object between workers and can handle an object at the worker. There are four kinds of objects(O0,O1,O2,O3).

The task is described as attribute-value pairs as shown in Fig. 6. For example, a task:"Carry the objectO0 from W1 to W2" is described as (command:carry object:O0 from:W1 to:W2 taskid:T1-2), and a task:"Handle O0 at W1 for 2 clocks" is described as (command:handle object:O0 where:W1 clock:2 taskid:T1-3). The values of the pairs are selected randomly, but the value of the taskid is generated as to be distinguishable from other values of taskid. The task is commanded to a randomly selected robot.

Each robot has different capabilities, and some objects can be handled only by particular robots (Table 1): robot R0 and R1 can handle object O0 and O1 only; R2 and R3 can handle O2 and O3. Thus, on receiving a request for service, a robot is required to negotiate a task with its peer robots.

The focus of evaluation is on the reduction of the communication cost. Thus, we extract the communication costs per task by each robot in each simulation-loop; and show the averaged costs as the result of the evaluation. The number of the simulation-loop is ten.

As comparison systems with LEMMING, *broadcast-based contract net system* and *random-based contract net system* are also evaluated. The broadcast-based contract net system always broadcasts task announcement messages. The random-based contract net system[1] randomly selects a robot for an addressee of the first task announcement message in each negotiation.

Definition and Calculation of Communication Cost: The communication cost of a message is defined as the number of the receivers of the message. For example, if a task announcement message is broadcast and there is 4 robots in the

---

[1] The random-based contract net system knows the names of all the robots in the environment in advance.

```
  "Carry OO from W1 to W2"
(command:carry object:OO from:W1 to:W2 taskid:T1-2)


  "Handle OO at W1 for 2 clocks"
(command:handle object:OO where:W1 clock:2 taskid:T1-3)
```

Fig. 6. Samples of tasks

robot	object
R0	00,01
R1	00,01
R2	02,03
R3	02,03

Table 1. Reference of robots and objects which they can carry and handle

environment, the communication cost of the message is 4; and if the message is sent to a robot, the cost is 1. This definition shows the assumption of this environment: each robot knows the names of all the robots in the environment, and broadcast is done by multicasting to the robots.

Definition of Weight for Similarity: The weight $W()$ for calculating similarity (described in the previous section) is defined as Table 2.

$W()$	command:	object:	from:	to:	where:	clock:	taskid:
command:	0	0	0	0	0	0	0
object:	0	1.0	0	0	0	0	0
from:	0	0	0	0	0	0	0
to:	0	0	0	0	0	0	0
where:	0	0	0	0	0	0	0
clock:	0	0	0	0	0	0	0
taskid:	0	0	0	0	0	0	0

Table 2. Weight $W()$ for similarity

Message Description: Fig. 7 show the descriptions of the messages for the task negotiation. Task Announcement message, Bid message, Award message, Report message are used for each contract, and Nack message is for future extension for directed contract[5].

Task Announcement message: (TYPE:ANNOUNCE CONTRACT:<contract identifier>
    FROM:<sender> TO:<addressee> TASK:<task>)
Bid message: (TYPE:BID   CONTRACT:<contract identifier>   FROM:<sender>
    TO:<addressee> PERFORMANCE:<performance>)
Award message: (TYPE:AWARD CONTRACT:<contract identifier>   FROM:<sender>
    TO:<addressee> TASK:<task>)
Nack message: (TYPE:NACK   CONTRACT:<contract identifier>   FROM:<sender>
    TO:<addressee> PERFORMANCE:<performance>)
Report message: (TYPE:REPORT CONTRACT:<contract identifier> FROM:<sender>
    TO:<addressee> PERFORMANCE:<performance> RESULT:<result>)

Fig. 7. Descriptions of the messages for Contract Net Protocol

Performance Measure: As the value of the performance, the time for executing task is used. The formula for estimated performance and actual performance are the follows:

< estimated performance >
= 1000
    − < estimated queued-time >
    − < estimated moving-time to the starting pos. >
    − < estimated execution-time >
< actual performance >
= 1000
    − < actual queued-time >
    − < actual moving-time to the starting pos. >
    − < actual execution-time >

The *estimated queued-time* means the estimated time in the wait-queue for the task's execution turn if the task is queued at that time(or the in-queued time, which equals to the bidding time). The *estimated moving-time to the starting pos.* means the estimated time for moving from the position where the former task is finished to the position where the estimating task starts. The *estimated execution-time* means the estimated time for executing the estimating task. The estimation of the moving-time and the execution-time are concerned with the speed of the robot and the geometrical distances.

The actual values also mean like these estimated values; but, in calculating the actual values, the in-queued time refers to the actual in-queued time(awarded time).

4.2 Results

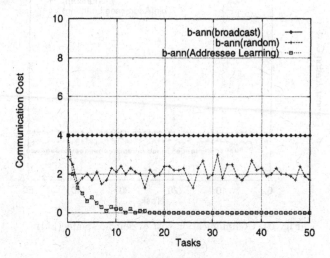

Fig. 8. Communication cost of broadcast

Fig. 8 shows the average communication cost of broadcast. These are plotted against the number of the experienced tasks with broadcast-based contract net system(solid line with diamond points), random-based contract net system(broken line with plus points), and LEMMING(dotted line with square points).

The broadcast-based system and the random-based system can not reduce the communication cost, but LEMMING can reduce it.

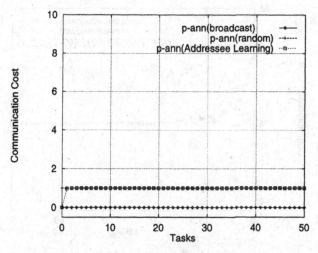

Fig. 9. Communication cost of point-to-point (announce)

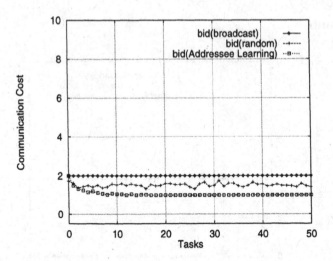

Fig. 10. Communication cost of point-to-point (bid)

Fig. 9,10 shows the average communication cost for task announcement and bidding by point-to-point communications, respectively. These are plotted against the number of the experienced tasks with broadcast-based contract net system, random-based contract net system, and LEMMING. The cost for awarding and reporting are omitted, because the cost for each process is always unity on all the comparing systems.

These figures shows that LEMMING needs the communication for the announcement message by point-to-point but reduces the cost for the bid message.

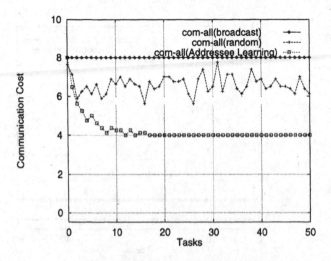

Fig. 11. Total communication cost

Fig. 11 shows the average total communication cost. These are plotted against the number of the experienced tasks with broadcast-based contract net system, random-based contract net system, and LEMMING.

This figure suggests that LEMMING can reduce the communication cost for task negotiation.

5   Extension

We have been extending LEMMING as to reduce communication cost more effectively[2] and to reduce searching cost of similar cases. We have also been applying LEMMING for a user friendly interface among multiple robots[3].

The extended LEMMING handles *directed contract*[5]. This extended LEMMING checks the result of Reasoner, and if the result is very suitable the LEMMING omits task announcement to send award message directly. If the award is not appropriate and the contractor cannot execute the awarded task, the contractor returns a Nack message to the manager. Thus, this extended LEMMING can negotiate a task only two messages(a award message and a report message). But the LEMMING has not been made effective checker of the result of Reasoner.

The performance of LEMMING depends on the weight($W()$) which is given by human now. We are now trying to let LEMMING learn the weight by itself.

To reduce searching cost of similar cases, the extended LEMMING can also forget such cases that are not selected as similar cases for a long time. As described before, the complexity of searching similar cases is $O(CM^2)$ where C is the number of the cases in Case Base, this forgetting which reduces C is effective.

To use multiple robots is difficult for human since a user has to select a proper robot for a task. But when each robot has LEMMING, the user does not have to do such selection and can use the robots more easily.

6   Conclusion

This paper described LEMMING, the learning system for reducing communication cost for task negotiation on Contract Net Protocol with Case-Based Reasoning(CBR). LEMMING learns to select a suitable robot for announcing a task by *Addressee Learning*. Thus, LEMMING can reduce the waste of the communication cost due to the irrelevant broadcast messages and bid messages. This paper evaluated LEMMING with some experiments, and our results suggest that LEMMING can reduce the cost of broadcast message and bid message per task. This evaluation further suggests that LEMMING can deal with task negotiation among multiple robots more efficiently than broadcast-based and random-based contract net systems.

References

1. Janet L. Kolodner. *Case-Based Reasoning*. Morgan Kaufmann, 1993.
2. Takuya Ohko and Yuichiro Anzai. Reducing communication load of contract net protocol by case-based reasoning. In *Proc. of the 9th Annual Conference of Japanese Society for Artificial Intelligence*, pages 283–286, 1995.
3. Takuya Ohko and Yuichiro Anzai. A user friendly interface for task assignment on multiple robots by contract net negotiation with case-based reasoning. In *Abridged Proc. of the 6th International Conference on Human-Computer Interaction(HCI'95)*, page 12, 1995.
4. Takuya Ohko, Kazuo Hiraki, and Yuichiro Anzai. LEMMING: A learning system for multi-robot environments. In *Proc. of the 1993 IEEE/RSJ International Conference on Intelligent Robots and Systems, Yokohama, Japan(IROS'93)*, volume 2, pages 1141–1146, 1993.
5. Reid G. Smith. The contract net protocol: High-level communication and control in a distributed problem solver. *IEEE Transactions on Computers*, C-29(12):357–366, 1980.
6. Stefan Wess and Christoph Globig. Case-based and symbolic classification — a case study —. In Stefan Wess, Klaus-Dietwe Althoff, and Michael M. Richer, editors, *Topics in Case-Based Reasoning(EWCBR-93)*, pages 76–91, 1993.

On Multiagent Q-Learning in a Semi-Competitive Domain*

Tuomas W. Sandholm**   and   Robert H. Crites***

{sandholm, crites}@cs.umass.edu
Computer Science Department
University of Massachusetts at Amherst
Amherst, MA 01003

Abstract. *Q-learning* is a recent *reinforcement learning* (RL) algorithm
that does not need a model of its environment and can be used *on-line*.
Therefore it is well-suited for use in repeated games against an unknown
opponent. Most RL research has been confined to single agent settings or
to multiagent settings where the agents have totally positively correlated
payoffs (team problems) or totally negatively correlated payoffs (zero-
sum games). This paper is an empirical study of reinforcement learning
in the iterated prisoner's dilemma (IPD), where the agents' payoffs are
neither totally positively nor totally negatively correlated. RL is considerably more difficult in such a domain. This paper investigates the
ability of a variety of Q-learning agents to play the IPD game against
an unknown opponent. In some experiments, the opponent is the fixed
strategy Tit-for-Tat, while in others it is another Q-learner. All the Q-
learners learned to play optimally against Tit-for-Tat. Playing against
another learner was more difficult because the adaptation of the other
learner creates a nonstationary environment in ways that are detailed in
the paper. The learners that were studied varied along three dimensions:
the length of history they received as context, the type of memory they
employed (lookup tables based on restricted history windows or recurrent neural networks (RNNs) that can theoretically store features from
arbitrarily deep in the past), and the exploration schedule they followed.
Although all the learners faced difficulties when playing against other
learners, agents with longer history windows, lookup table memories,
and longer exploration schedules fared best in the IPD games.

1   Introduction

Reinforcement learning (RL) is designed for cases where the learning system
is not provided with a target output for each input, but instead must select an

---
* An extended version of this paper appears in (Sandholm and Crites, 95).

** Supported by ARPA contract N00014-92-J-1698, Finnish Culture Foundation,
Honkanen Foundation, and Ella and George Ehrnrooth Foundation. The content
does not necessarily reflect the position or the policy of the Government and no
official endorsement should be inferred.

*** Supported by Air Force Office of Scientific Research Grant F49620-93-1-0269.

output for which it receives a scalar evaluation. It applies naturally to the case of an autonomous agent which receives sensations as inputs from its environment, and selects actions as outputs with the goal of affecting its environment in a way that maximizes utility. RL is based on the idea that the tendency to produce an action should be strengthened (*reinforced*) if it produces favorable results, and weakened if it produces unfavorable results. RL tasks can be divided naturally into two types. In non-sequential tasks, the agent must learn a mapping from situations to actions that maximizes the expected immediate payoff. Sequential tasks are more difficult because the actions selected by the agent may influence its future situations and thus its future payoffs. In this case, the agent interacts with its environment over an extended period of time, and it needs to evaluate its actions on the basis of their long-term consequences. Sequential tasks involve a credit assignment problem: a whole sequence of actions takes place before the long-term consequences are known. Credit for the consequences has to be allocated among the actions in the sequence. This is nontrivial, because the actions may interact and they may have different values with respect to the consequences.

The Q-learning algorithm works by estimating the values of state-action pairs. The value $Q(s, a)$ is defined to be the expected discounted sum of future payoffs obtained by taking action a from state s and following an optimal policy thereafter. Once these values have been learned, the optimal action from any state is the one with the highest Q-value. Q-values are estimated on the basis of experience—after being initialized to arbitrary values—as follows:

1. From the current state s, select an action a, receiving immediate payoff r and arriving at next state s'.
2. Update Q(s,a) based on this experience as follows:

$$\Delta Q(s, a) = \alpha[r + \gamma \max_b Q(s', b) - Q(s, a)] \tag{1}$$

where α is the learning rate and $0 \leq \gamma < 1$ is the discount factor. Go to 1.

This algorithm is guaranteed to converge to the correct Q-values with probability one if the environment is stationary and Markovian (i.e., the state-transition probabilities from the current state only depend on the current state and the action taken in it, not on the history that led to the current state), a lookup table is used to store the Q-values, no state-action pair is neglected forever, and the learning rate is decreased appropriately over time. Q-learning does not specify which action should be selected at each step, but requires that no action be neglected forever. In practice, a method is usually chosen that will ensure sufficient exploration while still favoring actions with higher value estimates. The Boltzmann distribution provides one such method, where the probability of selecting action a_i from state s is

$$p(a_i) = \frac{e^{Q(s,a_i)/t}}{\sum_a e^{Q(s,a)/t}} \tag{2}$$

where t is a computational temperature parameter that controls the amount of exploration. It is usually annealed (lowered) gradually over time.

Algorithms for sequential RL tasks have been studied mainly within a single agent context (Barto et al.,1983), (Sutton,1988), (Watkins,1989). Some of the newer work has applied reinforcement learning methods such as Q-learning to multiagent settings. In many of these studies the agents have had independent or rather easy tasks to learn. Sen et al. (1994) describe 2-agent block pushing experiments, where the agents try to make the block follow a line by independently applying forces to it. Tan (1993) reports on grid-world predator-prey experiments with multiagent reinforcement learning, focusing on the sharing of sensory information, policies, and experience among the agents. Unfortunately, just slightly harder predator-prey problems have uncovered discouraging results (Sandholm and Nagendraprasad,1993). Crites and Barto (1995) apply multiagent RL algorithms to elevator dispatching, where each elevator car is controlled by a separate agent. Littman and Boyan (1994) describe a distributed RL algorithm for packet routing, using a single, centralized Q-function, where each state entry in the Q-function is assigned to a node in the network which is responsible for storing and updating the value of that entry. This differs from the work described in this paper, where an entire Q-function, not just a single entry, is stored by each agent. Littman (1994) experiments with Q-learning agents that try to learn a mixed strategy that is optimal against the worst possible opponent in a zero-sum 2-player game. Markey (1993) uses a team of Q-learning agents to control a vocal tract model with ten degrees of freedom. Weiß(1993) presents Bucket Brigade based sequential reinforcement learning experiments in a simple blocks world problem, where cooperative agents with partial views share a goal but do not know what the goal is. Early on, Samuel (1959) applied RL to the game of checkers. Later, Tesauro (1992) has successfully applied RL to Backgammon. Shoham and Tennenholtz (1993) describe a simple learning algorithm called Cumulative Best Response that performs well in identical-payoff settings but performs poorly in the IPD. Despite some weak theoretical guarantees of eventual cooperation, in practice, agents using this learning rule usually fail to reach cooperation in hundreds of thousands of iterations. Other multiagent learning research has used purely heuristic algorithms for complex real-world problems such as learning coordination strategies (Sugawara and Lesser,1993) and communication strategies (Kinney and Tsatsoulis, 1993) with varying success.

Almost all of the research described above investigates settings where the agents have totally positively correlated payoffs (team problems) or totally negatively correlated payoffs (zero-sum games). This paper attempts to fill that gap by studying RL in the IPD, where the agents' payoffs are neither totally positively nor totally negatively correlated.

2   Prisoner's Dilemma

The *prisoner's dilemma* game is an abstraction of social situations where each agent is faced with two alternative actions: *cooperating*, i.e., doing the socially responsible thing, and *defecting*, i.e., acting according to self-interest regardless of how harmful this might be to other agents. This paper concentrates on the 2-agent prisoner's dilemma (PD) game, where the agents' payoffs for different action combinations are common knowledge. Characteristically, each agent is better off defecting regardless of the opponent's choice, but the sum of the agents' payoffs is maximized if both agents choose to cooperate—thus the dilemma. In game theoretic terms, defecting is a dominant strategy of the game and so the defect-defect action combination is the only *dominant strategy equilibrium* (and therefore also the only *Nash equilibrium*). On the other hand, *social welfare* is maximized at the cooperate-cooperate action combination, if social welfare is defined to be the equiweighted sum of the agents' payoffs. The payoff matrix of Table 1 defines a PD game if the following inequalities hold:

$$T > R > P > S, \quad 2R > T + S > 2P \tag{3}$$

		column player	
		cooperate (C)	defect (D)
row	cooperate (C)	R = 0.3, R = 0.3	S = 0.0, T = 0.5
player	defect (D)	T = 0.5, S = 0.0	P = 0.1, P = 0.0

Table 1. *Payoff matrix with row player's payoffs shown first. The numerical values are the ones used in the experiments. In general, T, R, P, and S could differ between the agents as long as they define a PD game.*

The PD game is a *noncooperative game*: no pregame negotiation is allowed, the agents cannot bindingly commit to any action, no enforced threats can be made, and no transfer of payoff is possible.

In practical situations, agents often encounter each other more than once. Correspondingly, some social interactions can be modeled by a sequence of PD games. This *supergame* of the PD game is called the *iterated prisoner's dilemma* (IPD) game. In supergames, an agent's policy (strategy) is a mapping from the entire history (all of its own and its opponent's moves) to an action. If for every possible history, the probability of some action (not necessarily the same action for every history) is 1 (probability of other actions is 0), the strategy is called *pure*. In a *mixed* strategy, an agent chooses its move stochastically from a distribution that is determined by the history.

This paper focuses on IPD games with an indefinite horizon. In such IPD games, it may be beneficial even for a selfish agent to cooperate on some iterations in the hope of invoking cooperation from its opponent. The goal of an agent at iteration n is to select actions that will maximize its discounted return:

$$\sum_{i=n}^{\infty} \gamma^{i-n} r_i$$

where r_i is the reward or payoff received on iteration i, and $0 \leq \gamma < 1$ is the discount factor.

Describing an intelligent strategy for a supergame is difficult because arbitrarily long input histories must be considered. Strategy designers have used two main approaches to address this problem:

- Use only a fixed number of previous moves as the context upon which the choice of next action is based, and
- Iteratively keep a tally of some (numeric) features that provide an abstract characterization of the entire history.

An example of the first approach is the pure strategy Tit-for-Tat (TFT), which cooperates on the first move and then does whatever the opponent did on the previous move. An example of the second approach is to compute at each time step the opponent's discounted cumulative score. A strategy has the desired property of being *collectively stable* if and only if it defects when that score exceeds a threshold (Axelrod, 1984). Both approaches to the problem of growing context suffer from the *hidden state problem*: the first approach ignores the older history, and the second approach can only give an abstraction of the true state - important details may be lost.

There is no single best strategy for the IPD game. Which strategy is best depends on the opponent's strategy, which the player obviously does not know. The *folk theorem of repeated games* (Kreps, 1990) states that any feasible payoffs that give each agent more than its minimax value can be supported in Nash equilibrium as long as the discount factor γ is sufficiently high. An agent's minimax payoff is the payoff that the agent gets when it uses its best strategy against its opponent's strategy that is worst for the agent. In the IPD, this corresponds to receiving a stream of P's (i.e. a stream of 0.1's in the example case with a discounted return of $\frac{0.1}{1-\gamma}$). TFT was chosen as an opponent for the learning players not only because it has performed well in IPD tournaments and evolutionary IPD experiments (Axelrod, 1984), but also because the optimal way to play against TFT is completely known. There are three different optimal ways to play against TFT depending on the discount factor γ (Axelrod, 1984):

- always cooperate; discounted return $V_c = \frac{R}{1-\gamma} = \frac{0.3}{1-\gamma}$
- alternate between defecting and cooperating; discounted return $V_a = \frac{T+\gamma S}{1-\gamma^2} = \frac{0.5}{1-\gamma^2}$
- always defect; $V_d = T + \frac{\gamma P}{1-\gamma} = 0.5 + \frac{0.1\gamma}{1-\gamma}$.

Thus, the agent playing against TFT should always cooperate if $\gamma \geq \frac{2}{3}$, alternate between defection and cooperation if $\frac{1}{4} \leq \gamma < \frac{2}{3}$, and always defect if $\gamma < \frac{1}{4}$. Each of the three ways of playing can be achieved by a number of strategies. For example, cooperation with TFT is realized by another TFT strategy or by a strategy that always cooperates no matter what the opponent does.

3 Q-Learning Players in the IPD

We generated a number of different types of Q-learning agents to challenge TFT and each other in IPD games. In each pairing of players in each experiment, the whole learning session was one long trial (300,000 PD iterations), i.e. the agent had only one chance to learn and evaluation took place during the last 100 iterations. The results are averaged over 100 IPD games for each pairing. Unless otherwise stated, the experiments were run with learning rate $\alpha = 0.2$ (chosen experimentally to give good performance) and discount factor $\gamma = 0.95$ (high to promote cooperation). The agents differed in the way they stored Q-values and in their exploration policies.

3.1 Storing Q-Values: Lookup Tables vs. Recurrent Neural Networks

If the state is considered to be the entire history, an agent is faced with a stationary environment (the other agent). An agent's learning method (algorithm and parameterization) is part of the agent's strategy in the IPD game. At each decision point, the state has increased in dimension with respect to the state at the previous decision point, so each state is visited at most once. Therefore the theoretical convergence results of Q-learning do not apply. Similarly, because each state is visited only once in a single supergame, an agent cannot distinguish whether its opponent is using a pure or a mixed strategy.

When the "state" is viewed as some window of previous moves (call this *sensation*, Fig. 1), the agent faces a hidden state problem. We addressed this

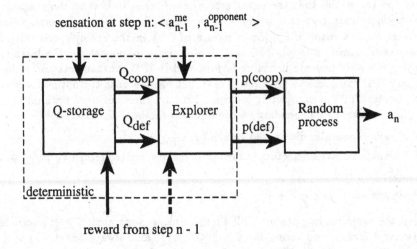

Fig. 1. *The architecture of a Q-learning agent for the PD game. Given the current sensation, Q-values for each action are used to determine action probabilities. These probabilities are then used to select an action. Q-values are updated based on the rewards received.*

problem in two different ways. The first set of agents used lookup tables to store their Q-values. The sensations of these agents were limited to w previous moves—i.e. w own moves and w of the opponent's moves. For example, given a window of only the last move ($w = 1$), four different sensations would be possible (CC, CD, DC, and DD). For each possible sensation, two Q-values need to be stored (corresponding to actions C and D).

The second set of agents had the same input sensations, but they stored the Q-values in a recurrent neural network (RNN) that can (at least in theory) store information of arbitrarily old actions, automatically learn which history features are important to keep track of, and generalize to previously unseen sensations, Fig. 2. Sensations were presented to the net in four bits because a unary encoding resulted in faster learning than a two bit binary encoding. The first bit was on if the opponent's previous action was cooperate, and the second bit was on if the action was defect. The third bit was on if the agent's own previous action was cooperate, and the fourth bit was on if its action was defect. We used a separate net for both actions, which has been shown empirically to enhance learning speed (Lin, 1993). Each net was constructed along the lines of Elman (1990): the net was a normal feedforward net except that the hidden-unit outputs were copied into context units, whose activations were fed back to the normal hidden-units on the next forward sweep. The copy connections from the normal hidden-units to the context units were fixed to one. This allowed the use of the vanilla backpropagation learning algorithm. In his experiments, Lin (1993) did not fix the copy connections, and was thus forced to do backpropagation through time. He did this by exhaustive unfolding in time in batch mode (i.e., weights were updated after each entire trial), which would have been impossible in the case of only one long trial as opposed to his many short trials of length 30 steps.

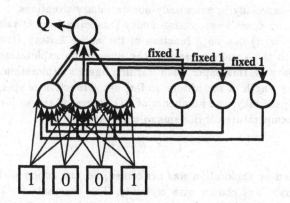

Fig. 2. *RNN as a Q-value storage. Each action had a separate RNN.*

The normal hidden-units were logistic units with outputs in the range between 0 and 1. The input units and context units did not do any processing - they simply passed on their input. The output unit (representing the estimated Q-value) was a linear unit. The normal hidden-units and the output unit received input from a bias unit (not shown in Fig. 2). The net was trained using the error backpropagation algorithm (Haykin, 1994) with the learning rate for logistic units set to 0.3 and their momentum set to 0.05. The learning rate for the linear output unit was set to 0.01. All of these values were chosen experimentally to enhance learning.

The output of a unit in a RNN depends not only on the input of the net, but also on the outputs of other units on the prior forward pass. Therefore, the updating of Q-values and the choice of an action must be done carefully so that both nets (one for each action) get exactly one forward pass per PD game iteration. For the action that was not taken in the previous time step this is simple, because no Q-value backup is required. To compute the new Q-estimate, one forward pass is done with the new sensation as input. For the action that was chosen on the previous time step, the first step is to save the activations. Then a forward pass with the new sensation is performed to determine this action's alternative Q-value to back up (the Q-update rule will choose the highest alternative over all actions). Next the activations are restored so that the net will be in the state that it was before the forward pass. Now the Q-update is done by changing the weights in the net by a backward pass. Last, a forward pass is done with the new weights and the new sensation to give the new Q-estimate for this action. This Q-estimate is used to choose the next action.

3.2 Exploration Methods

Agents must explore the consequences of their actions in order to be able to choose good actions later. It is not sufficient for an agent to always choose the action that it thinks best. It should try other actions as well to identify the environment—especially in potentially nonstationary situations.

In general, an agent's exploration policy (mapping from Q-values to action probabilities, Fig. 1) can be a function of the entire history (true state). So, with respect to the agent's sensation, the opponent's exploration policy may be nonstationary. In this paper, each learning agent's exploration policy was a function of the length of the history so far, not a function of specific events in the history. Specifically, the number n of PD games played so far was used to decrease the temperature for Boltzmann exploration:

$$t = 5 \cdot 0.999^n \tag{4}$$

If $t < 0.01$ then no exploration was performed, i.e. the action with the highest Q-value estimate was chosen with certainty. The constants for the annealing schedule $(5, 0.999, 0.01)$ were chosen experimentally. 5 and 0.01 are specific to the range of Q-values defined by the payoff matrix. In this domain the true Q-values (discounted payoffs) range between 0 (getting the sucker's payoff $S = 0.0$ all the time) and 10 (defecting on a cooperator all the time; payoff $T = 0.5$). An annealing schedule where t decreased linearly with n was also tested but was not as effective.

In all, there are four distinct reasons why an opponent may act differently at a certain sensation of the agent than it did earlier at the same sensation of the agent, Fig. 1:

- The opponent may be using a different sensation than the agent (e.g. longer time window or different features) in which case the agent cannot distinguish between two states that the opponent can. The opponent can use this extra context in the Q-storage-module (Fig. 1) which outputs the Q-values, in the Explorer-module which determines the mapping from Q-values to action probabilities, or in both of these. Once the system has reached stability this is a question of stochasticity with respect to the agent.
- The opponent may have learned, i.e. its mapping from sensations to Q-values may have changed. This may make the environment appear nonstationary.
- The opponent's exploration policy (mapping from Q-values to action probabilities) may have changed. The environment may thus appear nonstationary.
- The opponent's stochastic action selector may choose a different action even though its action probabilities have not changed. This makes the environment appear stochastic to the agent.

A player cannot distinguish which of these effects is causing the opponent to act differently. If the same sensation occurs multiple times, the agent may be able to differentiate between stochasticity and nonstationarity. The convergence proof of Q-learning applies to stochastic environments, but not to simultaneous learning due to nonstationarity.

4 Experiment 1: Learning against TFT

The first experiment was designed to see how the different learning agents performed against a player that used a fixed strategy (TFT). For $\gamma = 0.95$, lookup table based Q-learning agents using the last move as the sensation consistently learned to cooperate with TFT for a variety of parameter settings. RNN-based Q-learners also learned to cooperate with TFT as did a learner that had the same neural net architecture as the RNN but with no context units and no feedback connections. Lookup table based learners learned to cooperate with TFT in thousands of iterations, while RNN players required tens of thousands of iterations.

The next question was whether an agent could learn the optimal play against TFT for other values of γ as well. The lookup table based Q-learner with the Boltzmann exploration method was selected. At each setting of γ, 100 IPD games were run with 100,000 iterations each. For $\gamma = 0.05$, $\gamma = 0.1$, $\gamma = 0.15$, and $\gamma = 0.2$, the agent consistently learned to defect. For $\gamma = 0.25$, $\gamma = 0.3$,..., $\gamma = 0.65$, the agent learned to alternate between defecting and cooperating. For $\gamma = 0.7$, $\gamma = 0.75$,..., $\gamma = 0.95$, the agent learned to cooperate. Thus, the agent learned to play optimally against TFT in every one of the hundred IPD games at each setting of γ.

The Q-learning mechanism, though relatively slow, works extremely well against stationary policies such as TFT, which take into account a short window of previous moves. Playing against an agent with a stationary policy is analogous to single agent learning, because the learning agent perceives a stationary environment. The next sections discuss harder cases, where both agents learn simultaneously.

5   Experiment 2: Simultaneous Learning

Two types of learning agents were studied in the context of simultaneous learning: lookup table learners with Boltzmann exploration (LB) and RNNs with Boltzmann exploration (RB). All three pairings of these agents were tested, Fig. 3. CC means that both cooperated, CD means that the first agent cooperated, but the second defected, DC means that the first agent defected, but the second cooperated, and DD means that both defected.

Due to the exploration stopping threshold ($t = 0.01$), each agent stopped exploring after 6212 iterations. *Learning still continued* from that point on, however. The system always appeared to reach a stable state within the 300,000 iterations. Simultaneous learning was also studied by extending exploration to 62,143 iterations by increasing the exploration annealing factor from 0.999 to 0.9999, Fig. 3.

Final states often included *loops*, e.g. CC, CD, CC, CD, ... The loop length for lookup table learners is bounded above by 2^{m+n}, where m is the number of plays that one agent remembers and n is the number of plays that the other agent remembers. In theory, RNN players can have arbitrarily long loops due to their memory. In practice that did not tend to occur.

When two lookup table players played each other, one never totally took advantage of the other (e.g. CD, CD, CD, ...), but asymmetric loops did occur (e.g. CC, CD, CC, CD, ...). Between RNN players neither total advantage taking nor asymmetric loops occurred. When LB and RB played, surprisingly asymmetric loops only occurred to the *advantage of the lookup table player*.

Increasing α from 0.2 to 1.0 enhanced cooperation in the games RB-RB, but hindered cooperation in the games LB-LB and LB-RB (Sandholm and Crites, 95).

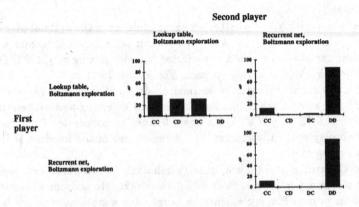

Fig. 3. *Percentages of plays at annealing rate 0.9999.*

The sum of the agents' payoffs was much higher in the game LB-LB than in LB-RB or RB-RB, Fig. 3. If even one of the players used a RNN as its Q-value storage, the outcome of the game was significantly less cooperative. This somewhat surprising result may be because the neural net players need more training examples than the lookup table players, because they are performing generalization in addition to the basic Q-learning, and are learning which history features to keep track of. Thus, neural net players may require a longer exploration phase than lookup table players. There is also a chance that some other network topology, some other learning algorithm, or some other learning rate and momentum parameters for backpropagation would have been more appropriate, although the parameters for these experiments were experimentally chosen to enhance cooperation.

6 Experiment 3: No Exploration

The impact of turning off the exploration was also analyzed. A lookup table learner that did not explore (LN) and a RNN learner that did not explore (RN) were tested against LB, against RB, against each other and against themselves. The non-exploring agents always picked the action with the highest current Q-value estimate. The results of games where at least one agent does no exploration depend heavily on the initialization of the Q-values. For example, if all Q-values are initialized with the same non-positive number, a non-exploring agent will always pick the action that it first picked in that state. This is because the Q-value corresponding to that action will be reinforced by a positive number (and thus exceed any other action's Q-value in that state), because the payoffs in the game are positive. In the experiments, the Q-values were initialized randomly from a uniform distribution from 0 to 1.

In the lookup table games LB-LN and LN-LN, neither player ever totally took advantage of the other, but asymmetric loops occurred to either player's advantage—more often to the the advantage of the exploring LB. The loops were longer (up to 4 plays) and more frequent than among exploring players. On some runs, RB could totally take advantage of RN, but never of another RB. In RN-RN, either player could be totally taken advantage of. Asymmetric loops occurred among RNN players when at least one of them did not explore. These loops were always to the advantage of the exploring player. When LN and RN played, asymmetric loops occurred either way, but only the RNN player could be totally taken advantage of. LN often had unbeneficial asymmetric loops against RB but few runs showed the reverse. LB often took advantage of RN, but rare asymmetric loops occurred in RN's favor.

The results suggest that exploration is crucial to avoid being taken advantage of by an exploring opponent. Yet if neither agent explores, the Q-value initializations determine the outcome, and cooperation occurs frequently. In games where at least one agent did not explore, the sum of the agents' payoffs was between the low payoffs of the games LB-RB and RB-RB and the high payoffs of the game LB-LB, Fig. 3.

7 Experiment 4: Extending Exploration

The hypothesis of this experiment was that agents will learn collectively better strategies if they are allowed to identify the system more thoroughly by extending the exploration process. This is not obvious in multiagent learning, because an agent's exploration introduces nonstationarity and stochasticity in the other agent's learning environment. Two LBs were matched with the annealing factor set to 0.999, 0.9999, 0.99999, 0.999999 and 0.9999999 (corresponding to 6212, 62143, 621458, 6214605, and 62146078 iterations of exploration). To allow roughly 300,000 iterations of learning after exploration had ceased in each case, the total number of iterations was increased accordingly.

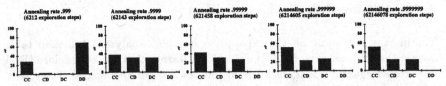

Fig. 4. *Percentages of plays for varying annealing rates.*

Defect-defect plays disappeared entirely as the exploration was prolonged even slightly, Fig. 4. Surprisingly, however, cooperate-cooperate plays also disappeared and gave way to asymmetric loops of length two. One half of the loop was CC and the other was CD (or symmetrically DC). Another interesting phenomenon was the fact that CD-DC loops occurred more frequently as the annealing factor for exploration was increased to 0.9999, but they became rarer as the annealing factor was further increased to 0.99999, and they disappeared as the annealing factor was increased to 0.999999 and 0.9999999. It appears that in the limit of extending the annealing schedule, CC plays occur 50% of the time, CD plays 25% of the time, and DC plays 25% of the time.

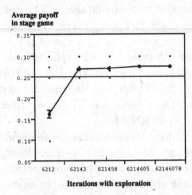

Fig. 5. *The average payoff within an iteration as a function of exploration length. Different payoffs are marked by dots. Error bars are presented one standard error above and below each mean.*

The average payoff of a stage game increases monotonically (with mostly diminishing returns) with longer exploration schedules, and appears to approach 0.275 (Fig. 5) which corresponds to the mentioned distribution of plays.

8 Experiment 5: Different Sensations

This experiment investigated what happens when LBs with different sensations play each other. The joint behavior of the agents was very sensitive to the annealing schedule (rates 0.999 and 0.9999 tested). Slower annealing tended to produce significantly more cooperation and other semi-cooperative loops and a wider variety of final looping patterns, while the faster annealing schedule increased defection.

Agents with history windows of 1, 2, and 3 moves were tested. With longer histories, a wider variety of patterns developed, and longer patterns developed. The longest looping pattern encountered was of length 8: CD, DC, CD, DC, CC, CC, CD, DD. It developed in the history 1 vs. 3 game with slow annealing. In the asymmetric contests, the agent with the longer history tended to fare slightly better than the agent with the shorter history (Fig. 6), but not as much as had been expected. Overall, there was clearly more cooperation when both agents used a history of one move, Fig. 4.

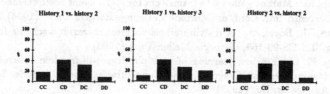

Fig. 6. *Percentages of plays at annealing rate 0.9999.*

9 Future Research

Future work should examine more closely the effect of exploration strategies on the types of patterns that develop. For example, what happens between agents using different annealing schedules or strategies other than Boltzmann exploration? Another interesting issue is learning among more than two agents. In the long run it is desirable to integrate sound learning methods into more complex agent architectures. Learning could help an agent adapt to the society of other agents and to the tasks at hand. Agents could learn pricing, timing and commitment strategies for competitive negotiations (Sandholm,1993), (Sandholm and Lesser,1995), deliberation control strategies to reduce computation overhead, variable and value ordering heuristics for cooperative distributed constraint satisfaction, and communication strategies, to name just a few potential applications.

Acknowledgment

We thank Andy Barto, Victor Lesser, and David Fogel for helpful comments.

References

1. Axelrod, R. : The evolution of cooperation. Basic Books, New York, NY (1984)
2. Barto, A. G., Sutton, R. S., Anderson, C. W. : Neuronlike adaptive elements that can solve difficult learning control problems. IEEE Trans. Systems, Man, and Cybernetics **13** (1983) 834–846
3. Crites, R. H., Barto, A. G. : Improving elevator performance using reinforcement learning. Advances in Neural Information Processing Systems 8 (1995) (to appear)
4. Elman, J. : Finding structure in time. Cognitive Science 14 (1990) 179–211
5. Haykin, S. : Neural networks: a comprehensive foundation. Macmillan, New York, NY (1994)
6. Kinney, M., Tsatsoulis, C. : Learning communication strategies in distributed agent environments. Working paper WP-93-4, Intelligent Design Lab, Univ. of Kansas (1993)
7. Kreps, D. : A course in microeconomic theory. Princeton Univ. Press, Princeton, NJ (1990)
8. Lin, L-J. : Reinforcement learning for robots using neural networks. Ph.D. dissertation, School of Comp. Sci., Carnegie Mellon Univ. (1993)
9. Littman, M. : Markov games as a framework for multi-agent reinforcement learning. Proc. Eleventh Intl. Conf. on Machine Learning, Rutgers Univ. (1994) 157–163
10. Littman, M., Boyan, J. : A distributed reinforcement learning scheme for network routing. TR CS-93-165, Carnegie Mellon Univ (1993)
11. Markey, K. L. : Efficient learning of multiple degree-of-freedom control problems with quasi-independent Q-agents. Proc. Connectionist Models Summer School. Erlbaum Associates, NJ. (1993)
12. Samuel, A. L. : Some studies in machine learning using the game of checkers. In Feigenbaum, E. A., Feldman, J., eds., Computers and thought. McGraw-Hill, New York, NY (1963)
13. Sandholm, T. W. : An implementation of the contract net protocol based on marginal cost calculations. AAAI-93, Washington, DC (1993) 256–262
14. Sandholm, T. W., Lesser, V. : Issues in automated negotiation and electronic commerce: extending the contract net framework. Proc. First Intl. Conf. on Multiagent Systems (ICMAS-95) (1995)
15. Sandholm, T. W., Crites, R. H. : Multiagent reinforcement learning in the iterated prisoner's dilemma. Biosystems, Special issues on the prisoner's dilemma. (1995) (to appear)
16. Sandholm, T. W., Nagendraprasad, M. V. : Learning pursuit strategies. Class project for CmpSci 689 Machine Learning, Computer Science Dept., Univ. of Mass., Amherst, January–May (1993)
17. Sen, S., Sekaran, M., Hale, J. : Learning to coordinate without sharing information. AAAI-94, Seattle, WA (1994) 426–431
18. Shoham, Y., Tennenholtz, M. : Co-learning and the evolution of coordinated multi-agent activity. (1993)
19. Sugawara, T., Lesser, V. : On-line learning of coordination plans. Comp. Sci. TR-93-27, Univ. of Mass., Amherst (1993)

20. Sutton, R. S. : Learning to predict by the methods of temporal differences. Machine Learning **3** (1988) 9–44
21. Tan, M. : Multi-agent reinforcement learning: independent vs. cooperative agents. Proc. Tenth Intl. Conf. on Machine Learning, Amherst, MA (1993) 330–337
22. Tesauro, G. J. : Practical issues in temporal difference learning. Machine Learning **8** (1992) 257–277
23. Watkins, C. : Learning from delayed rewards. PhD Thesis, Cambridge University, England (1989)
24. Weiß, G. : Learning to coordinate actions in multi-agent systems. IJCAI-93, Chambéry, France (1993) 311–316

Using reciprocity to adapt to others

Sandip Sen and Mahendra Sekaran

Department of Mathematical & Computer Sciences,
The University of Tulsa
Tulsa, OK 74104, USA
e-mail: sandip@kolkata.mcs.utulsa.edu, mahend@euler.mcs.utulsa.edu

Abstract. Interacting and adapting to other agents is an essential part of the behavior of intelligent agents. In most practical multiagent systems, it is likely that a single agent will interact with a number of agents representing different preferences and interests. Whereas it is recognized that if all agents were cooperating, peak system performance can be realized, it is impractical to assume benevolence from an arbitrary group of agents. More realistically, in an open system, agents should be self-interested. Can we then design environments where the best self-interested actions lead to cooperation between agents? In this paper, we investigate environments where reciprocative actions allow self-interested agents to maximize local as well as global utility. We argue that the traditional choice of deterministic reciprocity is insufficient, and propose a probabilistic reciprocity scheme to decide on whether or not to help another agent. We present experimental results to show that agents using this probabilistic reciprocity scheme can both approach optimal global behavior and resist exploitation by selfish agents. Thus the reciprocation scheme is found to be both efficient and stable and allows agents to adapt to others using past experience.

1   Introduction

Researchers involved in the design of intelligent agents that will interact with other agents in an open, distributed system are faced with the challenge of modeling other agents and their behavior [3, 5, 8]. If one can can assume that all agents will be cooperative in nature, efficient mechanisms can be developed to take advantage of mutual cooperation. These will lead to improved global as well as individual performance. But, in an open system, assumptions about cooperative agents or system-wide common goals are hard to justify. More often we will find different agents have different goals and motivations and no real inclination to help another agent achieve its objectives. So, agents need to adapt their behaviors depending on the nature or characteristics of the other agents in the environment.

Mechanisms for adaptation that use a lot of information and complex processing of that information consume a lot of computational resources [2, 9]. We are interested in developing adaptive mechanisms that are simple and impose little cognitive burden on the agents. In this paper, we assume agents to be self-motivated in their interactions with other agents, and that the interacting agents are uniquely identifiable. They may also help others in performing assigned tasks. We plan to develop a criteria for an agent to decide to help or not to help another agent when the latter requests for help. The decision criteria should be such that it allows an agent to perform effectively in the long run. This means that to be effective, an agent must be able to adapt its behavior depending on the behavior of other agents in the environment.

We investigate a simple decision mechanism using the principle of *reciprocity*, which means that agents help others who have helped them in the past or can help them in the future. In this paper, we use a multiagent domain where agents can exchange their tasks. We show that agents can use the principle of reciprocity to effectively adapt to the environment (for our discussion, the nature of the other agents determine the environment).

2 Reciprocity as an adaptive mechanism

We assume a multiagent system with N agents. Each agent is assigned to carry out T tasks. The jth task assigned to the ith agent is t_{ij}, and if agent k carried out this task independently of other tasks, the cost incurred is C_{ij}^k. However, if agent k carried out this task together with its own task t_{kl}, the cost incurred for task t_{ij} is C_{ij}^{kl}. Also, the cost incurred by agent k to carry out its own task t_{kl} while carrying out task t_{ij} for agent i is C_{kl}^{kij}. In this paper, we allow an agent to carry out a task for another agent only in conjunction with another of its own tasks.

We now identify the scopes for cooperation. If an agent, k, can carry out the task of another agent, i, with a lower cost than the cost incurred by the agent who has been assigned that task ($C_{ij}^i > C_{ij}^{kl}$), the first agent can cooperate with the second agent by carrying out this task. If agent k decides to help agent i, then it incurs an extra cost of C_{ij}^{kl} but agent i saves a cost of C_{ij}^i. The obvious question is why should one agent incur any extra cost for another agent. If we consider only one such decision, cooperation makes little sense. If, however, we look at a collection of such decisions, then reciprocal cooperation makes perfect sense. Simple reciprocity means that an agent k will help another agent i, if the latter has helped the former in the past. But simple reciprocity by itself does not promote cooperative behavior. This is because, no one is motivated to take the first cooperative action, and hence nobody ever cooperates!

In practice, reciprocity also involves a predictive mechanism. An agent helps another agent, if it expects to receive some benefit from the latter in the future. Developing a domain-independent predictive model is a very difficult problem. In absence of such a general predictive mechanism we propose a much simpler but equally effective stochastic choice mechanism to circumvent the problem of simple reciprocity. We will define S_{ik} and W_{ik} as respectively the savings obtained from and extra cost incurred by agent i from agent k over all of their previous exchanges. Also, let $B_{ik} = S_{ik} - W_{ik}$ be the balance of these exchanges (obviously, $B_{ik} = -B_{ki}$). We now present the probability that agent k will carry out task t_{ij} for agent i while it is carrying out its task t_{kl}. This probability is calculated as:

$$Pr(i, k, j, l) = \frac{1}{1 + \exp^{\frac{C_{ij}^{kl} - \beta * C_{avg}^k - B_{ki}}{\tau}}},$$

where C_{avg}^k is the average cost of tasks performed by agent k (this can be computed on-line or preset), and β and τ are constants. This gives a sigmoidal probability distribution in which the probability of helping increases as the balance increase and is more for less costly tasks. We include the C_{avg} term because while calculating the probability of helping, relative cost should be more important than absolute cost (if the average cost of an agent is 1000, incurring an extra cost of 1000 is less likely than incurring an extra cost of 10). Due to the stochastic nature of decision-making some initial requests for cooperation will be granted whereas others will be denied. This will break the deadlock that prevented simple reciprocity from providing the desired system behavior.

We present a sample probability distribution in Figure 1. The constants β and τ can be used to make agents more or less inclined to cooperate. The factor β can be used to move the probability curve left (more inclined to cooperate) or right (less inclined to cooperate). At the onset of the experiments B_{ki} is 0 for all i and k. At this point there is a 0.5 probability that an agent will help another agent by incurring an extra cost of $\beta * C_{avg}^k$ (we assume that the average cost incurred is known; an approximate measure is sufficient for our calculations). The factor τ can be used to control the steepness of the curve. For a very steep curve approximating a step function, an agent will almost always accept cooperation requests with extra cost less than $\beta * C_{avg}^k$, but will rarely accept cooperation requests with an extra cost greater than that value. Similar analyses of the effects of β and τ can be made for any cooperation decision after agents have experienced a number of exchanges. In essence, β and τ can be used to choose a cooperation level [4] for the agents at the onset of the experiments. The level of cooperation or the inclination to help another agent, however, dynamically changes with problem solving experience.

Our probabilistic scheme is different from a simple, deterministic tit-for-tat [1] strategy, e.g., agent k may decide to help agent i even if the later had refused help in the previous time-step. The decision is based only on the balance, not on when requests for help were accepted or denied. A deterministic strategy like tit-for-tat is unsuitable for most practical problems because of several reasons:

- In Prisoner's dilemma [6] or other formal games, the participants are assumed to repeatedly play the same game. In real life, the probability of identical situations being repeated is small.
- As a corollary to the above fact, it then becomes necessary to compare different situations. Tit-for-tat provides no mechanism for comparing favors. In realistic scenarios, an agent needs to evaluate a request for help against the amount of help received from the requesting agent in the past. Disproportionate requests for help are scarcely granted. So, the evaluation mechanism

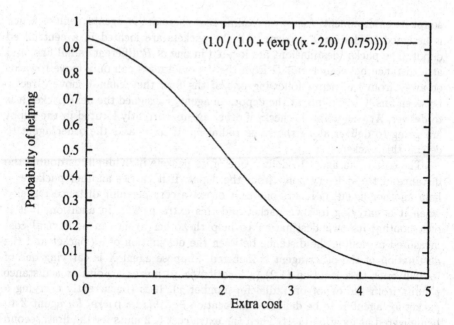

Fig. 1. Probability distribution for accepting request for cooperation.

depends less on when the help was received (though chronology does play a role) and more on the estimated amounts of help received and requested.

- Axelrod has shown that if initially agents decide to help each other, agents following tit-for-tat strategy will always help one another,i.e., they decide to cooperate [1]. However, the initial choice is quite arbitrary and cannot be justified. Once can as easily envision players using the tit-for-tat strategy but deciding not to help another agent the first time they interact. Under those initial conditions, a group of tit-for-tat players perform at the level of completely selfish players (the evolution of selfishness!). Interestingly enough, in the prisoner's dilemma game, not only is tit-for-tat a stable strategy, but so is a strategy of complete selfishness.

Our proposed mechanism for deciding on helping other agents allows comparison of favors, and thus is a more realistic and useful solution to the decision problem. It also allows the agent designer to choose the level of risk inclination/averseness of the agents.

3 A package delivery problem

In this section, we present a simple package delivery problem which we will use to demonstrate the effectiveness of our proposed mechanism to allow an agent to adapt its environment. Again we assume that there are N agents, each of which is assigned to deliver T packets. All the packets are located in a centralized depot. The packet destinations are located in one of R different radial fins, and at a distance between 1 and D from the depot. Agents can only move towards or away from the depot following one of the fins; they cannot move directly between fins. On arriving at the depot, an agent is assigned the next packet it is to deliver. At this point, it checks if other agents currently located in the depot are going to deliver along the same radial fin. If so, it asks the other agent to deliver this packet.

The cost of an agent to deliver one of its packets individually is double the distance of the delivery point from the depot. If it carries another package to help another agent, it incurs one unit of extra cost per unit distance traveled when it is carrying its own packet and this extra packet. In addition, if it is overshooting its own destination to help the other agent, an additional cost measured as double the distance between the destination of its packet and the destination of the other agent is incurred. Suppose agent X is carrying one of its deliveries to a location (1,2) (a location (x, y) means a point at a distance y units from the depot on radial fin number x). It is concurrently carrying a packet for agent Y to be delivered at location (1,3) and a packet for agent Z to be delivered at location (1,4). Then the extra cost is 2 units for the first, second and third unit distances traveled, and 1 unit for going from (1,3) to (1,4), and two units to come back from (1,4) to (1,2) for a total of 9 units; 5.5 units are charged to agent Z and 3.5 units are charged to agent Y.

We impose the following limitations on agents helping other agents:

1. An agent will request for help only if the cost incurred by the helping agent is less than the savings obtained by the helped agent. Only agents involved in the exchange need to share their destinations, so this information is not broadcast globally.
2. Though an agent can help several agents at the same time, it can carry at most one packet for each of these other agents at the same time.

4 Experimental results

In this section, we present experimental results on the package delivery problem with agents using the reciprocity mechanism described in Section 2 to decide whether or not to honor a request for cooperation from another agent. We vary the number of agents and the number of packets to be delivered by each agent to show the effects of different environmental conditions. The other parameters for the experiments are as follows: $R = 4$, $D = 3$, $\tau = 0.75$, and $\beta = 0.5$. Each of our experiments are run on 10 different randomly generated data sets, where a data set consist of an ordered assignment of package deliveries to agents. All the agents are assigned the same number of deliveries. The evaluation metric is the average cost incurred by the agents to complete all the deliveries.

We used this domain to also investigate the effects of agent characteristics on overall system performance. We experimented with the following types of agents:

Philanthropic agents: Agents who will always accept a request for cooperation. Philanthropic agents will produce the best system performance. To aid this process, we impose the restriction that if two philanthropic agent are assigned deliveries on the same fin, the one going further away from the depot takes over the delivery of the agent who is going a shorter distance. In this way, the system incurs minimal extra cost.

Selfish agents: Agents who will request for cooperation (some of which will be accepted) but never accept a cooperation request. Selfish agents can benefit in the presence of philanthropic agents by exploiting their benevolence.

Reciprocal agents: Agents that uses the balance of cost and savings to stochastically decide whether to accept a given request for cooperation.

Individual agents: Agents who deliver their assigned packets without looking for help from others. They will also not accept any cooperation requests.

We expect the individual and the philanthropic agents to provide the two extremes of system performance. The individual agents should travel on the average the longest distance to complete their deliveries (because no one is cooperating), whereas the philanthropic agents should travel the least. We expect reciprocal agent behaviors to lie in between. The frequency of occurrence of cooperation possibilities should determine which of the two ends of the spectrum is occupied by the reciprocal agents. The following are the key research questions that confronted us:

- Can reciprocative agents match the performance of philanthropic agents?
- Can selfish agents exploit reciprocative agents?

It would seem that in the long run reciprocal agents should perform better because with sufficient interactions they become philanthropic towards each other, a possibility denied to the selfish agents. In order to gain a further understanding of agent interactions, we have run a set of experiments with both homogeneous and heterogeneous agent groups. Results from these groups and their analysis is presented in the next section.

4.1 Homogeneous groups

As a starting point, we wanted to evaluate the performance of each of the above-mentioned types of agents when they were placed in a group where all the other agents were of the same type, i.e., the groups were *homogeneous* in composition with respect to the types of agent in the group.

We chose the number of agents, N, as 100 and varied the number of deliveries per agent from 100 to 500 in increments of 100. Different experiments were performed on homogeneous sets of individual, reciprocal, and philanthropic agents. Results from these set of experiments are presented in Figure 2. As expected, the performance of the individual agents was the worst, and the philanthropic agents were the best. The interesting thing is that the performance of the reciprocal agent is almost identical to that of philanthropic agents. That is, when a reciprocal agent is placed in a group of other reciprocal agents it adapts over time to behave like a philanthropic agent, and this adaptation benefits everybody. This is a significant result because we have been able to show that under proper environmental conditions (frequent interactions with possibilities of cooperation), self-motivated behavior based on reciprocity can produce mutually cooperative behavior that leads to near-optimal system performance. In addition, with more packages to deliver, the savings in distance traversed is more with reciprocal and philanthropic agents over individual agents. The ratio of corresponding points on the two curves should be the same, however, as it is determined by the probability of another agent being able to help one agent with its delivery. For the package delivery problem described in Section 3 this probability is largely determined by the number of radial fins, R, the maximum distance traversed from the depot, D, and the number of agents, N.

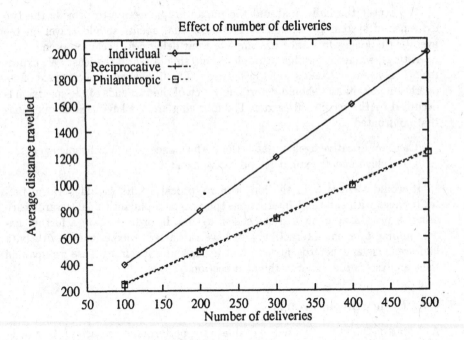

Fig. 2. Average distance traversed by each agent to complete all deliveries.

We also performed a similar set of experiments by fixing the number of deliveries per agent at 500 and varying the number of agents from 25 to 50 to 75 to 100. Results from these set of experiments are presented in Figure 3. As above, the performance of the individual agents was the worst, and the philanthropic agents was the best (approximately one-third savings is obtained). The performance of the reciprocal agents was very close to that of the philanthropic agents, and it improved with more agents (with more agents there is more scope of cooperation). Relational agents perform less efficiently than philanthropic agents as occasionally they turn down globally beneficial cooperation requests that will affect local problem solving (involve incurring additional cost for an agent with whom there is a already a large negative balance).

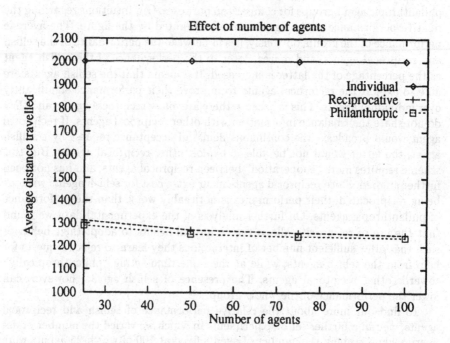

Fig. 3. Average distance traversed by each agent to complete all deliveries.

4.2 Heterogeneous groups

After having addressed the question about the relative efficiencies of philanthropic and reciprocative agents, we then decided the answer the second research question of the vulnerability of a group of reciprocal agents to exploitation by selfish agents. We wanted to find out if the reciprocative agents are a stable group. Axelrod defines a group to be stable against another individual (using a different strategy than that used by the individuals in the group), if the latter cannot outperform the average group performance when it interacts with the group members. We were interested in group stability in a more general form. Can reciprocal agents in a heterogeneous group outperform the selfish agents in the group? If that is the case, all self-interested agents will ultimately prefer to use the strategy of reciprocation, i.e., become reciprocative agents.

We expected that selfish agents should be able to obtain some help from reciprocal agents, and hence would perform better than individual agents. But they would not be able to match the performance of reciprocal agents. For these set of experiments, we fixed the number of agents at 100 and the number of deliveries at 500. We varied the percentage of selfish agents in the group. Results are presented in Figure 4, which also contains the results from individual and philanthropic agent groups for comparison purposes. Our intuitions regarding the relative performance of the agents are corroborated by the figure. The average performance of the group, obviously, lies in between the performance of the selfish and reciprocal agents, and moves closer to the performance of the selfish agent as the percentage of the latter is increased. It appears that the selfish agents are able to exploit the reciprocal agents to improve their performance significantly over individual agents. This is because there are many reciprocal agents and they do not share their balance information with other reciprocal agents. If reciprocal agent would broadcast the continuous denial of acceptance request by a selfish agent, the latter would not be able to exploit other reciprocal agents. But this scheme requires more "cooperation" between reciprocal agents, and has not been further studied. Since reciprocal agents incur extra cost for selfish agents without being reciprocated, their performance is noticeably worse than the performance of philanthropic agents. On further analysis of the experimental data we found that the use of reciprocity allows the reciprocal agents to adopt their behavior such that after sufficient number of interactions they learn to reject requests for help from the selfish agents, while at the same time acting "philanthropically" towards other reciprocal agents. The presence of selfish agents, however, can lower the performance of the whole group.

To find out more about the relative performance of selfish and reciprocal agents, we ran a further set of experiments in which we varied the number of deliveries while keeping the number of agents fixed at 100 of which 25 agents were selfish in nature. Results from these set of experiments are presented in Figure 5. A noteworthy result was that with few deliveries to make, selfish agents outperformed reciprocal agents. This can be explained by the fact that the number of reciprocal agents were large enough compared to the number of deliveries, and this allowed selfish agents to exploit reciprocal agents for most of its deliveries. This in turn affected the performance of the reciprocal agents, as they could not recover from the extra cost incurred to help these selfish agents. With sufficient deliveries to make, however, reciprocal agents turned out to be clear winners. This lends further credence to our claim that it is ultimately beneficial for an agent to be reciprocative rather than selfish.

5 Conclusions

In this paper, we have shown that self-motivated behavior can evolve cooperation among a group of autonomous agents. Under appropriate environmental conditions, such a group of agents can also achieve near-optimal global performance. This can be achieved by using reciprocity as an aid to adaptation to

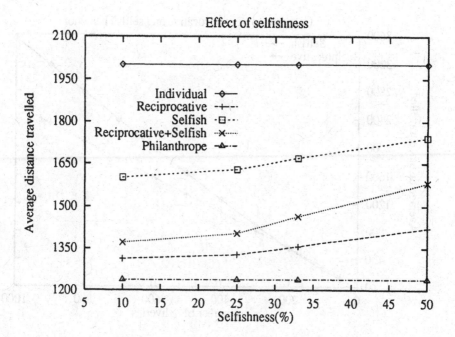

Fig. 4. Average distance traversed by each agent to complete all deliveries as the percentage of selfish agent in a group of reciprocal agents is varied. The individual and the philanthropic agent results do not contain selfish agents and are presented for comparison.

other agents. This allows agents to realize scopes for cooperation while avoiding wasting efforts on helping unresponsive agents. This is a significant result because in an open, distributed environment, an autonomous agent is likely to face a multitude of agents with different design philosophies and attitudes. Assuming benevolent or cooperative agents is impractical in these situations. Our analysis and experiments show that agents can use reciprocal behavior to adapt to the environment, and improve individual performance. Since reciprocating behavior produces better performance in the long run over selfish or exploitative behavior, it is to the best interest of all agents to be reciprocative. Our results hold for domains where cooperation always leads to aggregate gains for the group.

In this paper, we concentrated on tasks that can be individually solved by agents. Our work on a extension of the current system that addresses tasks which require joint action by several agents has yielded very similar results [7].

Investigating the effects of relaxing the requirements for the global cooperation constraint (constraint 1 in the last paragraph of Section 3) will be interesting. Also, we now take help from the first person that agrees to help. We also plan to study the performance of the mechanism when the agent goes through

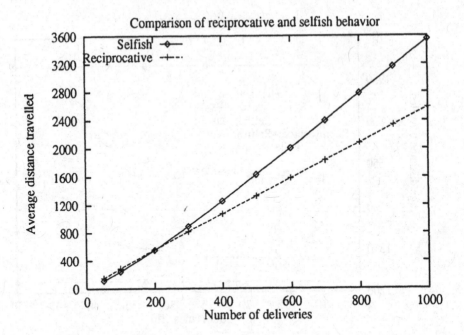

Fig. 5. Average distance traversed by each agent to complete all deliveries with different number of deliveries.

all the offers for help and chooses to take help from the agent with which its got the most negative balance.

The results in this paper hold when the extra work done by the helping agent is less than the savings in work obtained by the agent being helped. We would like to further evaluate and characterize the assumptions which allow reciprocal behavior to be stable. In addition, for the problem domain presented in this paper, we plan to come up with a formal criteria for deciding whether a reciprocative strategy is stable. This criterion will involve the probability of interaction between two agents, the distribution of task costs, etc.

We also plan to investigate more complex and realistic domains such as distributed monitoring, distributed information gathering, etc. to further evaluate the strengths and limitations of our proposed mechanism.

Acknowledgements

This research was partially supported by NSF Research Initiation Award IRI-9410180.

References

1. Robert Axelrod. *The Evolution of Cooperation*. Basic Books, 1984.
2. L. B. Booker. Classifier systems that learn internal world models. *Machine Learning*, 3:161–192, 1988.
3. Les Gasser. Social conceptions of knowledge and action: DAI foundations and open systems semantics. *Artificial Intelligence*, 47(1-3):107–138, 1991.
4. Claudia Goldman and Jeffrey S. Rosenschein. Emergent coordination through the use of cooperative state-changing rules. In *Proceedings of the Twelfth National Conference on Artificial Intelligence*, pages 408–413, 1994.
5. Carl Hewitt. Open information systems semantics for distributed artificial intelligence. *Artificial Intelligence*, 47(1-3):79–106, 1991.
6. A. Rapoport. Prisoner's dilemma. In J. Eatwell, M. Milgate, and P. Newman, editors, *The New Palgrave: Game Theory*, pages 199–204. Macmillan, London, 1989.
7. Mahendra Sekaran and Sandip Sen. To help or not to help, 1995.
8. S. Sian. Adaptation based on cooperative learning in multi-agent systems. In Y. Demazeau and J.-P. Müller, editors, *Decentralize AI*, volume 2, pages 257–272. Elsevier Science Publications, 1991.
9. C. Watkins. *Learning from Delayed Rewards*. PhD thesis, King's College, Cambridge University, 1989.

Multiagent coordination with learning classifier systems

Sandip Sen and Mahendra Sekaran

Department of Mathematical & Computer Sciences,
The University of Tulsa
Tulsa, OK 74104, USA
e-mail: sandip@kolkata.mcs.utulsa.edu, mahend@euler.mcs.utulsa.edu

1 Introduction

Researchers in the field of Distributed Artificial Intelligence (DAI) [4] have developed a variety of agent coordination schemes under different assumptions about agent capabilities and relationships. Most of these schemes rely on shared knowledge or authority relationships between agents. These kinds of information may not be available or may be manipulated by malevolent agents. We have used reinforcement learning [3] as a coordination mechanism that imposes little cognitive burden on agents and does not suffer from the above-mentioned shortcomings [15, 16].

In this paper, we evaluate a particular reinforcement learning methodology, a genetic algorithm based machine learning mechanism known as classifier systems [13] for developing action policies to optimize environmental feedback. Action policies that provide a mapping between perceptions and actions can be used by multiple agents to learn coordination strategies without having to rely on shared information. These agents are unaware of the capabilities of other agents and may or may not be cognizant of goals to achieve. We show that through repeated problem-solving experience, these agents can develop policies to maximize environmental feedback that can be interpreted as goal achievement from the viewpoint of an external observer. Experimental results from a couple of multiagent domains show that classifier systems can be more effective than the more widely used Q-learning scheme for multiagent coordination.

2 Coordination of multiple agents

Multiagent systems are a particular type of DAI system, in which autonomous intelligent agents inhabit a world with no global control or globally consistent knowledge. These agents may still need to coordinate their activities with others to achieve their own local goals. They could benefit from receiving information about what others are doing or plan to do, and from sending them information to influence what they do.

Almost all of the coordination schemes developed to date assume explicit or implicit sharing of information. In the explicit form of information sharing, agents communicate partial results [9], speech acts [7], resource availabilities [18], etc. to other agents to facilitate the process of coordination. In the implicit form of information sharing, agents use knowledge about the capabilities of other agents [10, 11] to aid local decision-making.

We believe that the less an agent depends on shared information, and the more flexible it is to the on-line arrival of problem-solving and coordination knowledge, the better it can adapt to changing environments. As flexibility and adaptability are key aspects of intelligent and autonomous behavior, we are interested in investigating mechanisms by which agents can acquire and use coordination knowledge through interactions with its environment (that includes other agents) without having to rely on shared information.

In our ongoing research effort to identify such coordination schemes, we compare the performance of classifier systems and the widely used Q-learning algorithm on a resource sharing problem and a robot navigation problem. We show that classifier systems perform competitively with the Q-learning algorithm [22] to develop effective coordination schemes even when multiple agents are learning concurrently.

Previous proposals for using learning techniques to coordinate multiple agents have mostly relied on using prior knowledge [6], or on cooperative domains with unrestricted information sharing [17]. Even previous work on using reinforcement learning for coordinating multiple agents [20, 23] have relied on explicit information sharing. We, however, concentrate on systems where agents share no problem-solving knowledge. We show that although each agent is independently using reinforcement learning techniques to optimizing its own environmental reward, global coordination between multiple agents can emerge without explicit or implicit information sharing. These agents can therefore act independently and autonomously, without being affected by communication delays (due to other agents being busy) or failure of a key agent (who controls information exchange or who has more information), and do not have to be worry about the reliability of the information received (Do I believe the information received? Is the communicating agent an accomplice or an adversary?). The resultant systems are, therefore, robust and general-purpose. Our assumptions are similar to that used by Sandholm and Crites [21], and by Sen, Sekaran and Hale [16]; the individual goals of agents in the problem domains discussed in this paper are much more loosely coupled than in their problems.

3 Reinforcement learning

In reinforcement learning problems [3] reactive and adaptive agents are given a description of the current state and have to choose the next action from a set of possible actions so as to maximize a scalar *reinforcement* or *feedback* received after each action. The learner's environment can be modeled by a discrete time, finite state, Markov decision process that can be represented by a 4-tuple $\langle S, A, P, r \rangle$ where $P : S \times S \times A \mapsto [0, 1]$ gives the probability of moving from state s_1 to s_2 on performing action a, and $r : S \times A \mapsto \Re$ is a scalar reward function. Each agent maintains a policy, π, that maps the current state into the desirable action(s) to be performed in that state. The expected value of a discounted sum of future rewards of a policy π at a state x is given by $V_\gamma^\pi \stackrel{\text{def}}{=} E\{\sum_{t=0}^\infty \gamma^t r_{s,t}^\pi\}$, where $r_{s,t}^\pi$ is the random variable corresponding to the reward received by the learning agent t time steps after if starts using the policy π in state s, and γ is a discount rate ($0 \leq \gamma < 1$).

Various reinforcement learning strategies have been proposed using which agents can develop a policy to maximize rewards accumulated over time. For evaluating the classifier system paradigm for multiagent reinforcement learning, we compare it with the Q-learning [22] algorithm, which is designed to find a policy π^* that maximizes $V_\gamma^\pi(s)$ for all states $s \in S$. The decision policy is represented by a function, $Q : S \times A \mapsto \Re$, which estimates long-term discounted rewards for each state–action pair. The Q values are defined as $Q_\gamma^\pi(s,a) = V_\gamma^{a;\pi}(s)$, where $a; \pi$ denotes the event sequence of choosing action a at the current state, followed by choosing actions based on policy π. The action, a, to perform in a state s is chosen such that it is expected to maximize the reward,

$$V_\gamma^{\pi^*}(s) = \max_{a \in A} Q_\gamma^{\pi^*}(s,a) \text{ for all } s \in S.$$

If an action a in state s produces a *reinforcement* of R and a transition to state s', then the corresponding Q value is modified as follows:

$$Q(s,a) \leftarrow (1 - \beta)\, Q(s,a) + \beta\, (R + \gamma \max_{a' \in A} Q(s',a')). \tag{1}$$

The above update rule is similar to Holland's bucket-brigade [13] algorithm in classifier systems and Sutton's temporal-difference [19] learning scheme. The similarities of Q-learning and classifier systems have been analyzed in [8].

Classifier systems are rule based systems that learn by adjusting rule strengths from feedback and by discovering better rules using genetic algorithms. In this paper, we will use simplified classifier systems where all possible message action pairs are explicitly stored and classifiers have one condition and one action. These assumptions are similar to those made by Dorigo and Bersini [8]; we also use their notation to describe a classifier i by (c_i, a_i), where c_i and a_i are respectively the condition and action parts of the classifier. $S_t(c_i, a_i)$ gives the strength of classifier i at time step t. We first describe how the classifier system performs and then discuss two different feedback distribution schemes, namely the Bucket Brigade algorithm (BBA), and the Profit Sharing Plan (PSP).

All classifiers are initialized to some default strength. At each time step of problem solving, an input message is received from the environment and matched with the classifier rules to form a matchset, $\mathcal{M}$. One of these classifiers is chosen to fire and based on its action, a feedback may be received from the environment. Then the strengths of the classifier rules are adjusted. This cycle is repeated for a given number of time steps. A series of cycles constitute a *trial* of the classifier system. In the BBA scheme, when a classifier is chosen to fire, its strength is increased by the environmental feedback. But before that, a fraction α of its strength is removed and added to the strength of the classifier who fired in the last time cycle. So, if classifier i fires at time step t, produces external feedback of R, and classifier j fires at the next time step, the following equations gives the strength update of classifier i:

$$S_{t+1}(c_i, a_i) = (1 - \alpha) * S_t(c_i, a_i) + \alpha * (R + S_{t+1}(c_j, a_j)).$$

We now describe the profit sharing plan (PSP) strength-updating scheme [12] used in classifier systems. In this method, problem solving is divided into episodes in between receipts of external reward. A rule is said to be active in a period if it fired in at least one of the cycles in that episode. At the end of episode e, the strength of each active rule i in that episode is updated as follows:

$$S_{e+1}(c_i, a_i) = S_e(c_i, a_i) + \alpha * (R_e - S_e(c_i, a_i)),$$

where R_e is the external reward received at the end of the episode. We have experimented with two methods of choosing a classifier to fire given the matchset. In the more traditional method, a classifier $i \in \mathcal{M}$ at time t is chosen with a probability given by $\frac{S_t(c_i, a_i)}{\sum_{d \in \mathcal{M}} S_t(c_d, a_d)}$. We call this fitness proportionate PSP or PSP(FP). In the other method of action choice, the classifier with the highest fitness in $\mathcal{M}$ is chosen 90% of the time, and a random classifier from $\mathcal{M}$ is chosen in the rest 10% cases (Mahadevan uses such an action choosing mechanism for Q-learning in [14]). We call this a semi-random PSP or PSP(SR).

For the Q-learning algorithm, we stop a run when the algebraic difference of the policies at the end of neighboring trials is below a threshold for 10 consecutive trials. With this convergence criterion, however, the classifier systems ran too long for us to collect reasonable data. Instead, every 10th trial, we ran the classifier system (both with BBA and PSP) with a deterministic action choice over the entire trial. We stopped a run of the classifier system if the differences of the total environmental feedback received by the system on neighboring deterministic trials were below a small threshold for 10 consecutive deterministic trials.

We study the performance of classifier systems and Q-learning on two different domains. In the resource sharing domain, agents receive feedback only at the end of each trial (delayed), and only one of the agents is learning (the other agent has a fixed load distribution). In the robot navigation domain, agents receive feedback after each step (immediate), and both of the agents learn concurrently.

4 Resource sharing problem

We designed a tightly-coupled multiagent resource sharing problem where environmental feedback is received only after a sequence of agent actions. In our version of the resource sharing problem, agents learn to distribute their load on a shared resource effectively, so that they receive maximum utility from the resource. Furthermore, we assume that if agents are not aware of the maximum load limit of the resource at any point of time, they will have to learn to distribute their load over a time-window without exceeding the load limit. Agents in this domain can be considered to be indifferent because they are only interested in their own goals, but are not necessarily adversarial. Competitive learning has been studied by many researchers [1], and studies have only served to highlight the complexity and the difficulties involved. We intended to compare the performance of Q-learning with other reinforcement learning schemes. Since, previous research on classifier systems has not been focussed on studying their capability to evolve coordination schemes in multiagent systems, we decided to choose classifier systems in our study. Using the resource sharing task, we intend to compare the performance of Q-learning and classifier systems in evolving effective coordination schemes in a competitive domain. Furthermore, we evaluate these techniques for scaling up to situations where multiple agents are learning simultaneously from situations where only one of the agents is learning to adjust its actions against a fixed set of actions from other agents.

4.1 Problem description

Our resource sharing problem assumes two agents sharing a common resource or channel, with each of them trying to distribute their load on the system so as to achieve maximum utility. A maximum load of L can be applied on the system at any point in time (loads in excess of this do not receive any utility;there are no penalties however for exceeding the load limit). The utility obtained from the resource for a given applied load is as in Figure 1. There is a time window within which the agents have to operate and utilize their allotted load hours. Related work on adaptive load balancing has been reported in [2], but they do not use reinforcement learning. In their version of the problem there are many resources, and agents have to finish their jobs using available resources. They use a set of selection rules using which agents select a resource for a job.

This domain can be used to study the behavior of reinforcement learning mechanisms in two different multiagent scenarios: learning in multiagent systems, and concurrent learning. The first category encompasses those domains in which there are multiple agents present in the system, but not necessarily all of them are learning at the same time. The second category is a subset of the first category where all the agents present in the system are learning concurrently. This illustrates a form of competitive learning. We conducted experiments using both of these scenarios.

4.2 Learning in Multiagent systems

In the first version of the problem, it is assumed that one agent has already applied some load distributed over a fixed time period, and the other agent is learning to distribute its load on the system without any knowledge of the current distribution. A single trial consists of an episode of applying loads until T time steps are completed or until the agent has exhausted the allotted K load-hours, whichever occurs earlier. Through repetitive trials, the agents are expected to learn to distribute their load on the system in an optimal fashion. Figure 2 presents the load distribution used by the first agent as well as one of

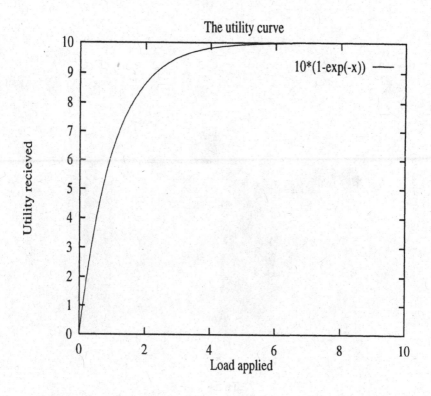

Fig. 1. Curve depicting the utility received for a given load.

several optimal load distributions for the second agent in the particular problem we have used for experiments ($T = 10$ in this problem).

The second agent can use K load-hours of the channel. If it applies a load of k_t load-hours on the system at time step t, when the first agent has applied l_t load-hours, the utility it receives is $u(l_t, k_t) = U(\max(L, k_t + l_t)) - U(\max(L, l_t))$, where U is the utility function in Figure 1, and $L = 10$ is the maximum load allowed on the system at any time instance. The total feedback it gets at the end of T time steps is $\sum_{t=1}^{T} u(l_t, k_t)$. This problem requires the second agent to distribute its load around the loads imposed by the first agent in order to obtain maximum utility. The problem is that the second agent has no direct information about the load distribution on the system. This is a typical situation in reinforcement learning problems where the agent has to choose its actions based only on scalar feedback.

Since the resource sharing problem produces rewards only after a series of actions are performed we used the PSP method of payoff distribution with the classifier system. Though BBA can also be used for payoff distribution in this problem, our initial experiments showed that PSP performed much better than

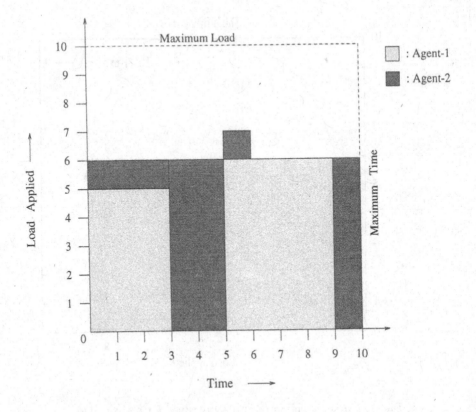

Fig. 2. A resource sharing problem.

BBA on this problem. The parameter values are $\beta = 0.5$, $\gamma = 0.95$ for Q-learning and $\alpha = 0.5$ for PSP.

In this set of experiments the fitness-proportionate PSP did not converge even after 150,000 trials. Experimental results comparing Q-learning and semi-random PSP, PSP(SR), based classifier systems on the resource sharing problem is displayed in Figure 3. Results are averaged over 50 runs of both systems. Though both methods find the optimal load distribution in some of the runs, more often than not they settle for a less than optimal, but reasonably good, distribution. PSP takes about twice as long to converge but produces a better load distribution on the average. The difference in performance is found to be significant at the 99% confidence level using a two-sample t-procedure. We believe this happens because all the active rules directly share the feedback at the end of a trial in PSP. In Q-learning, however, the external feedback is passed back to policy elements used early in a trial, over successive trials. Interference with different action sequence (the same action might produce different feedback based on the current load on the system) sharing the same policy element (state-action pair) can produce convergence to sub-optimal solutions.

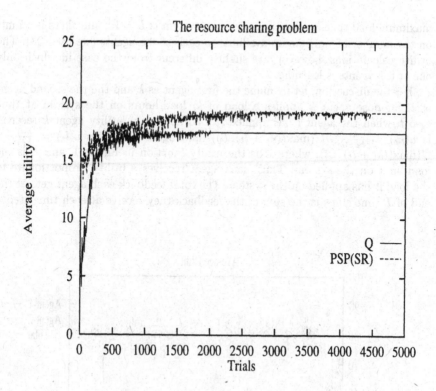

Fig. 3. Comparison of PSP and Q-learning on the resource sharing problem.

Typical solutions produced by PSP and Q-learning differed in one important characteristic. PSP solutions will save some of the load for the last empty time-slot, whereas Q-learning solutions use up all the available load before that. Since PSP is able to utilize the last empty time slot on the channel, it produces better utility than Q-learning.

The above results show two things: 1) an agent can effectively use a classifier system to coordinate its actions effectively with no knowledge about the actions of the other agent using the common resource, 2) the semi-random action choice mechanism can be a more effective method for classifier systems than the commonly used fitness-proportionate action choice scheme.

4.3 Concurrent Learning

To study the behavior of multiagent systems when both the agents are learning concurrently, we redefined the resource sharing problem so that both the agents are simultaneously applying their loads on the resource.

Apart from the fact that both the agents are learning at the same time, the domain specifications of the problem are very similar to the previous case. The maximum load that can be applied on the system is $L = 10$, and there is a limit on the number of work-hours available to each of the agents (we used 25). The utility calculations, however, are slightly different from the case in which only one of the agents is learning.

For the discussion, let us name the first agent as k and the the second agent as l. Suppose agent k applies a load of k_t load-hours on the system at time step t, when the agent l has applied l_t load-hours; the utility agent k receives is $u(k_t) = \frac{k_t}{k_t+l_t} * U(\max((k_t + l_t), L))$, and agent l receives $u(l_t) = \frac{l_t}{k_t+l_t} * U(\max((k_t + l_t), L))$, where U is the utility function in Figure 1, and L is the load-limit on the system. Thus, each agent receives a utility proportionate to the load it has applied on the system. The total feedback each agent gets at the end of T time steps is the sum of the feedback they receive at each time step.

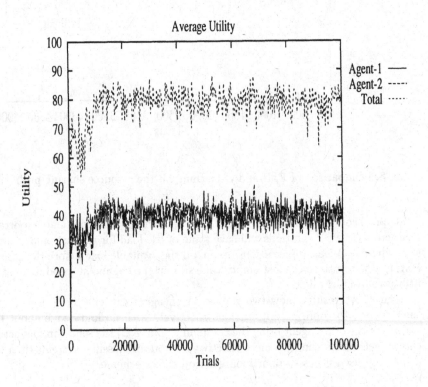

Fig. 4. Performance of Q-learning on the resource sharing problem.

Since the resource sharing problem produces rewards only after a series of actions are performed we used the PSP method of payoff distribution with the classifier system. Though BBA can also be used for payoff distribution in this problem, our initial experiments showed that PSP performed much better than

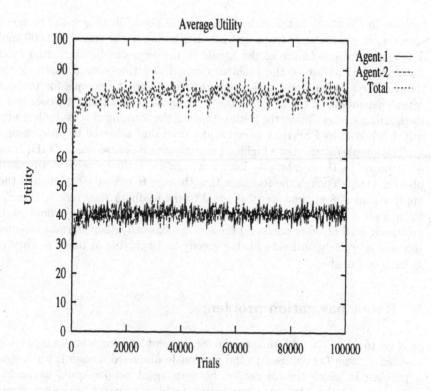

Fig. 5. Performance of PSP on the resource sharing problem.

BBA on this problem. To study the performance of reinforcement learning algorithms on this problem, we compared the performance of Q-learning and semi-random PSP. The learning parameter values used were $\beta = 0.5$, $\gamma = 0.95$ for Q-learning and $\alpha = 0.5$ for PSP. The time window was set to 10, the load limit on the resource, L, was set to 10, and the agents were each allowed to apply 25 load hours on the resource. Though there are probably many possible load distributions possible under this setting, one of the optimal utility values that can be obtained by each agent is approximately 50.

Experimental results indicate that both the learning mechanisms learn to distribute their load on the system at a reasonably high performance level, but not in an optimal fashion. An interesting observation is that none of the agents benefit at the expense of the other agent, and both receive approximately the same utility from their load distributions. So, the solutions generated by the reinforcement learning schemes may not be optimal, but are good and fair. The performance of the Q-learning algorithm is shown in Figure 4 and PSP is shown in Figure 5.

The performance curves of both the learning mechanisms clearly indicate the increase in the utility obtained by each agent as the trials progress. The agents, however, do not converge to an optimal distribution at the end of 100,000 trials. The reason for the failure of the agents to converge can be attributed to the *tightly-coupled* nature of the problem domain and the delayed feedback they receive. For a given state, each agent receives different feedback for the same action, depending on the action of the other agent at that time. A closer look at the learning curves during the initial stages of the learning process indicate that utility achieved by PSP rises more rapidly than that achieved by Q-learning.

The sample distributions highlight one important characteristic of the knowledge learned by the agents: they learn not to overload the resource at any particular time step. Though the feedback that the agents receive when each of them apply a load of 8 at time step t is equal to the feedback they receive if each of them apply a load of 5, they learn to prefer the latter because they could use the remaining load at other points on the system. Basically, they learn to distribute the load effectively, instead of being greedy and applying as much as they can as early as possible.

5   Robot navigation problem

In order to study the performance of reinforcement learning schemes on a loosely coupled domain (as opposed to the previously discussed domain), we designed a problem in which the interaction between agent actions could be made to occur infrequently. The robot navigation problem provides us with a domain where the interactions among the agents can be varied continuously (loosely-coupled to tightly-coupled) and feedback can be immediate or delayed. We study the performance of both Q-learning and classifier systems on this domain with immediate feedback.

5.1   Problem Description

We designed a problem in which four agents, A, B, C, and D, are to find the optimal path in a grid world, from given starting locations to their respective goals, A', B', C', and D'. The agents traverse their world using one of the five available operators: *north, south, east, west,* or *hold.* Figure 6 depicts potential paths that each of the agents might choose during their learning process. The goal of the agents is to learn moves that quickly take them to their respective goal locations without colliding with other agents.

Each agent receives feedback based on its move: when it makes a move that takes it *towards* its goal, it receives a feedback of 1; when it makes a move that takes it *away* from its goal, it receives a feedback of -1; when it makes a move that results in *no change* of its distance from its goal (*hold*), it receives a feedback of 0; and when it makes a move that results in a *collision*, the feedback is computed as depicted in Fig 7. All agents learn at the same time by updating their individual policies.

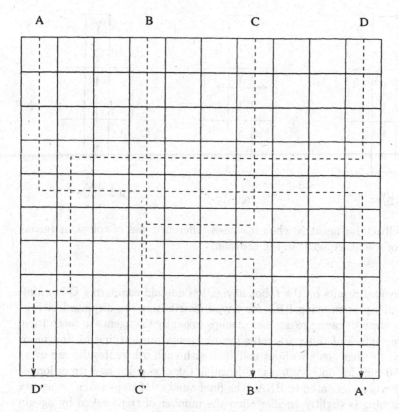

Fig. 6. A robot navigation problem.

5.2 Experimental Results

The robot navigation task is a domain in which the agent interactions could be varied very easily. When the goal locations and start locations are in adjacent locations on the grid, it models a very *tightly coupled* system, and when the start and goal locations of the agents are spread over the grid, it models a very *loosely-coupled* system. Even for a scenario where the agents are put in different corners of the grid (*loosely-coupled*), at some point the agent interactions might overlap, and the system models a *tightly-coupled* one at that point in time. This variability allows us to experiment with loosely and tightly coupled situations in the same domain.

Since the robot navigation problem that we chose to study produces feedback after each time step, we have used the BBA method of payoff distribution with the classifier system. The system parameters are $\beta = 0.5$, and $\gamma = 0.8$ for Q-learning and $\alpha = 0.1$ for BBA.

The system is said to have attained convergence when the agents reach the goal location and stay there through the length of the trial for 10 consecutive trials.

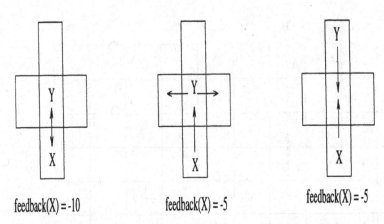

feedback(X) = -10   feedback(X) = -5   feedback(X) = -5

Fig. 7. Feedback for agent X when it causes different types of collisions (given the action of the other agent in the collision).

Experimental results on the robot navigation domain comparing Q-learning and a classifier system using BBA for payoff distribution are displayed in Figure 8. Plots show the average number of steps taken by the agents to reach their goals. Lower values of this parameter means agents are learning to find more direct paths to their goals without colliding with each other. Results are averaged over 50 runs for both systems. Q-learning takes as much as 5 times longer to converge when compared to BBA. The final number of steps taken by agents using Q-learning is slightly smaller than the number of steps taken by agents using BBA. We believe that if we make the convergence criteria more strict for the BBA, a better solution can be evolved with more computational effort.

The interesting aspect of this experiment is that all the agents were learning simultaneously and hence it was not obvious that they would find good paths. Typical solutions, however, show that agents stop at the right positions to let others pass through. This avoids collisions. The paths do contain small detours, however, and hence are not optimal.

The performance of BBA when $\alpha=0.5$ (comparable to β used in Q-learning) was not very different when compared to that presented in Figure 3. It is interesting to note that when experiments were tried setting the β in Q-learning to 0.1 (comparable to α in BBA), the system did not attain convergence.

6   Conclusions

In this paper we have addressed the problem of developing multiagent coordination strategies with minimal domain knowledge and information sharing between agents. We have compared classifier system based methods and Q-learning algorithms, two reinforcement learning paradigms, to investigate a resource sharing and a robot navigation problem. Our experiments show that the classifier based methods perform very competitively with the Q-learning algorithm, and are able

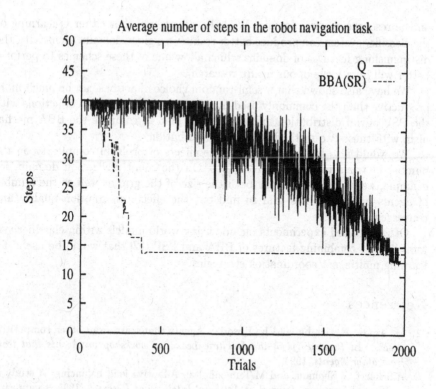

Fig. 8. Comparison of BBA and Q-learning on the robot navigation problem.

to generate good solutions to both problems. PSP works well on the resource sharing problem, where an agent is trying to adapt to a fixed strategy used by another agent, and when environmental feedback is received infrequently. When both the agents were learning concurrently, though both the schemes performed reasonably well, no one scheme outperforms the other. The sample distributions clearly indicates that the agents learn not to overload the resource at any particular time step, though they are not aware of the maximum load that can be applied on the systems and other system characteristics. Results are particularly encouraging for the robot navigation domain, where all agents are learning simultaneously. A classifier system with the BBA payoff distribution allows agents to coordinate their movements with others without deviating significantly from the optimal path from their start to goal locations.

This paper demonstrates that classifier systems can be used effectively to achieve near-optimal solutions more quickly than Q-learning, as illustrated by the experiments conducted in the robot navigation task. If we enforce a more rigid convergence criteria, classifier systems achieve a better solution than Q-learning through a larger number of trials, as illustrated by the results obtained on the resource sharing domain. We believe however, that either Q-learning or the classifier system can produce better results in a given domain. Identifying the distinguishing features of domains which allow one of these schemes to perform better will be a focus of our future research.

We have also shown that a semi-random choice of actions can be much more productive than the commonly used fitness-proportionate choice of actions with the PSP payoff distribution mechanism. We plan to compare the BBA mechanism with these two methods of payoff distribution.

We would also like to investigate the effects of problem complexity on the number of trials taken for convergence. On the robot navigation domain, for example, we would like to vary both the size of the grid as well as the number of agents moving on the grid to find out the effects on solution quality and convergence time.

Other planned experiments include using world models within classifier systems [5] and combining features of BBA and PSP [12] that would be useful for learning multiagent coordination strategies.

References

1. M. Asada, E. Uchibe, and K. Hosoda. Agents that learn from other competitive agents. In *Proceedings of the Machine Learning workshop on Agents that learn from other Agents*, 1995.
2. A.Schaerf, Y.Shoham, and M.Tennenholtz. Adaptive load balancing: A study in multiagent learning. *Journal of Artificial Intelligence Research*, 1995. to appear.
3. Andrew B. Barto, Richard S. Sutton, and Chris Watkins. Sequential decision problems and neural networks. In *Proceedings of 1989 Conference on Neural Information Processing*, 1989.
4. Alan H. Bond and Les Gasser. *Readings in Distributed Artificial Intelligence*. Morgan Kaufmann Publishers, San Mateo, CA, 1988.
5. L. B. Booker. Classifier systems that learn internal world models. *Machine Learning*, 3:161–192, 1988.
6. P. Brazdil, M. Gams, S. Sian, L. Torgo, and W. van de Velde. Learning in distributed systems and multi-agent environments. In *European Working Session on Learning*, Lecture Notes in AI, 482, Berlin, March 1991. Springer Verlag.
7. Philip R. Cohen and C. Raymond Perrault. Elements of a plan-based theory of speech acts. *Cognitive Science*, 3(3):177–212, 1979.
8. Marco Dorigo and Hugues Bersini. A comparison of Q-learning and classifier systems. In *Proceedings of From Animals to Animats, Third International Conference on Simulation of Adaptive Behavior*, 1994.
9. Edmund H. Durfee. *Coordination of Distributed Problem Solvers*. Kluwer Academic Publishers, 1988.
10. Mark S. Fox. An organizational view of distributed systems. *IEEE Transactions on Systems, Man, and Cybernetics*, 11(1):70–80, January 1981. (Also published in *Readings in Distributed Artificial Intelligence*, Alan H. Bond and Les Gasser, editors, pages 140–150, Morgan Kaufmann, 1988.).
11. M.R. Genesereth, M.L. Ginsberg, and J.S. Rosenschein. Cooperation without communications. In *Proceedings of the National Conference on Artificial Intelligence*, pages 51–57, Philadelphia, Pennsylvania, 1986.

12. John Grefenstette. Credit assignment in rule discovery systems. *Machine Learning*, 3(2/3):225–246, 1988.
13. John H. Holland. Escaping brittleness: the possibilities of general-purpose learning algorithms applied to parallel rule-based systems. In R.S. Michalski, J.G. Carbonell, and T. M. Mitchell, editors, *Machine Learning, an artificial intelligence approach: Volume II*. Morgan Kaufmann, Los Alamos, CA, 1986.
14. Sridhar Mahadevan. To discount or not to discount in reinforcement learning: A case study comparing R learning and Q learning. In *Proceedings of the Tenth International Conference on Machine Learning*, pages 205–211, 1993.
15. Mahendra Sekaran and Sandip Sen. Learning with friends and foes. In *Sixteenth Annual Conference of the Cognitive Science Society*, pages 800–805, 1994.
16. Sandip Sen, Mahendra Sekaran, and John Hale. Learning to coordinate without sharing information. In *National Conference on Artificial Intelligence*, pages 426–431, 1994.
17. S. Sian. Adaptation based on cooperative learning in multi-agent systems. In Y. Demazeau and J.-P. Müller, editors, *Decentralize AI*, volume 2, pages 257–272. Elsevier Science Publications, 1991.
18. Reid G. Smith. The contract net protocol: High-level communication and control in a distributed problem solver. *IEEE Transactions on Computers*, C-29(12):1104–1113, December 1980.
19. Richard S. Sutton. *Temporal Credit Assignment in Reinforcement Learning*. PhD thesis, University of Massachusetts at Amherst, 1984.
20. Ming Tan. Multi-agent reinforcement learning: Independent vs. cooperative agents. In *Proceedings of the Tenth International Conference on Machine Learning*, pages 330–337, June 1993.
21. T.W.Sandholm and R.H.Crites. Multiagent reinforcement learning in the iterated prisoner's dilemma. *Biosystems*, 1995. to appear.
22. C.J.C.H. Watkins. *Learning from Delayed Rewards*. PhD thesis, King's College, Cambridge University, 1989.
23. Gerhard Weiß. Learning to coordinate actions in multi-agent systems. In *Proceedings of the International Joint Conference on Artificial Intelligence*, pages 311–316, August 1993.

Subject Index

Springer-Verlag
and the Environment

We at Springer-Verlag firmly believe that an international science publisher has a special obligation to the environment, and our corporate policies consistently reflect this conviction.

We also expect our business partners – paper mills, printers, packaging manufacturers, etc. – to commit themselves to using environmentally friendly materials and production processes.

The paper in this book is made from low- or no-chlorine pulp and is acid free, in conformance with international standards for paper permanency.

Lecture Notes in Artificial Intelligence (LNAI)

Vol. 869: Z. W. Raś, M. Zemankova (Eds.), Methodologies for Intelligent Systems. Proceedings, 1994. X, 613 pages. 1994.

Vol. 872: S Arikawa, K. P. Jantke (Eds.), Algorithmic Learning Theory. Proceedings, 1994. XIV, 575 pages. 1994.

Vol. 878: T. Ishida, Parallel, Distributed and Multiagent Production Systems. XVII, 166 pages. 1994.

Vol. 886: M. M. Veloso, Planning and Learning by Analogical Reasoning. XIII, 181 pages. 1994.

Vol. 890: M. J. Wooldridge, N. R. Jennings (Eds.), Intelligent Agents. Proceedings, 1994. VIII, 407 pages. 1995.

Vol. 897: M. Fisher, R. Owens (Eds.), Executable Modal and Temporal Logics. Proceedings, 1993. VII, 180 pages. 1995.

Vol. 898: P. Steffens (Ed.), Machine Translation and the Lexicon. Proceedings, 1993. X, 251 pages. 1995.

Vol. 904: P. Vitányi (Ed.), Computational Learning Theory. EuroCOLT'95. Proceedings, 1995. XVII, 415 pages. 1995.

Vol. 912: N. Lavrăč S. Wrobel (Eds.), Machine Learning: ECML – 95. Proceedings, 1995. XI, 370 pages. 1995.

Vol. 918: P. Baumgartner, R. Hähnle, J. Posegga (Eds.), Theorem Proving with Analytic Tableaux and Related Methods. Proceedings, 1995. X, 352 pages. 1995.

Vol. 927: J. Dix, L. Moniz Pereira, T.C. Przymusinski (Eds.), Non-Monotonic Extensions of Logic Programming. Proceedings, 1994. IX, 229 pages. 1995.

Vol. 928: V.W. Marek, A. Nerode, M. Truszczynski (Eds.), Logic Programming and Nonmonotonic Reasoning. Proceedings, 1995. VIII, 417 pages. 1995.

Vol. 929: F. Morán, A. Moreno, J.J. Merelo, P.Chacón (Eds.), Advances in Artificial Life. Proceedings, 1995. XIII, 960 pages. 1995.

Vol. 934: P. Barahona, M. Stefanelli, J. Wyatt (Eds.), Artificial Intelligence in Medicine. Proceedings, 1995. XI, 449 pages. 1995.

Vol. 941: M. Cadoli, Tractable Reasoning in Artificial Intelligence. XVII, 247 pages. 1995.

Vol. 946: C. Froidevaux, J. Kohlas (Eds.), Symbolic Quantitative and Approaches to Reasoning under Uncertainty. Proceedings, 1995. X, 430 pages. 1995.

Vol. 954: G. Ellis, R. Levinson, W. Rich. J.F. Sowa (Eds.), Conceptual Structures: Applications, Implementation and Theory. Proceedings, 1995. IX, 353 pages. 1995.

Vol. 956: X. Yao (Ed.), Progress in Evolutionary Computation. Proceedings, 1993, 1994. VIII, 314 pages. 1995.

Vol. 957: C. Castelfranchi, J.-P. Müller (Eds.), From Reaction to Cognition. Proceedings, 1993. VI, 252 pages. 1995.

Vol. 961: K.P. Jantke. S. Lange (Eds.), Algorithmic Learning for Knowledge-Based Systems. X, 511 pages. 1995.

Vol. 981: I. Wachsmuth, C.-R. Rollinger, W. Brauer (Eds.), KI-95: Advances in Artificial Intelligence. Proceedings, 1995. XII, 269 pages. 1995.

Vol. 984: J.-M. Haton, M. Keane, M. Manago (Eds.), Advances in Case-Based Reasoning. Proceedings, 1994. VIII, 307 pages. 1995.

Vol. 990: C. Pinto-Ferreira, N.J. Mamede (Eds.), Progress in Artificial Intelligence. Proceedings, 1995. XIV, 487 pages. 1995.

Vol. 991: J. Wainer, A. Carvalho (Eds.), Advances in Artificial Intelligence. Proceedings, 1995. XII, 342 pages. 1995.

Vol. 992: M. Gori, G. Soda (Eds.), Topics in Artificial Intelligence. Proceedings, 1995. XII, 451 pages. 1995.

Vol. 997: K. P. Jantke, T. Shinohara, T. Zeugmann (Eds.), Algorithmic Learning Theory. Proceedings, 1995. XV, 319 pages. 1995.

Vol. 1003: P. Pandurang Nayak, Automated Modeling of Physical Systems. XXI, 232 pages. 1995.

Vol. 1010: M. Veloso, A. Aamodt (Eds.), Case-Based Reasoning Research and Development. Proceedings, 1995. X, 576 pages. 1995.

Vol. 1011: T. Furuhashi (Ed.), Advances in Fuzzy Logic, Neural Networks and Genetic Algorithms. Proceedings, 1994. VIII, 223 pages. 1995.

Vol. 1020: I. D. Watson (Ed.), Progress in Case-Based Reasoning. Proceedings, 1995. VIII, 209 pages. 1995.

Vol. 1036: G. Adorni, M. Zock (Eds.), Trends in Natural Language Generation. Proceedings, 1993. IX, 382 pages. 1996.

Vol. 1037: M. Wooldridge, J.P. Müller, M. Tambe (Eds.), Intelligent Agents II. Proceedings, 1995. XVI, 437 pages, 1996.

Vol. 1038: W. Van de Velde, J.W. Perram (Eds.), Agents Breaking Away. Proceedings, 1996. XIV, 232 pages, 1996.

Vol. 1040: S. Wermter, E. Riloff, G. Scheler (Eds.), Connectionist, Statistical, and Symbolic Approaches to Learning for Natural Language Processing. Proceedings, 1995. IX, 468 pages. 1996.

Vol. 1042: G. Weiß, S. Sen (Eds.), Adaption and Learning in Multi-Agent Systems. Proceedings, 1995. X, 238 pages. 1996.

Vol. 1047: E. Hajnicz, Time Structures. IX, 244 pages. 1996.

Vol. 1050: R. Dyckhoff, H. Herre, P. Schroeder-Heister (Eds.), Extensions of Logic Programming. Proceedings, 1996. VIII, 318 pages. 1996.

Lecture Notes in Computer Science